By the Editors of Consumer Guide™

Prescription

DRUGS

for People

Over 50

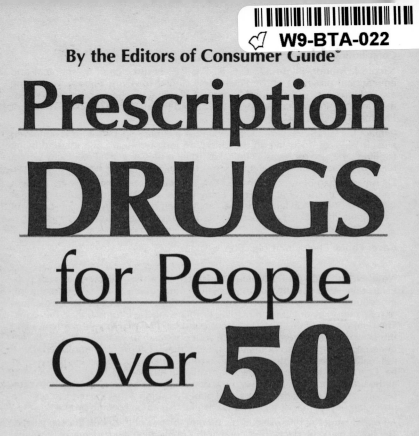

Nicole J. Brandt, Pharm.D., C.G.P., B.C.P.P.

Jennifer L. Hardesty, Pharm.D.

Amie Taggart Blaszczyk, Pharm.D.

Publications International, Ltd.

Contributing Writers:

Nicole J. Brandt, Pharm.D., C.G.P., B.C.P.P., is director of the clinical and educational programs of the Peter Lamy Center for Drug Therapy and Aging at the University of Maryland School of Pharmacy, where she also oversees the Geriatric Pharmacotherapy Pathway and Residency in the Department of Pharmacy Practice and Science.

Jennifer L. Hardesty, Pharm.D., F.A.S.C.P., is a clinical specialist for Woodhaven Health Services, focusing on the elderly in long-term care and assisted-living facilities. She also serves as a clinical assistant professor at the Peter Lamy Center for Drug Therapy and Aging at the University of Maryland School of Pharmacy.

Dr. Amie Taggart Blaszczyk, Pharm.D., is the geriatric pharmacotherapy resident and clinical instructor at the Peter Lamy Center for Drug Therapy and Aging at the University of Maryland. She is an active member of the American Society of Consultant Pharmacists and participates in many senior outreach events.

Cover Photo: PhotoDisc Collection.

Contents

Introduction

In the twenty-first century, people are living longer due at least in part to the development of more and better medicines. A variety of drug therapies is now available to target many diseases that were once considered incurable or untreatable. But this very same increase in medication options means that we, as consumers, must often make daunting decisions about our own health care and, specifically, about which medications to take. And the older we get, the more medications we are likely to need, so the more such decisions we are likely to face.

When it comes to deciding which medications are most appropriate for you, the best strategy is to use a team approach, with you, your doctor(s) and/or other health-care professionals, and your pharmacist working together. Each brings an expertise essential to determining the best drug treatment for you. Your doctor knows how to diagnose and treat medical conditions. Your pharmacist understands medications, dosages, side effects, and interactions. And you know your body better than anyone else. Because it is your health in the balance, it's up to you to work with your team and be informed and knowledgeable about all your medications—both prescription and over the counter—and how they're affecting your body. That's where this book can help.

Prescription Drugs for People Over 50 is a complete guide to medications for mature adults. It takes into account the unique concerns and physical realities of mature consumers who use prescription drugs. All medications carry certain risks. But those risks tend to be greater in older adults. One reason for this is that as the body ages, physical changes occur that affect how well the body absorbs, metabolizes, and eliminates drugs.

In addition, the more drugs you take, the more likely you are to have negative side effects from them. And in general, older adults take more medications than any other age group: A full two-thirds of people over 65 take medications daily. People over 65 represent only a little more than 12 percent of the population, but they take more than 30 percent of prescription medicines and approximately 40 percent of over-the-counter drugs.

And all too often, older adults don't fully understand the instructions for using their prescriptions. They may stop taking a drug too soon because they feel better or because the side effects are unexpected or troublesome. Or they may simply forget to take their pills. Research indicates that about 50 percent of people using prescription drugs don't take their medications correctly. Each year, older Americans report more than 9 million adverse drug reactions, resulting in thousands of hospitalizations.

To avoid such reactions, you should understand how to use your drugs properly and know what they are designed to do, how they work, what side effects they can cause, how they interact with each other, and how your body should react when you use them.

Prescription Drugs for People Over 50 provides essential, up-to-date information on hundreds of the most commonly prescribed drugs, including listings of possible side effects and how serious they are; instructions for use and warnings, such as whether a drug should be taken with food or on an empty stomach and whether the drug will affect your ability to drive a car; and the availability of a generic equivalent. This book also contains information about storing medications properly, administering various forms of drugs correctly, reading product labels, choosing a pharmacist, and saving money on your prescriptions.

Of course, this book is not a substitute for consulting your doctor and pharmacist; they should be your primary sources of information about how to use a prescribed drug. Rather, this book is an accurate and quick home reference guide that offers helpful information any time you need it. By staying informed, you'll be able to make choices to help ensure your years after 50 are long, active, and healthy.

TAKING MEDICATIONS CORRECTLY

Prescription medications can cure or manage many diseases if taken correctly; however, when taken incorrectly, they may be ineffective or, worse, may cause more damage than if you had taken no drugs at all. Getting the right dose at the right time in the right way is crucial. This is especially true for older adults, who tend to be more sensitive than people in other age groups to the effects of medication. The proper method of administering your medication will depend, in part, on the form (liquid, pill, patch, etc.) that has been prescribed for you. Review the following instructions to be sure you are administering your prescribed medication correctly.

Oral Liquids

One common method for delivering medication is as a liquid that is meant to be swallowed. Keep the following in mind when using an oral liquid:

- If the medication label says "Shake Well," be sure to shake the container thoroughly before measuring each dose. Certain liquids are suspensions, in which the drug particles are "suspended," or floating throughout the liquid. Suspensions must be shaken well to evenly distribute the drug particles throughout the liquid.

- Measure each dose of liquid medication with a medicine-dosing spoon or medicine-dosing cup, not a flatware teaspoon or tablespoon or a drinking cup from your kitchen. Home utensils vary greatly in the amount of liquid they hold. Your pharmacy carries an assortment of inexpensive medicine-dosing spoons and cups; one may even come free with your prescription. If your medication comes with a special dosing device, use only that device for measuring that drug, unless your pharmacist directs otherwise.

Topical Liquids, Creams, and Ointments

Certain medications come in a liquid, cream, or ointment form to be applied to the skin. To use one of these topical products:

- Apply it with clean fingers, a small cotton ball, a cotton-tipped swab, or a small gauze pad. Don't use a large gauze pad, because too much of the medication will be absorbed into it.

- Never stick your finger or a swab or other object down into the bottle, because you may contaminate the medication. Instead, pour or squeeze a small amount of the medication onto a swab or pad or onto your clean fingers.

- Once you have applied a topical product, do not cover the area with an "occlusive" dressing—one that does not allow air to pass through—unless specifically instructed to do so.

- For nitroglycerin ointment, measure an exact dose by squeezing a line of ointment along the measuring paper enclosed in the package. Spread it on your chest or upper arm in a thin, uniform layer at least 2 inches by 3 inches, then cover it with the measuring paper. Use another site for the next application to avoid irritation.

Capsules, Tablets, and Oral Powders

Most medications for adults come in pill form. Many people, however, have trouble swallowing pills, especially large ones. Pills can get stuck in the esophagus (the tube that connects your mouth to your stomach) and begin to dissolve there. This can lead to irritation, chest pains, and vomiting. The following tips may help make swallowing pills easier. If you still have difficulty, however, tell your doctor or pharmacist; another form of the drug may be available.

- Drink lots of water with each individual pill. Take a swallow of water before taking each pill, then wash down the medication with more water. This will help prevent stomach upset and other side effects.

- Don't take a pill lying down. Sit or stand up straight, and stay that way until you feel the pill go all the way down to your stomach (ideally, stay upright for at least 30 minutes).

- If you feel a pill lodged in your esophagus, drink more water or eat some soft food, such as pudding or a banana.

- If you have difficulty swallowing a pill, ask your pharmacist if you can empty the capsule or break or crush the tablet into a spoon and mix it with a small amount of applesauce, chocolate syrup, or another soft food. *Be sure to get your pharmacist's approval first.* Some pills are less effective when mixed with food; others have a special coating or delayed-release action and would lose effectiveness or even become toxic if crushed.

- Chewable tablets can be dissolved in water if you don't like their taste.

- Some drugs come in a powder or pill form that must be mixed with liquid before swallowing. Ask your pharmacist which liquids you may use.

- Some tablets, such as nitroglycerin, are sublingual—they should be placed under the tongue and allowed to dissolve. They are absorbed through the lining of the mouth.

Eyedrops, Eye Ointments, and Gels
Before administering eye medication, wash your hands. Then follow the instructions on the next page. Do not touch the dropper to your eye or to anything else,

because the dropper can easily become contaminated and transfer germs back to the medication.

1. Remove contact lenses or glasses, then either lie down or tilt your head back.

2. With one hand, gently pull down your lower eyelid to form a pocket.

3. With the other hand, place a drop or line of ointment or gel between your lower lid and eyeball.

4. Close your eyes (don't rub or squeeze them shut), and apply gentle pressure for two to three minutes to the inside corner (next to the nose) of the treated eye so the medicine doesn't drain away through the tear duct. Blot excess medication with a tissue.

5. Wait at least 5 minutes before applying another drop (if prescribed) or another drug to the eye; your eye can only hold one drop at a time. Wait 15 minutes before inserting contact lenses.

Nose Drops and Sprays
Blow your nose before using any nasal medication. Do not touch the dropper to the nasal membranes, because the dropper can easily become contaminated and transfer germs back to the medicine.

To administer nose drops:

1. Lie down or tilt your head back.

2. Squirt the prescribed number of drops into each nostril.

3. Stay in that position until you feel the medication spreading to your sinus passages.

To administer nose spray:

1. Sit upright with your head bent slightly forward.

2. Aim the sprayer into your nostril without letting it touch the inside of your nose. Squeeze the bottle, and do not release the squeeze until you remove the sprayer from your nostril; otherwise, nasal mucus and bacteria may be pulled down into the medication bottle.

3. After each prescribed spray, lean your head back until you feel the medication reach your sinuses.

Eardrops
To apply eardrops properly:

1. Warm the bottle by holding it or rolling it between your hands; never use boiling water or a microwave.

2. Shake the bottle before use if directed to do so.

3. Lie on your side or tilt your head to the side so the affected ear is facing upward.

4. Use one hand to pull the top of the earlobe toward the top and back of your head; this will allow the medicine to reach your eardrum.

5. With the other hand, squeeze the prescribed number of drops into the ear, being careful not to touch the dropper to your ear, which can contaminate the dropper and the remaining medicine.

6. Maintain that position for a few moments to allow the drops to move down into the ear canal.

Rectal Suppositories

Before inserting a rectal suppository, wash your hands. If you are administering a suppository to someone else or if you have long fingernails, wear latex medical gloves. Then follow these steps:

1. Unwrap the suppository.

2. If the suppository is soft, chill it in cold water for a few minutes to firm it up; this will make it easier to insert. Likewise, coating the suppository with a water-soluble lubricant such as K-Y Jelly—do not use petroleum jelly, or Vaseline—may make it easier to insert; however, check with your doctor or pharmacist to be sure it is okay to do so. Another option to help ease insertion is to moisten the rectal area with cool tap water first.

3. Lie on your side, and push the suppository (pointed end first) into the rectum. If it slips back out, reinsert it deeper in the rectum, then hold the buttocks together for a few moments to keep the suppository in.

4. Stay on your side for about 15 minutes. Try not to have a bowel movement for at least 1 hour.

Vaginal Creams, Tablets, and Suppositories

Read the directions that come with the prescribed vaginal medication first; they can vary slightly among products or brands. For example, some products come with an applicator that you attach to the tube and fill with medication, while others come with prefilled applicators. Then wash your hands, prepare the applicator (if necessary), and proceed with the insertion as follows:

1. Lie on your back, with your knees drawn up toward your chest.

2. Insert the applicator into the vagina as far as it will go comfortably.

3. Push the plunger to empty the cream, tablet, or suppository into the vagina.

4. Remove the applicator, and wash it thoroughly in warm soapy water.

Often, these creams are prescribed to treat vaginal infections that also cause itching or burning of the skin just outside the vagina. In such cases, the cream should be spread on the affected skin, using a clean finger, in addition to being inserted into the vagina with the applicator. The cream may stain clothing if it is applied externally or if it leaks from the vagina, so consider wearing a feminine pad to protect undergarments and clothing.

Patches

If a patch has been prescribed for you, choose the application site with care. DO NOT apply it to irritated or broken skin. DO NOT apply it right after bathing, before the skin is completely dry. And be sure to alternate the application site as directed to prevent skin irritation.

Before handling the patch, wash your hands. Remove the patch from its wrapper, and IMMEDIATELY apply it to your skin. Hold the patch in place for about ten seconds, making sure the edges of the patch are making good contact with the skin. Then wash your hands again.

Inhalants

If an inhalant medicine has been prescribed for you, you will need instruction for how to use an inhaler. It is important that you ask your pharmacist or doctor to demonstrate proper technique before you begin using an inhaler and any time you have any questions or uneasiness about using it. A device called a spacer can make an inhaler easier to use; if you have difficulty using your inhaler, ask your pharmacist and doctor about adding a spacer, and be sure its correct use is demonstrated for you. Also, if more than one inhalant medicine has been prescribed for you, be sure you know which one to use first. Follow these instructions, unless your pharmacist directs you otherwise:

1. Hold the inhaler according to the specific instructions found on the package.

2. Place the tip of the inhaler approximately one inch (about two finger-widths) in front of your opened mouth.

3. Without taking a deep breath first, exhale as completely as you can.

4. Begin to inhale through your mouth, and as you get to the middle of the inhaled breath, press down on the top of the inhaler until it releases a puff of medicine. (Beginning to inhale before the medicine is released will ensure that the medicine is pulled down into your lungs, where it is needed, rather than remaining in your mouth.) Be sure to keep your tongue down as you inhale, so it doesn't block the mist.

5. Close your mouth, and hold your breath for as long as possible (at least 10 to 15 seconds). This helps the medicine reach all the tiny air sacs in your lungs.

6. Exhale through your nose.

7. Rinse your mouth with warm water afterward to help prevent dryness. It is especially important to rinse your mouth with warm water after using a steroid inhaler, because rinsing can help prevent thrush—an overgrowth of fungus in the mouth, which can result from steroid use.

In addition to discussing proper drug administration with your doctor and pharmacist and following the instructions provided here, you can find illustrated directions on the Web site of the American Society of Health-System Pharmacists at www.safemedication.com.

Special Needs

Arthritis, poor eyesight, or memory lapses can make it difficult for some older adults to take their medications correctly. There are some coping tips and practical aids that can make medication use safer and easier for those with special needs.

Arthritis—Arthritis can make it difficult to open child-resistant caps on medications, so ask your pharmacist to put your pills in oversized, easy-to-open bottles. Be extremely diligent about keeping these bottles out of the reach of children, however.

Poor Eyesight—Large-type labels are not available at all pharmacies, but you can keep a magnifying glass (which many pharmacies sell) with your medicines. It also helps to read medication labels under bright light.

Forgetfulness, Memory Impairment, or Dementia— Anyone who needs to take medication on a regular basis should develop a system for remembering their drugs. One of the best methods is to make medication use part of your daily routine, like brushing your teeth. Some people use meals or bedtime to remember drugs; they reach for their medications each morning as they sit down to breakfast or at night as they get ready for bed.

Memory aids such as charts and calendar pillboxes can also help, especially if you take multiple drugs each day. Another option is to sort pills into separate cups for each part of the day. You can even devise your own reminders, such as turning each medicine bottle upside down after taking a pill and turning them right-side-up before going to bed at night. Some people set the pills for the next morning inside each bottle cap at night, then they put the caps back on the bottles after they take their doses. You can also set an alarm clock to remind yourself of medication time.

Those with serious memory impairments will need a family member or hired assistant to keep track of medications. Adult day care, supervised living facilities, and home health nurses can provide assistance. An estimated 23 percent of all nursing home admissions are due to the inability to remember medication schedules.

For anyone who takes medication on an ongoing basis, it's a good idea to keep a medication record card—listing every medication you take—in your wallet or purse in case of emergency. And for those with potentially life-threatening conditions—such as diabetes, heart disease, or severe allergies—a medical alert bracelet or necklace worn at all times can literally be a lifesaver.

STORING MEDICATIONS PROPERLY

Most medications should be stored in a cool place with low humidity that is out of direct sunlight. A bathroom cabinet is not a good place to store drugs because it is too hot and humid. A bedroom or hall cabinet is better.

If you have young children in your home or if they visit occasionally, don't leave your pills lying around where young hands can reach them. Keep medications in a cabinet with a plastic childproof lock securing the handles; the lock keeps little hands out yet can be easily removed when children leave. And don't forget about medications in your purse; be sure the purse is placed where children cannot get to it, especially if your medicine bottles do not have childproof lids.

Don't keep medications by your bedside (one exception is nitroglycerin for those with angina)—if you're sleepy, you may take them when you shouldn't or administer the wrong dose. Do not set drugs on a windowsill, where sunlight or heat can degrade them. And do not transfer drugs to unlabeled bottles—you might forget what's in them.

Check with your pharmacist to find out how best to dispose of your medications when they have passed their expiration date; don't just toss them in the trash or flush them down the toilet. While some out-of-date drugs are merely less effective, others may be harmful. If you have a chronic condition for which you keep a large supply of medication on hand, ask your pharmacist how long you can safely store it.

When traveling, keep medication in your purse or a bag that you carry with you at all times. Do not leave it in the car, where outdoor temperatures can destroy it. For airline travel, carry your medication onboard with you, so lost luggage or a delayed flight won't prevent you from taking your medicine on time. Talk to your doctor or pharmacist about how to travel with medicines that require refrigeration. For some medicines that are generally kept chilled, such as insulin, a few hours outside the refrigerator won't do any harm, but others may break down or degrade even in that short period of time.

PREVENTING SIDE EFFECTS
Every drug has side effects. For older adults, however, side effects are often more severe. Sometimes even "mild" medications can trigger unexpected and uncomfortable symptoms.

How a drug affects an individual depends on a number of factors, including the patient's age, health, weight, and metabolism and the presence of allergies or kidney or liver disease. Sometimes side effects are the result of an overdose or of combining one drug with another or with alcohol. Some, however, occur simply as a result of the way a drug works in the body.

Older adults are more susceptible to side effects than are younger adults because their bodies metabolize or eliminate many drugs more slowly. With age, kidney functions and some liver functions slow down. Because of this slowing, the effective dose for an older adult is often smaller, and the usual adult dose may actually cause unwanted side effects. Older adults may also be more prone to side effects from some medications because of subtle changes that occur in the body's cells.

Some common side effects of medications are confusion, tiredness, dizziness, constipation, stomach upset, sleep changes, diarrhea, incontinence, blurred vision, mood changes, and rashes.

The following steps can help prevent or minimize these and other possible side effects of medication use.

Take as few drugs as possible—Not every ailment needs a drug to fix it. A change in diet or exercise habits may work as well as or better than a drug. To ease constipation, for example, eat whole grains, fresh fruits, and vegetables; drink six to eight 8-ounce glasses of water each day; and add some physical activity to your daily routine. For mild osteoarthritis, try a heating pad or gentle stretching to ease stiffness and soreness. Ask your doctor, pharmacist, or other health-care professional what nondrug therapies might be appropriate for you.

Coordinate your medications—If you have several different doctors, make sure each knows what the other has prescribed for you. Ask if there's a single drug that can treat more than one of your medical conditions. For example, your blood pressure medicine might also be good for your heart disease, eliminating the need for an additional medication. Always use the same pharmacy, especially if you are seeing more than one doctor; that way, your entire prescription history will be in one place, and you and your pharmacist can detect and prevent duplications and drug interactions.

Keep a medication list with you—You should keep a list of all of your medications—both prescription and over the counter—with you at all times. This way, should an emergency occur, medical personnel will be able to avoid giving you any medications that might interact dangerously with your current medicines.

Know your body—Don't automatically attribute a new symptom to aging; it may be an unwanted side effect from a medication you're taking. Be sure to inform your doctor of any new symptoms. You may need to try a number of different drugs to find one that works best for you while causing the fewest side effects.

Know your medications—Make sure you understand what each of your medications is supposed to do, what side effects you can expect, which side effects are serious, how to store the medicine, what to do if you miss a dose, and how long you will need to take it. Make sure you understand all the explanations and instructions. Don't be embarrassed to ask questions—it is the duty of health-care professionals to explain your medications in terms you understand. Write down all your questions, and don't leave the doctor's office or pharmacy until they are all addressed. If a question arises after your visit, telephone the doctor or pharmacist for an answer.

Keep your doctor appointments—By attending follow-up appointments, you give your health-care provider the chance to evaluate your medication for unwanted side effects as well as effectiveness.

Get a medication check-up—Whenever you visit your general practitioner, bring all your prescription containers and ask the doctor to review them. In addition, have your pharmacist review all the medications you take— including over-the-counter drugs—at least once a year.

Confirm your continued need for a medication—At your regular visits, ask the doctor, "When can I stop taking this drug?" and "How do we know this drug is still working?" Some prescribers don't always think to eliminate drugs as reliably as they think to add them to your regimen.

Use one pharmacy, and develop a relationship with your pharmacist—A good pharmacist will inform you of possible side effects and precautions, how to take medications properly, and whether there's a less expensive generic version of a drug available. Your pharmacist may also have more time to talk with you about your drugs than your doctor does. And, as previously mentioned, developing a relationship with a single pharmacist or pharmacy, where your entire medication history is kept on file, can help you avoid potentially dangerous drug interactions and duplication.

Watch your diet—Food can have a direct impact on your medication. Some drugs are better absorbed when taken with a fatty meal. Others lose effectiveness when taken with milk or high-protein meals. Ask your pharmacist what foods and/or liquids you can and cannot have with your medications.

Follow directions—The timing of the doses is important for many drugs. "Four times a day" is not necessarily the same as "every six hours." Ask your pharmacist to explain when and how you should take each drug. Read the label every time you take the medication to remind yourself and prevent mistakes.

Don't forget doses—Use a calendar, a pillbox, or whatever system works for you to keep track of doses, and take them on time. You may experience fewer side effects if you do, and the drug will be more effective.

Be diligent—Check your pills and bottles every time you leave the pharmacy, even if you've been taking the drug for years. Query the pharmacist if a medication looks different. And, for every medicine you take, be sure your pharmacist or doctor has provided you with the answers to the following questions:

- What is the generic name of this drug? Is it a brand-name product, and if so, what is its brand name?

- What is it designed to do, and how will I know if it is working?

- What is the dosing schedule, and how do I take it?

- What should I do if I forget a dose?

- What side effects should I expect?

- How long will I be on this drug?

- How should I store this drug?

- Should I take this drug on an empty stomach or with food? Is it safe to drink alcohol while I'm being treated with this drug?

- Are there any activities, foods, beverages, or other medications I should avoid while taking this drug?

USING OVER-THE-COUNTER DRUGS WISELY

Over-the-counter (OTC) medications—those obtained without a prescription—provide relief for a variety of minor ailments such as aches and pains, colds and allergies, dry skin or itchy eyes, and minor digestive troubles. While OTC drugs are generally safe when used according to directions, they all have side effects and can potentially interact with your prescription medications. Some OTC products can also have a negative effect on certain medical conditions you may have. For example:

- Decongestants (in cold medications) can cause problems for those with high blood pressure, thyroid problems, or diabetes.

- Antihistamines (in allergy medications) can cause side effects for those with prostate problems, constipation, or certain types of glaucoma.

- Aspirin can cause side effects for people with asthma, gout, ulcers, or bleeding disorders.

- Nonsteroidal anti-inflammatory drugs (NSAIDs), such as ibuprofen (as in Motrin and Advil) and naproxen (in Aleve), can cause dangerous side effects in people with stomach ulcers, kidney problems, high blood pressure, or fluid retention.

Therefore, you need to be just as cautious and informed about your use of OTC medications as you are about your prescribed drugs.

Ask Questions About OTC Drugs

It is essential that you keep both your doctor and pharmacist up-to-date about all the OTC medicines, vitamins, minerals, herbs, and supplements (as well as prescription drugs) you take. Bring a current list of these products with you each time you visit the doctor and pharmacy, and be sure you get answers to the following questions:

- What kind of interactions might occur among the items on the list? Will any of them interact with or have an effect on my prescription medication(s), my medical condition(s), the foods I eat, or my daily activities?

- What is the recommended dose for me? (Older adults may be able to use half the usual dose and still get the desired effect but without as many side effects.)

- Can OTC products replace any of my prescription medications?

Always Read the OTC Label

The labels on OTC products contain a wealth of valuable information that can help you minimize or prevent side effects and dangerous interactions and ensure that you are getting the greatest benefit and value from the medications. And as a result of a regulation issued by the U.S. Food and Drug Administration (FDA), the labels on most OTC products must use a consistent format, cleaner design, and larger type that make the labels easier to read and follow. The regulation also requires that simpler, clearer language be used to make label information easier for consumers to understand. The information you'll find on the OTC label includes:

- **Active Ingredient.** Under this heading you'll find the name of the substance(s) responsible for the product's therapeutic, or beneficial, effect and the amount(s) in a single unit (such as one tablet or capsule) of the drug.

- **Purpose.** This refers to the product's action or category, such as fever reducer, cough suppressant, antihistamine, or antacid.

- **Uses.** Here you'll find a listing of the symptoms or medical conditions—such as runny nose, itching, headache, or heartburn—the product will treat or prevent.

- **Warnings.** Listed under "Warnings," you'll find information such as when or by whom the product should not be used; what situations or conditions might require you to get your doctor's advice before using the product; possible side effects or interactions; and when you should stop taking the product and/or call your doctor. Other precautions found here include a warning to seek medical guidance before using the drug if you are pregnant or breast-feeding, what to do in case of overdose, and a reminder to keep the drug out of children's reach.

- **Directions.** Here you'll find specific instructions, by age group, on how much of the drug to take, how to take it, how often, and for how long.

- **Other Information.** This section includes proper storage requirements and, where applicable, information about the amounts of certain ingredients (such as calcium, potassium, or sodium) that can have health effects.

- **Inactive Ingredients.** Here you will find a listing of ingredients in the product that are included for nontherapeutic effects, such as colorings, flavorings, stabilizers, preservatives, or carriers. This section is especially useful for people who have allergies.

Other important information you'll find on the label or packaging includes:

- The product's **expiration date** (the date after which you should not use the product), when applicable. Be sure to check that the date has not passed before you purchase the product.

- The **lot or batch code,** which is a number that the manufacturer can use to identify the specific product and trace its manufacturing history.

- The **name and address of the manufacturer, packer, or distributor** of the product.

- The **net amount or quantity of the package's contents,** which refers to how much of the product is in each package.

If you read the label on an OTC product and still have questions about the medicine or about whether it's appropriate and safe for you, talk to your pharmacist, doctor, or other health-care professional.

SAVING MONEY ON PRESCRIPTIONS

Many older adults pay for drugs out of pocket. Older adults also use more medications than any other age group, resulting in high pharmacy bills. You may be able to save on medications in a number of ways:

- Buy in bulk. Many drugs are cheaper in quantities of 100 or more. If you take the same drug dose on an ongoing basis, ask your doctor to prescribe a larger quantity. However, buy only as much of the medication as you can use before it expires.

- When trying a new prescription, ask your doctor for free samples. Pharmaceutical companies give lots of samples to physicians to promote their drugs. If samples are not available, ask the pharmacist to fill only enough medicine for a week or two. Don't buy a month's worth of expensive pills until you're sure your body will tolerate them. Many pharmacies have free delivery services so that you won't need to make an extra trip if the new medicine does work out.

- Ask if senior citizens get a discount.

- Ask if a less expensive generic equivalent will work just as well. Many patients fear that a generic isn't as good as "the real thing." This is not true. Generics contain the same medicines as their brand-name counterparts but are much cheaper because the generic companies don't have to pay for advertising or for research and development of new drugs.

- Shop around. Call a few pharmacies to see what they charge for your medication. Be sure you tell the pharmacist the name of the medication, the strength required, and the quantity you want. If you find a drug cheaper somewhere else, your regular pharmacist might match the price if you ask. Don't be "penny wise and pound foolish," though, by spreading your prescriptions among pharmacies all over town. Using one pharmacy is still the best way to avoid duplications and harmful interactions.

- When buying an OTC drug, ask your pharmacist to suggest the least expensive effective product. The pharmacist can often recommend a discount product that works just as well as a more expensive one.

- Check drug prices available through AARP (formerly American Association for Retired Persons) and disease-related organizations (for diabetes or arthritis, for example). Let your regular pharmacist know if you obtain medicine from these sources so they can be added to your drug profile.

- Investigate patient-assistance programs and discuss them with your doctor. Some helpful Web sites to check out are www.needymeds.com and www.pparx.org.

CHOOSING A PHARMACIST

A knowledgeable and helpful pharmacist can provide valuable information to anyone who is taking medication. Most pharmacists don't examine patients, but they can act as medical consultants to help prevent drug-interaction problems, side effects, and duplication of medications. You should choose a pharmacist based on much of the same criteria you would use to choose a physician: competence, service, convenience, and cost. Having all your prescriptions filled at one pharmacy means a centralized record of your medications exists no matter how many doctors you visit.

A pharmacist may have either a five-year bachelor of science (B.S.) degree in pharmacy or a six-year doctor of pharmacy degree (Pharm.D.). In addition to earning a pharmacy degree, the pharmacist must pass an exam from a state's board of pharmacy to be licensed to practice in that state.

Many pharmacies use technicians to help fill prescriptions. Some may have no formal pharmaceutical training, but every prescription they fill must be double-checked by a pharmacist. Some states allow more technicians per pharmacist than others.

When choosing a pharmacy, observe the way it operates. Is it clean and neat? Is it efficient? Can they find your order quickly, or do they seem disorganized? Is there a short or long wait for medicines? Does the pharmacy offer computer printouts with drug information, and can their computer system keep track of all the medications you take? Is the pharmacist available for private consultation? Does the pharmacist spend as much time with you as you need, or do you feel rushed out the door? Does the pharmacy have a free delivery service?

Large pharmacies often offer extended hours on weekends and even during the night. They carry many other household products, so one-stop shopping is easier. The drawback to a large pharmacy is that it will have a large staff, and you may never be served by the same pharmacist twice, or the staff may be too busy to talk with you about the special problems a medication poses.

A small pharmacy, however, is likely to have only one or two pharmacists on staff. They may get to know you individually, remember your special health needs, and alert you to potential problems with a given medication. They may also have more time to spend with you explaining how to take your medications. The drawback to a small pharmacy is that it is probably open only during regular business hours, and it may not stock nonmedical items, such as soap or razors.

Find a conveniently located pharmacy. If your drugstore is located across the street from your doctor's office or near where you live, you'll fill your prescriptions more easily than if you had to drive a long distance. Some pharmacies have drive-through windows so you can stay in the car while waiting. And many pharmacies have free delivery, making location less important.

An important consideration in purchasing medicine is cost. If you have an insurance plan that is honored at a certain pharmacy, then going there will definitely save money. If you have no drug insurance or it covers a percentage of your drugs no matter where you shop, you may want to choose your pharmacist based mainly on the cost of your drugs. Large pharmacies can usually offer lower prices than smaller pharmacies, but call around to check. Always balance the cost of the medicine with the availability of the pharmacist. Again, most experts recommend that you establish a relationship with your pharmacist just like you would with your doctor, because all three of you are important members of your health-care team.

BUYING PRESCRIPTION DRUGS ONLINE

The Internet has changed the way many of us live, including how we work and shop. The growth of the Internet has enabled consumers to purchase medicines online. There are online pharmacies that provide legitimate prescription services. Unfortunately, there are also questionable sites, which can make purchasing medicines online risky.

Some of the potential risks of buying medication from an illegal or questionable Web site include:

- Receiving fake, unapproved, outdated, or substandard products

- Little or no quality control in terms of the packaging, storage, and purity of product ingredients

- The possibility of an incorrect diagnosis from sites that inappropriately provide diagnoses and/or prescribe medications without having a health-care professional see the patient

- Obtaining an inappropriate medicine, such as one not suitable for the patient's condition or one that will interact dangerously with a patient's other medications or medical conditions

- Lack of assurance of confidentiality and other security issues

Here are some basic dos and don'ts to help you purchase medicines online safely:

DO talk to your health-care professional before using any medication for the first time. Take only medications that have been prescribed by your physician or other authorized health-care provider.

DO check with the National Association of Boards of Pharmacy, or NABP (www.nabp.net, 847-391-4406), to determine if a Web site is a licensed pharmacy in good standing. Some sites display the NABP VIPPS™ (Verified Internet Pharmacy Practice Sites) seal, which confirms that the site meets state and federal standards.

DO use sites that provide convenient access to a licensed pharmacist who can answer your questions and that can verify that a licensed pharmacist is actually filling the prescriptions.

DO buy only from Web sites that require a prescription from your physician or authorized health-care provider and that can verify the prescription before dispensing a medication. Look for a written verification policy posted on the site. You want to be sure you are getting what you are paying for from a legitimate source.

DO steer clear of Web sites that include undocumented case histories claiming "amazing" results.

DO avoid sites that do not identify with whom you are dealing and do not provide a U.S. address and phone number to contact if there's a problem.

DO beware of Web sites that advertise a "new cure" for a serious disorder or a quick cure-all for a wide range of medical problems. Remember: If it sounds too good to be true, it probably is.

DO look for easy-to-understand privacy and security policy statements.

DON'T buy from online sites that offer to sell you a drug that has not been approved by the FDA, sell you a prescription drug without a prescription, or prescribe a drug for you for the first time without requiring you to have your doctor examine you and write a prescription for the drug first.

DON'T purchase from foreign Web sites at this time, because it is illegal to import drugs from these sites, and they place you at greater risk for medical, legal, and financial difficulties. The FDA can't help you if you get ripped off.

DON'T do business with a Web site that doesn't offer you access to a registered pharmacist who can answer your questions.

DON'T buy from Web sites that use terms that sound impressive to disguise a lack of good science or those that claim the government, the medical profession, or research scientists have conspired to suppress a product.

DON'T buy from Web sites that lack a posted customer service policy.

DON'T give out any personal information—including Social Security number, credit card number, or health history—unless you are confident it is a legitimate business that will not share your personal information without your permission.

USING THIS BOOK
There are several ways to find information in this book. The drug profiles are listed in alphabetical order by generic name. If you know the brand name of your drug

but not its generic name, you can use the Brand Names Index (or the Canadian Brand Names Index if you live in Canada) to find the generic name. You can also simply refer to the General Index, which lists page numbers for both the generic and brand-name products profiled in this book.

There are several things to keep in mind when reading a profile. First, this book should never supersede your doctor's or pharmacist's instructions. Under "Administration," you'll find instructions on how the drug is usually prescribed and taken. However, your doctor or pharmacist may give you different instructions. Always follow your doctor's and/or pharmacist's instructions.

Second, under "Precautions," you'll find situations that warrant talking to your doctor about your treatment. These are not the only situations in which you should raise questions. Tell your doctor or pharmacist about all your health problems, medications, and concerns before you start taking a medication. Remember, during long-term therapy, new concerns may arise; *talk to your doctor or pharmacist whenever you have questions.*

Finally, under the heading "Side Effects," you'll find lists of side effects that should prompt you to contact your doctor or other health-care provider immediately, as well as lists of the most commonly reported side effects of each drug. It's important to note that not everyone who takes a specific medication will experience all—or even any—of the side effects that are listed, even the commonly reported ones. And while the side effects that are commonly reported may not require a doctor's attention, it is important to know that they may still impair your ability to perform certain activities or make you feel uncomfortable, at least temporarily (sometimes these side effects diminish or disappear as your body adjusts to the medication).

Indeed, you will find warnings regarding these side effects and advice to help you minimize them in the "Special Notes" section of each drug profile. In addition, many of the profiles have statements that are printed in bold. These are "black box warnings," the strongest advisory statement the FDA requires drug manufacturers to put on packaging. A black box warning means medical studies have shown that the drug carries a significant risk of serious or even life-threatening side effects. Black box warnings are serious and deserve your full attention, as well as the attention of your doctor and your pharmacist, so be sure to discuss with them any concerns you have.

If you have questions about any other side effect or find a side effect difficult to tolerate despite following the coping advice, you should certainly discuss it with your pharmacist and doctor. They may be able to suggest additional ways for you to prevent, minimize, or cope with a drug's side effects. And, if necessary, your doctor may be able to prescribe a substitute medication to see if you tolerate it any better.

albuterol

Brand Names:

AccuNeb	Ventolin
Proventil	Ventolin HFA
Proventil HFA	Volmax
Proventil Repetabs	VoSpire ER

Generic Available: yes

Type of Drug: bronchodilator

Used for: Treatment of asthma, emphysema, and chronic bronchitis.

How This Medication Works: Causes the passageways in the lungs to dilate.

Dosage Form and Strength:

- tablets (2 mg, 4 mg, 8 mg)
- syrup (2 mg/5 mL)
- inhaler (90 mcg/inhalation or 108 mcg/inhalation)
- nebulizer solution (0.63 mg/3 mL, 1.25 mg/3 mL)

Storage:

- room temperature
- protect from moisture—do not store in bathroom or kitchen

Administration:

- When using the inhaler, allow at least 2 minutes between inhalations (puffs).
- If you use more than one inhaler, it is important to administer them in the correct order. If you are using albuterol and another inhaler, use the

albuterol first. Wait at least 5 minutes before
inhaling the second medication.
- Have your doctor or pharmacist demonstrate proper
  use of the inhaler, and make sure they have you
  practice your technique in front of them.
- If your inhaler has not been used for more than
  2 weeks, prime it by shaking it and spraying 2 test
  sprays in the air before administering your dose.
- Take a missed dose as soon as possible. However,
  if it is almost time for the next dose, skip the missed
  dose and return to your regular dosing schedule.

Precautions:
Do not use if:
- you are allergic to albuterol, epinephrine,
  metaproterenol, salmeterol, or terbutaline.

Talk to your doctor if:
- you have diabetes, heart disease, high blood
  pressure (hypertension), problems with circulation
  or blood vessels, seizures, or thyroid disease.
- you are taking any other medications,
  especially for heart disease, high blood
  pressure (hypertension), migraine headaches, or
  depression.

Side Effects:
*Contact your health-care provider immediately if you
experience:*
- skin rash, itching, or hives.
- difficulty breathing or increased wheezing.
- bluish coloring of the skin.
- swelling of the face, lips, or eyelids.
- fainting or dizziness.

- chest discomfort or pressure.
- irregular heartbeat.
- hallucinations.

Commonly reported side effects:
- nervousness
- tremor or trembling
- coughing
- unpleasant taste
- flushing or redness of the face
- headache
- palpitations
- increase in blood pressure or pulse
- nausea and/or vomiting
- insomnia

Time Required for Drug to Take Effect:

Inhaled medications start to work within 60 seconds of a dose, and tablets within about 2 to 3 hours.

Symptoms of Overdose:

- chest discomfort or pressure
- irregular heartbeat
- severe nausea and/or vomiting
- severe difficulty breathing
- severe tremor or trembling
- unusual paleness and coldness of skin

Special Notes:

- If you are using albuterol as treatment for acute attacks or to prevent exercise-induced asthma, keep your inhaler with you at all times.
- Sometimes a spacer device is used with your inhaler. A spacer helps the drug get beyond the mouth or throat and into the lungs.

- Consult your physician or pharmacist before using any over-the-counter drugs.
- Limit caffeine while taking this drug; it can aggravate nervousness and fast heart rate.
- Keep track of how many inhalations are left, and get your medication refilled about 1 week before you expect to run out.

alendronate

Brand Names: Fosamax, Fosamax Plus D

Generic Available: no

Type of Drug: biphosphonate

Used for: Prevention and treatment of osteoporosis and treatment of Paget's disease of the bone.

How This Medication Works: Reduces rate of bone loss (resorption), which makes bones stronger.

Dosage Form and Strength:
- tablets (5 mg, 10 mg, 35 mg, 40 mg, 70 mg)
- Plus D tablets (70 mg alendronate/2,800 IU cholecalciferol)
- solution (70 mg/75 mL)

Storage:
- room temperature
- tightly closed
- protect from light

Administration:
- For osteoporosis, the usual dose is 5 or 10 mg daily or 35 or 70 mg weekly. For Paget's disease, usual dose is 40 mg daily for 6 months.
- Take in the morning with an 8-ounce glass of water at least 30 minutes before food, beverages, or other medication.
- Stay upright for 30 minutes after taking a dose.
- Take a missed dose as soon as possible. However, if it is almost time for the next dose, skip the missed dose and return to your regular dosing schedule.

Precautions:
Do not use if:
- you have had a severe allergic reaction to alendronate or etidronate.
- you have severe kidney disease.
- you have low calcium levels (hypocalcemia).
- you have trouble swallowing.
- you can't sit upright for at least 30 minutes.

Talk to your doctor if:
- you have kidney disease or ulcers.
- you are taking any other medication, especially calcium supplements.

Side Effects:
Contact your health-care provider immediately if you experience:
- chest or stomach pain.
- throat pain or pain when swallowing.
- low calcium levels (hypocalcemia).
- severe nausea or vomiting.
- jaw pain or severe joint pain.

Commonly reported side effects:
- temporary increase in bone pain
- constipation or diarrhea
- headache
- muscle pain
- abdominal discomfort

Time Required for Drug to Take Effect: For osteoporosis, 3 to 6 weeks. For Paget's, 3 to 6 months.

Symptoms of Overdose: No information currently available; contact local poison control center.

Special Notes:
- Consult your doctor about taking supplements of calcium and vitamin D.
- If you use a calcium supplement, take it at least 2 hours after your dose of alendronate.

alfuzosin

Brand Name: Uroxatral

Generic Available: no

Type of Drug: alpha-1 blocker

Used for: Treatment of an enlarged prostate.

How This Medication Works: Relaxes the muscles of the prostate, improving urinary symptoms.

Dosage Form and Strength: 24-hour tablets (10 mg)

Storage:
- room temperature
- protect from moisture—do not store in bathroom or kitchen

Administration:
- Usually taken once daily.
- Take 30 minutes after the same meal every day.
- Swallow tablet whole; do not crush or chew.
- Drink plenty of noncaffeinated liquids, unless told otherwise by your health-care provider.
- Take a missed dose as soon as possible. However, if it is almost time for the next dose, skip the missed dose and return to your regular dosing schedule.

Precautions:
Do not use if:
- you are allergic to alfuzosin.
- you are taking medications for erectile dysfunction, including sildenafil (Viagra), tadalafil (Cialis), or vardenafil (Levitra).

Talk to your doctor if:
- you are taking blood pressure medications.
- you are taking other alpha-blocker medicines, such as prazosin (Minipress), terazosin (Hytrin), or doxazosin (Cardura).
- you are taking certain medicines to treat yeast infections, including itraconazole (Sporanox) and ketoconazole (Nizoral).
- you are taking protease inhibitors.
- you have a history of angina or liver disease.

Side Effects:

Contact your health-care provider immediately if you experience:
- signs of a life-threatening reaction, which include wheezing; chest tightness; itching; or swelling of face, lips, tongue, or throat.
- a rash.
- severe dizziness or if you pass out.
- new or worsening chest pain.
- a severe headache.
- urinary symptoms that worsen or if you cannot pass urine.

Commonly reported side effects:
- dizziness
- headache
- nasal congestion or runny nose
- abnormal ejaculation

Time Required for Drug to Take Effect: Starts to work within 8 hours of first dose, but it may require 1 week of treatment to reach maximum effectiveness.

Symptoms of Overdose:
- headache
- low blood pressure
- dizziness

Special Notes:
- May cause drowsiness, dizziness, or impaired judgment. Be careful driving or engaging in tasks that require alertness until you know how your body responds to this drug.

- Dizziness may occur with the first few doses you take, or if you have forgotten several doses and restart the therapy; use caution.
- Be careful in hot weather—drink plenty of fluids to prevent dehydration.
- Check your blood pressure on a regular basis (talk with your physician about how often).
- This medication is usually prescribed to men; if you are a woman and have been prescribed this medication, talk with your health-care provider to be sure this is the right medication for you.
- Do not consume grapefruit or grapefruit juice while taking this drug.
- Do not take saw palmetto in combination with this medication, unless the same health-care provider prescribes both.

allopurinol

Brand Names: Aloprim, Zyloprim

Generic Available: yes

Type of Drug: antigout

Used for: Treatment of gout and kidney stones and reduction of uric acid levels.

How This Medication Works: Inhibits the formation of uric acid.

Dosage Form and Strength: tablets (100 mg, 300 mg)

Storage:
- room temperature
- tightly closed
- protect from light and moisture—do not store in bathroom or kitchen

Administration:
- Only for prevention of gout attacks, not for acute attacks, which it may actually worsen.
- Drink plenty of liquids (eight 8-ounce glasses daily) while taking this drug, unless your health-care provider instructs otherwise.
- May be taken without regard to meals, but take with food or milk if stomach upset occurs.
- Your doctor may start you on a lower dose and increase it slowly to minimize side effects.
- Take a missed dose as soon as possible. However, if it is almost time for the next dose, skip the missed dose and return to your regular dosing schedule.

Precautions:
Do not use if:
- you are allergic to allopurinol.

Talk to your doctor if:
- you have diabetes, high blood pressure (hypertension), or kidney disease.
- you are taking any other medications, especially anticoagulants (such as warfarin), azathioprine, or mercaptopurine.

Side Effects:
Contact your health-care provider immediately if you experience:
- skin rash, hives, or itching.

- blood in urine or stool.
- nausea and/or vomiting.
- muscle aches or numbness.
- difficult or painful urination.
- difficulty breathing.
- swelling or weight gain.
- unusual bleeding or bruising.
- yellowing of the skin or eyes.

Commonly reported side effects:
- diarrhea
- drowsiness
- headache
- nausea and/or vomiting
- hair loss

Time Required for Drug to Take Effect: Starts
to work within 1 to 2 hours of first dose, but it usually takes 1 to 3 weeks of treatment to reach maximum effectiveness.

Symptoms of Overdose: No specific symptoms.

Special Notes:
- You may be required to have blood tests to determine the amount of uric acid in your blood.
- Check with your physician or pharmacist before using any over-the-counter medications while taking this drug.
- This drug may cause drowsiness. Use caution when driving or operating dangerous machinery.
- Do not consume alcohol while taking this drug.
- Avoid taking too much vitamin C while on this drug. It may increase the risk of kidney stones.

- Do not take an antacid within 6 hours of taking this drug; it may make this drug less effective.

alprazolam

Brand Names:
Niravam
Xanax
Xanax XR

Generic Available: yes

Type of Drug: antianxiety (benzodiazepine)

Used for: Treatment of anxiety, panic disorders, and post-traumatic stress syndrome.

How This Medication Works: Depresses central nervous system to reduce anxiety or control panic.

Dosage Form and Strength:
- tablets (0.25 mg, 0.5 mg, 1 mg, 2 mg)
- oral solution (1 mg/mL)
- extended-release tablets (0.5 mg, 1 mg, 2 mg, 3 mg)

Storage:
- room temperature
- tightly closed

Administration:
- Regular tablets and solution usually taken 2 to 3 times daily; extended-release tablets once daily.
- Swallow extended-release tablets whole; do not crush, break, or chew.

- Shake liquid well before using.
- May be taken without regard to meals.
- Take a missed dose as soon as possible. However, if it is almost time for the next dose, skip the missed dose and return to your regular dosing schedule.

Precautions:

Do not use if:
- you have had an allergic reaction to alprazolam or to other medications in the benzodiazepine family, such as diazepam, lorazepam, or oxazepam.

Talk to your doctor if:
- you are taking other medications that may depress the central nervous system.
- you have asthma or other lung problems, kidney disease, liver disease, or narrow-angle glaucoma.
- you have been told that you snore.
- you take ketoconazole or itraconazole.

Side Effects:

Contact your health-care provider immediately if you experience:
- confusion.
- difficulty concentrating.
- seizures.
- hallucinations.
- a rash.

Commonly reported side effects:
- dizziness or drowsiness
- slurred speech
- blurred vision

- dry mouth
- change in sexual desire or ability

Time Required for Drug to Take Effect: Starts
to work within hours of taking a dose.

Symptoms of Overdose:
- continuing or worsening confusion or slurred speech
- severe weakness or drowsiness
- shortness of breath

Special Notes:
- Do not stop taking this drug without first talking with your doctor.
- This drug may be habit-forming if you use it for a long period of time.
- This medication may cause drowsiness. Avoid activities requiring mental alertness, such as driving a car or operating dangerous machinery.
- Do not drink alcohol while taking this drug.
- Benzodiazepines have been associated with falls and should be used with extra caution in the elderly.
- Sound-alike/look-alike warning: Xanax may be confused with Xopenex, Zantac, or Zyrtec.

amiodarone

Brand Names: Cordarone, Pacerone

Generic Available: yes

Type of Drug: antiarrhythmic

Used for: Treatment of seriously abnormal heart rhythms (atrial fibrillation, ventricular tachycardia). **This medication has a heightened risk of causing significant patient harm when used incorrectly.**

How This Medication Works: Slows heart rate by decreasing the effect of chemicals on the heart muscle.

Dosage Form and Strength:
- tablets (100 mg, 200 mg, 400 mg)
- solution (50 mg/mL)

Storage:
- room temperature
- tightly closed
- protect from moisture—do not store in bathroom or kitchen

Administration:
- Usually taken once or twice daily.
- You may have to take several tablets daily for the first few weeks. This is called a loading dose.
- May be taken with food if stomach upset occurs.
- Take a missed dose as soon as possible. However, if it is almost time for the next dose, skip the missed dose and return to your regular dosing schedule.

Precautions:
Do not use if:
- you are allergic to amiodarone.
- you have a slow heartbeat without a pacemaker.

Talk to your doctor if:
- you are taking warfarin, digoxin, phenytoin, procainamide, quinidine, theophylline, or any medicine in the beta-blocker family (such as atenolol, metoprolol, and propranolol).
- you have ever had heart block or a very slow heartbeat.
- you have liver or lung disease.

Side Effects:

Contact your health-care provider immediately if you experience:
- chest pain or belly pain.
- nervousness or shakiness.
- wheezing, cough, and shortness of breath.
- severe nausea and/or vomiting.
- dark urine or yellowing of the eyes or skin.
- a rash.

Commonly reported side effects:
- dry eyes
- nausea and/or vomiting
- constipation
- loss of appetite
- lack of coordination, dizziness, or fatigue
- insomnia
- tremor

Time Required for Drug to Take Effect: Starts working within 2 to 3 days of first dose, but it takes 3 to 6 weeks of treatment to reach maximum effectiveness.

Symptoms of Overdose:
- extremely slow heartbeat

- low blood pressure, marked by light-headedness or dizziness

Special Notes:
- Your doctor should monitor your thyroid, liver function, and lung function while you are taking amiodarone. Talk with your doctor to ensure proper monitoring.
- Use a sunblock with at least SPF 15 when outside because amiodarone may increase your sensitivity to the sun.
- A blue-gray discoloration of sun-exposed skin may develop during long-term treatment. This cosmetic change causes no physical harm and slowly fades in most cases after treatment ends; but you should still inform your doctor if you develop this discoloration.
- Do not consume grapefruit or grapefruit juice while taking this drug.

amitriptyline

Brand Name: Elavil

Generic Available: yes

Type of Drug: tricyclic antidepressant

Used for: Treatment of depression and chronic pain, and prevention of migraine headaches.

How This Medication Works: Increases the action of the chemicals norepinephrine and serotonin in the brain.

Dosage Form and Strength: tablets (10 mg, 25 mg, 50 mg, 75 mg, 100 mg, 150 mg)

Storage:
- room temperature
- tightly closed

Administration:
- Usually taken at bedtime.
- May be prescribed 2 to 3 times daily, depending on the dose and your response to the medicine.
- May be taken with or without food.
- Take a missed dose as soon as possible. However, if it is almost time for the next dose, skip the missed dose and return to your regular dosing schedule.

Precautions:
Do not use if:
- you are allergic to amitriptyline or any other tricyclic antidepressant, such as imipramine.
- you are also taking a monoamine oxidase (MAO) inhibitor, such as phenelzine or selegiline.

Talk to your doctor if:
- you have closed-angle glaucoma, heart disease, urinary or prostate problems, severe constipation, breathing problems, seizures, or diabetes.
- you are taking cimetidine, clonidine, methyldopa, or any sedative, muscle relaxant, antihistamine, decongestant, or stimulant, or if you drink alcohol.

Side Effects:
Contact your health-care provider immediately if you experience:
- **the desire to harm yourself.**

- fainting or dizziness leading to falls.
- rapid heartbeat.
- chest pain.
- confusion or hallucinations.
- severe constipation or difficulty urinating.
- a rash.
- severe sedation.
- fever.
- restlessness and agitation.

Commonly reported side effects:
- drowsiness
- dry mouth
- mild constipation
- weight gain
- unpleasant taste
- stomach upset

Time Required for Drug to Take Effect: May
take 4 to 8 weeks of treatment for full antidepressant benefit; certain types of pain may improve with 1 to 2 weeks of treatment.

Symptoms of Overdose:
- confusion or hallucinations
- seizures
- extreme sedation
- rapid heartbeat
- difficulty breathing
- inability to urinate
- severe constipation
- dilated pupils

Call 911 immediately if you suspect an overdose.

Special Notes:

- Suicidal thoughts are a serious symptom of depression. If you are planning to harm yourself, call 911 immediately.
- Know which "target symptoms" (restlessness, worry, fear, or changes in sleep or appetite) you are being treated for and be prepared to tell your doctor if your target symptoms are improving, worsening, or unchanged.
- Avoid driving or other tasks requiring alertness until you see how this medicine affects you.
- Check with your physician or pharmacist before using any over-the-counter medications while taking this drug.
- Do not discontinue or increase your dose without first talking with your doctor.
- If you have diabetes, you may need to check your blood glucose more frequently.
- Use a sunblock with at least SPF 15 when outside because amitriptyline may increase your sensitivity to the sun.

amlodipine

Brand Name: Norvasc

Generic Available: yes

Type of Drug: calcium channel blocker

Used for: Treatment of high blood pressure (hypertension), and relief of angina (chest pain or pressure).

How This Medication Works: Inhibits smooth muscle contraction and causes blood vessels to dilate.

Dosage Form and Strength: tablets (2.5 mg, 5 mg, 10 mg)

Storage:
- room temperature
- protect from moisture—do not store in bathroom or kitchen

Administration:
- Do not take more often than once every 24 hours unless directed to by your health-care provider.
- Take at the same time every day.
- Take with food or water if stomach upset occurs.
- Take a missed dose as soon as possible. However, if it is almost time for the next dose, skip the missed dose and return to your regular dosing schedule.

Precautions:
Do not use if:
- you have ever had an allergic reaction to amlodipine or another calcium channel blocker, such as felodipine.

Talk to your doctor if:
- you have heart disease, kidney or liver disease, or problems with circulation or your blood vessels.
- you are taking any other medications, especially medications for the heart or blood pressure such as carbamazepine, cyclosporin, or warfarin.

Side Effects:

Contact your health-care provider immediately if you experience:

- skin rash or itching.
- difficulty breathing.
- chest pressure or discomfort.
- fainting.
- swelling of the ankles, feet, or lower legs.

Commonly reported side effects:

- low blood pressure, marked by light-headedness or dizziness
- headache
- sexual dysfunction (impotence)
- flushing
- drowsiness or fatigue
- nausea
- constipation

Time Required for Drug to Take Effect: Starts
to work within 1 to 2 days of first dose, but it may take 2 to 4 weeks of treatment for maximum effect.

Symptoms of Overdose:

- nausea and/or vomiting
- weakness or dizziness
- slow heartbeat or palpitations
- confusion, slurred speech
- loss of consciousness

Special Notes:

- Amlodipine is not a cure, and you may have to take this medication for a long time.
- To avoid dizziness, rise slowly over several minutes from a sitting or lying position.

- If you notice dizziness, avoid driving and other activities that require mental alertness.
- Constipation, a minor side effect, may be relieved by drinking more water, eating foods that are high in fiber (vegetables, fruits, bran), and exercising.
- Check with your physician or pharmacist before using any over-the-counter medications while taking this drug.
- Avoid becoming dehydrated or overheated. Drink plenty of fluids, especially in hot weather.
- Do not consume grapefruit or grapefruit juice while taking this drug.

amlodipine and benazepril combination

Brand Name: Lotrel

Generic Available: no

Type of Drug: antihypertensive combination (calcium channel blocker and angiotensin-converting enzyme [ACE] inhibitor)

Used for: Treatment of high blood pressure (hypertension).

How This Medication Works: Amlodipine inhibits smooth muscle contraction and causes blood vessels to dilate. Benazepril lowers blood pressure by decreasing production of angiotensin, a strong chemical that causes blood vessels to constrict.

Dosage Form and Strength: capsules
(2.5 mg amlodipine/10 mg benazepril, 5 mg/10 mg,
5 mg/20 mg, 5 mg/40 mg, 10 mg/20 mg, 10 mg/40 mg)

Storage:
- room temperature
- protect from light and moisture—do not store in
  bathroom or kitchen

Administration:
- Usually taken once daily.
- Take at a similar time each day.
- May be taken without regard to meals, but take
  with food if stomach upset occurs.
- Take a missed dose as soon as possible. However,
  if it is almost time for the next dose, skip the
  missed dose and return to your regular dosing
  schedule.
- Do not take more than once every 24 hours,
  unless instructed to by your health-care provider.

Precautions:
Do not use if:
- **you are pregnant or could become pregnant.**
- you have an allergy to amlodipine, benazepril, or
  any calcium channel blocker (such as felodipine)
  or ACE inhibitor (such as lisinopril, enalapril, or
  ramipril).
- you have bilateral renal artery stenosis.

Talk to your doctor if:
- you have severe aortic stenosis.
- you have severe liver or kidney disease.
- you have low blood pressure.
- you become dehydrated.

- you take allopurinol, lithium, potassium supplements, or spironolactone.

Side Effects:

Contact your health-care provider immediately if you experience:

- signs of a life-threatening reaction, which include fever; wheezing; chest tightness; and itching or swelling of face, lips, tongue, or throat.
- severe dizziness or fainting.
- severe headache.
- severe swelling of feet, ankles, or legs.
- a rash.

Commonly reported side effects:

- dizziness or light-headedness
- headache
- constipation
- abnormal taste
- mild swelling of feet, ankles, or legs
- cough

Time Required for Drug to Take Effect: Starts lowering blood pressure within 24 hours of first dose.

Symptoms of Overdose:

- low blood pressure
- slow pulse
- nausea and/or vomiting
- confusion

Special Notes:

- Do not use potassium-containing salt substitutes while taking this drug.

- Follow a diet plan and exercise program recommended by your health-care provider.
- To avoid dizziness, rise slowly over several minutes from a sitting or lying position.
- More liquids, regular exercise, and a fiber-containing diet may help with constipation.
- Notify your health-care provider if you develop a persistent cough that becomes bothersome.
- Talk to your doctor about the need for bloodwork while you take this drug.

amoxicillin

Brand Names:

Amoxil

Moxilin

Polymox

Trimox

Generic Available: yes

Type of Drug: antibiotic

Used for: Treatment of bacterial infections.

How this Medication Works: Kills bacteria by damaging their cell walls.

Dosage Form and Strength:

- tablets (125 mg, 250 mg, 400 mg, 500 mg, 875 mg)
- capsules (250 mg, 500 mg)
- suspension (125 mg/5 mL, 250 mg/5 mL, 400 mg/5 mL)

Storage:

Capsules and tablets:

- room temperature

- tightly closed
- protect from moisture—do not store in bathroom or kitchen

Suspension:
- refrigerated
- tightly closed

Administration:
- Usually taken 3 times daily.
- May be taken without regard to meals.
- Take at even intervals, every 8 hours.
- Take until completely gone, even if symptoms disappear.
- Shake liquid form well before measuring dose.
- Tablets may be chewed thoroughly and swallowed.
- Take a missed dose as soon as possible. However, if it is almost time for the next dose, skip the missed dose and return to your regular dosing schedule.

Precautions:
Do not use if:
- you are allergic to amoxicillin or penicillin.

Talk to your doctor if:
- you have an allergy to cephalosporins, such as cephalexin, cefaclor, cefadroxil, or cefuroxime.
- you are taking allopurinol, warfarin, or other antibiotics.

Side Effects:
Contact your health-care provider immediately if you experience:
- a rash or hives.

- severe diarrhea.
- shortness of breath or wheezing.
- vaginal itching or discomfort.
- unusual bleeding or bruising.

Commonly reported side effects:
- diarrhea
- abnormal taste
- dry mouth
- nausea

Time Required for Drug to Take Effect: Starts
killing bacteria within hours after first dose, but you
must finish the prescribed amount of medicine, even if
symptoms disappear.

Symptoms of Overdose:
- hallucinations
- seizures
- lethargy or confusion
- coma

Special Notes:
- Do not use for infections other than the one for
  which it was prescribed.
- Discard liquid after 7 days (14 days, if refrigerated).
- Long-term use may lead to bacterial resistance.
- Eating yogurt with active cultures may help relieve
  mild diarrhea. Contact your health-care provider
  if diarrhea persists.

ampicillin

Brand Name: Principen

Generic Available: yes

Type of Drug: antibiotic

Used for: Treatment of bacterial infections.

How This Medication Works: Kills bacteria by damaging their cell walls.

Dosage Form and Strength:
- capsules (250 mg, 500 mg)
- suspension (125 mg/5 mL, 250 mg/5 mL, 500 mg/5 mL)

Storage:
Capsules:
- room temperature
- tightly closed
- protect from moisture—do not store in bathroom or kitchen

Suspension:
- refrigerated
- tightly closed

Administration:
- Usually taken 3 to 4 times daily.
- Take on an empty stomach, 1 hour before or 2 hours after meals.
- Take at even intervals (every 6 or 8 hours).
- Take until completely gone, even if symptoms disappear.
- Take a missed dose as soon as possible. However, if it is almost time for the next dose, skip the missed dose and return to your dosing schedule.
- Shake liquid well before measuring dose.

Precautions:

Do not use if:
- you are allergic to ampicillin or penicillin.

Talk to your doctor if:
- you are allergic to any of the cephalosporins, such as cephalexin, cefaclor, cefadroxil, or cefuroxime.
- you are taking another antibiotic, allopurinol, or warfarin.

Side Effects:

Contact your health-care provider immediately if you experience:
- a rash or hives.
- severe diarrhea.
- shortness of breath or wheezing.
- vaginal itching or discomfort.
- unusual bleeding or bruising.

Commonly reported side effects:
- diarrhea
- abnormal taste
- dry mouth
- nausea

Time Required for Drug to Take Effect:

Begins to kill bacteria within hours after first dose, but you must finish the prescribed amount of medicine, even if symptoms disappear.

Symptoms of Overdose:
- hallucinations
- seizures
- lethargy
- confusion
- coma

Special Notes:
- Do not use for infections other than the one for which it was prescribed.
- Discard suspension after 7 days (after 14 days, if kept refrigerated).
- Long-term use may lead to bacterial resistance to ampicillin.
- Eating yogurt with active cultures may help relieve mild diarrhea. Contact your health-care provider if diarrhea persists.

anastrozole

Brand Name: Arimidex

Generic Available: no

Type of Drug: antineoplastic agent (aromatase inhibitor)

Used for: Treatment of breast cancer in postmenopausal women.

How This Medication Works: Prevents estrogen from feeding estrogen-hungry cancer cells, and decreases the spread of the cancer.

Dosage Form and Strength: tablets (1 mg)

Storage:
- room temperature
- protect from moisture—do not store in bathroom or kitchen

Administration:
- Usually taken once daily.
- May be taken without regard to meals, but take with food if stomach upset occurs.
- Take a missed dose as soon as possible. However, if it is almost time for the next dose, skip the missed dose and return to your regular dosing schedule.

Precautions:
Do not use if:
- you have a hypersensitivity to anastrozole.
- you are or may be pregnant.

Talk to your doctor if:
- you have high blood pressure or high blood cholesterol levels.
- you are taking tamoxifen.
- you have any circulation problems or history of blood clots.

Side Effects:
Contact your health-care provider immediately if you experience:
- signs of a life-threatening reaction, which include fever; wheezing; chest tightness; and itching or swelling of face, lips, tongue, or throat.
- chest pain or pressure or difficulty breathing.
- swelling or pain in the legs or arms.
- severe headache.
- signs or symptoms of depression, suicidal thoughts, or nervousness.
- severe nausea, vomiting, or diarrhea.
- vaginal itching or discharge.

Commonly reported side effects:
- flushing
- tiredness or weakness
- headache
- joint pain
- cough
- dizziness or drowsiness

Time Required for Drug to Take Effect: Starts working within 24 hours of first dose, but it takes up to 2 weeks of treatment to reach maximum effectiveness.

Symptoms of Overdose: severe irritation of the stomach, including stomach pain and bleeding

Special Notes:
- Total and LDL cholesterol levels may increase in patients receiving anastrozole.
- Anastrozole may be associated with a reduction in bone mineral density; talk to your health-care provider about osteoporosis prevention.
- Avoid herbal products such as black cohosh, hops, licorice, red clover, thyme, and dong quai while taking anastrozole.
- The safety and effectiveness of this medication in premenopausal women has not been established.

aspirin

Brand Names:

Ascriptin	Bufferin
Bayer	Ecotrin

Generic Available: yes

Type of Drug: antiplatelet agent

Used for: Prevention of strokes and heart attacks; treatment of pain, inflammation, and fever.

How This Medication Works: Prevents platelets from becoming sticky and clumping together to form clots. Also blocks production and release of chemicals that cause pain and inflammation.

Dosage Form and Strength: tablets (81 mg, 162 mg, 325 mg, 500 mg, 650 mg)

Storage:
- room temperature
- protect from light and moisture—do not store in bathroom or kitchen

Administration:
- Usually taken once daily for prevention of heart attack and stroke.
- Take with food to reduce stomach upset.
- Swallow enteric-coated and long-acting products whole; do not chew, break, or crush.
- Chew or crush chewable tablet well.
- Take a missed dose as soon as possible. However, if it is almost time for the next dose, skip the missed dose and return to your regular dosing schedule.

Precautions:
Do not use if:
- you are allergic to aspirin.
- you experience allergic-type reactions, including asthma or itching, to nonsteroidal

anti-inflammatory drugs (such as Motrin, Advil, or Naprosyn).
- you have the syndrome consisting of asthma, rhinitis, and nasal polyps.

Talk to your doctor if:
- you use other aspirin-containing products; other pain medicines; blood thinners; or garlic, ginseng, ginkgo, or vitamin E supplements.
- you have liver disease.
- you drink more than 3 alcoholic beverages a day.
- you have stomach discomfort, ulcers, or a history of ulcers.
- you take ibuprofen, because ibuprofen might interfere with aspirin's effectiveness.

Side Effects:

Contact your health-care provider immediately if you experience:
- severe stomach pain, dark and tarry stools, or vomiting of material that looks like coffee grounds.
- a change in strength on one side of your body greater than on the other side, difficulty speaking or thinking, or a change in balance or vision.
- unusual bruising or bleeding.
- chest pain or pressure.
- ringing in the ears.

Commonly reported side effects:
- stomach discomfort or heartburn
- nausea and/or vomiting

Time Required for Drug to Take Effect: Starts
working within hours of taking a dose.

Symptoms of Overdose:
- low blood pressure
- feelings of dizziness
- flushing
- sweating
- unusual bruising or bleeding
- stomach pain

Special Notes:
- Tell your dentist, surgeon, and other health-care providers that you use this medicine.
- While taking this drug, consult your health-care provider or pharmacist before using any other over-the-counter medications.
- Avoid taking additional over-the-counter products that contain aspirin.
- Limit alcohol intake while on this medication.

aspirin and extended-release dipyridamole combination

Brand Name: Aggrenox

Generic Available: no

Type of Drug: antiplatelet agent

Used for: Prevention of strokes.

How This Medication Works: Prevents platelets from becoming sticky and clumping together to form clots, which can cause a stroke.

Dosage Form and Strength: capsules (200 mg extended-release dipyridamole/25 mg aspirin)

Storage:
- room temperature
- protect from light and moisture—do not store in bathroom or kitchen

Administration:
- Usual dose is 1 capsule in the morning and 1 in the evening.
- Swallow capsules whole; do not chew, break, or crush.
- May be taken without regard to meals, but take with food if stomach upset occurs.
- Take a missed dose as soon as possible. However, if it is almost time for the next dose, skip the missed dose and return to your regular dosing schedule.

Precautions:
Do not use if:
- you have a hypersensitivity to aspirin or dipyridamole.
- you experience allergic-type reactions, including asthma or itching, to nonsteroidal anti-inflammatory drugs (such as Motrin, Advil, or Naprosyn).
- you have the syndrome consisting of asthma, rhinitis, and nasal polyps.

Talk to your doctor if:
- you use other aspirin-containing products; other pain medicines; blood thinners; or garlic, ginseng, ginkgo, or vitamin E supplements.

- you have liver disease.
- you drink more than 3 alcoholic beverages a day.
- you have stomach discomfort, ulcers, or a history of ulcers.
- you take ibuprofen, because ibuprofen might make this drug less effective.

Side Effects:

Contact your health-care provider immediately if you experience:

- severe stomach pain, dark and tarry stools, or vomiting of material that looks like coffee grounds.
- a change in strength on one side of your body greater than on the other side, difficulty speaking or thinking, change in balance, or change in vision.
- unusual bruising or bleeding.
- chest pain or pressure.

Commonly reported side effects:

- headache
- stomach discomfort or heartburn
- nausea and/or vomiting
- diarrhea
- fatigue

Time Required for Drug to Take Effect: Starts working within hours of taking a dose.

Symptoms of Overdose:

- low blood pressure
- dizziness
- flushing, sweating
- unusual bruising or bleeding
- stomach pain

Special Notes:

- Tell your dentist, surgeon, and other health-care providers that you use this medicine.
- While taking this drug, consult your health-care provider or pharmacist before using any over-the-counter medications, and avoid taking additional over-the-counter products that contain aspirin.
- Limit alcohol intake while on this medication.

atenolol

Brand Name: Tenormin

Generic Available: yes

Type of Drug: beta-adrenergic blocking agent, or beta-blocker

Used for: Relief of angina (chest pain or pressure), and treatment of high blood pressure (hypertension) and heart attacks.

How This Medication Works: Inhibits certain hormones that increase heart rate and blood pressure.

Dosage Form and Strength: tablets (25 mg, 50 mg, 100 mg)

Storage:

- room temperature
- protect from moisture—do not store in bathroom or kitchen

Administration:
- For high blood pressure and angina, usually taken once daily.
- Take at the same time every day.
- In cases of heart attack, limited to hospital use.
- May be taken with or without food.
- Take a missed dose as soon as possible. However, if it is almost time for the next dose, skip the missed dose and return to your regular dosing schedule.

Precautions:
Do not use if:
- you have ever had an allergic reaction to atenolol or another beta-blocker, such as metoprolol or propranolol.

Talk to your doctor if:
- you are taking any other medications.
- you have lung disease or diabetes.

Side Effects:
Contact your health-care provider immediately if you experience:
- skin rash or itching.
- difficulty breathing.
- confusion, hallucinations, or nightmares.
- palpitations or irregular heartbeat.
- depression or sad mood.
- swelling of feet, ankles, or lower legs.
- chest pressure or discomfort.
- unusual bleeding or bruising.

Commonly reported side effects:
- insomnia

- cold hands and feet
- low blood pressure, marked by dizziness or light-headedness
- drowsiness
- nervousness, anxiety
- nausea
- diarrhea
- constipation
- sexual dysfunction

Time Required for Drug to Take Effect: Starts
to work within 1 to 2 hours of first dose but may take 2 weeks of treatment to reach maximum effectiveness.

Symptoms of Overdose:
- slow or irregular heartbeat
- fainting or severe dizziness
- difficulty breathing or wheezing
- seizures
- blue tint to nail beds or palms

Special Notes:
- **Do not stop taking this medication without consulting your doctor first, because serious side effects may occur.**
- To avoid dizziness while taking this drug, rise slowly over several minutes from a sitting or lying position.
- If you notice dizziness, avoid activities that require mental alertness such as driving a car or operating dangerous machinery.
- Atenolol is not a cure, and you may have to take this medication for a long time.

- Check with your physician or pharmacist before using any over-the-counter medications while taking this drug.
- Older patients may be more sensitive to cold temperatures while on this medication.

atorvastatin

Brand Name: Lipitor

Generic Available: no

Type of Drug: antihyperlipidemic agent (HMG-CoA reductase inhibitor)

Used for: Treatment of high blood cholesterol levels, and prevention of heart attack and stroke.

How This Medication Works: Reduces LDL (bad) cholesterol production in the body.

Dosage Form and Strength: tablets (10 mg, 20 mg, 40 mg, 80 mg)

Storage:
- room temperature
- protect from moisture—do not store in bathroom or kitchen

Administration:
- Usually taken once daily.
- Take at a similar time each day.
- May be taken without regard to meals, but take with food if stomach upset occurs.

- Take a missed dose as soon as possible. However, if it is almost time for the next dose, skip the missed dose and return to your regular dosing schedule.
- Take this medicine even if you feel well. Most people with this condition do not feel sick.

Precautions:

Do not use if:
- you are allergic to atorvastatin.
- you have severe liver disease.
- you are or may be pregnant.

Talk to your doctor if:
- you have active liver disease or increased liver enzymes.
- you take other cholesterol medications, niacin, cyclosporine, erythromycin, oral antifungals, verapamil, or amiodarone.

Side Effects:

Contact your health-care provider immediately if you experience:
- severe muscle pain or weakness.
- yellowing of the skin or eyes.
- flulike symptoms.
- unusual bruising or bleeding.
- a rash.

Commonly reported side effects:
- headache
- mild aches and pains
- stomach pain
- flatulence
- constipation or diarrhea

Time Required for Drug to Take Effect: Starts lowering cholesterol within 72 hours of first dose, but it may take 2 to 4 weeks of treatment to reach maximum effectiveness.

Symptoms of Overdose: No specific symptoms.

Special Notes:

- Follow a diet plan and exercise program recommended by your health-care provider.
- Do not take colestipol or cholestyramine within 4 hours of taking this medicine.
- Do not consume grapefruit or grapefruit juice while taking this drug.
- Limit alcohol intake while on this medication.
- Use a sunblock with at least SPF 15 when outside because this drug may increase your sensitivity to the sun.
- You will need periodic bloodwork to check liver function and cholesterol levels while you are taking this medication.

benazepril

Brand Name: Lotensin

Generic Available: yes

Type of Drug: antihypertensive (angiotensin-converting enzyme [ACE] inhibitor)

Used for: Treatment of high blood pressure (hypertension), heart failure, and kidney problems due to diabetes.

How This Medication Works: Lowers blood
pressure by decreasing the body's production of angiotensin, a strong chemical that causes blood vessels to
constrict.

Dosage Form and Strength: tablets (5 mg,
10 mg, 20 mg, 40 mg)

Storage:
- room temperature
- protect from light and moisture—do not store in
  bathroom or kitchen

Administration:
- Usually taken once or twice daily.
- Take at a similar time each day.
- May be taken without regard to meals, but take
  with food if stomach upset occurs.
- Take a missed dose as soon as possible. However,
  if it is almost time for the next dose, skip the missed
  dose and return to your regular dosing schedule.

Precautions:
Do not use if:
- **you are pregnant or could become pregnant.**
- you have an allergy to benazepril or other ACE
  inhibitor (such as lisinopril, enalapril, or ramipril).
- you have bilateral renal artery stenosis.

Talk to your doctor if:
- you have severe aortic stenosis.
- you have severe liver or kidney disease.
- you have low blood pressure.
- you become dehydrated.

- you are taking allopurinol, lithium, potassium supplements, or spironolactone.

Side Effects:

Contact your health-care provider immediately if you experience:

- signs of a life-threatening reaction, which include fever; wheezing; chest tightness; and itching or swelling of face, lips, tongue, or throat.
- severe dizziness or fainting.
- severe headache.
- a rash.

Commonly reported side effects:

- dizziness or light-headedness
- headache
- constipation
- abnormal taste
- mild swelling of feet, ankles, or legs
- cough

Time Required for Drug to Take Effect: Starts working within 24 hours of first dose.

Symptoms of Overdose:

- low blood pressure
- slow pulse
- nausea and/or vomiting
- confusion

Special Notes:

- Do not use potassium-containing salt substitutes while taking this drug.
- Follow a diet plan and exercise program recommended by your health-care provider.

- To avoid dizziness, rise slowly over several minutes from a sitting or lying position.
- Notify your health-care provider if you develop a persistent cough that becomes bothersome.
- Talk to your doctor about the need for bloodwork while you take this drug.

benztropine

Brand Name: Cogentin

Generic Available: yes

Type of Drug: antiparkinsonian (anticholinergic)

Used for: Treatment of Parkinson's disease and parkinsonism.

How This Medication Works: Blocks the action of the brain chemical acetylcholine, restoring the balance between it and the brain chemical dopamine.

Dosage Form and Strength: tablets (0.5 mg, 1 mg, 2 mg)

Storage:
- room temperature
- tightly closed

Administration:
- Usually taken once or twice daily.
- May be taken with food to avoid upset stomach.

- Take a missed dose as soon as possible. However, if it is almost time for the next dose, skip the missed dose and return to your regular dosing schedule.

Precautions:
Do not use if:
- you ever had an allergic reaction to benztropine.
- you have narrow-angle glaucoma (angle-closure type), colitis, severe constipation, prostate problems, myasthenia gravis, or tardive dyskinesia.

Talk to your doctor if:
- you are taking medicine for anxiety, depression, hallucinations, another mental condition, insomnia, dizziness, seasickness, upset stomach, cramping (muscle relaxants), hiatal hernia, allergies, irregular heartbeat, or pain.
- you have dry mouth, constipation, urinary retention, breathing problems, liver or kidney disease, or rapid heartbeat.
- you are taking metoclopramide or an antipsychotic, such as haloperidol or thioridazine.

Side Effects:
Contact your health-care provider immediately if you experience:
- severe constipation.
- difficulty urinating or painful urination.
- seizures.
- severe agitation or confusion.
- hallucinations.
- hot, dry, flushed skin.

- fever.
- severe muscle weakness or cramping.

Commonly reported side effects:
- dilated pupils or blurred vision
- dizziness
- drowsiness
- nausea and/or vomiting
- dry mouth
- mild constipation

Time Required for Drug to Take Effect: Relief
of symptoms occurs within 1 to 2 hours of dose.

Symptoms of Overdose:
- fever
- severe constipation
- inability to urinate
- seizures
- severe confusion, agitation, or hallucinations
- hyperactivity, combativeness
- severe muscle weakness or cramping
- coma, stupor

Special Notes:
- Anticholinergic drugs should be used cautiously in older adults, because these patients may be more sensitive to side effects.
- Many other medicines have similar side effects. To avoid compounding these effects, have your doctor and pharmacist check all medicines you use, including over-the-counter products.
- Do not drink alcohol while taking this drug.

- Avoid being out in hot weather for long periods, because this drug may increase your risk of heatstroke, which is a medical emergency.
- Do not stop taking this drug without consulting your doctor first.

bicalutamide

Brand Name: Casodex

Generic Available: no

Type of Drug: antineoplastic agent (antiandrogen)

Used for: Treatment of prostate cancer.

How This Medication Works: Slows prostate cancer growth by lowering the body's testosterone levels.

Dosage Form and Strength: tablets (50 mg)

Storage:
- room temperature
- protect from light and moisture—do not store in bathroom or kitchen

Administration:
- Usually taken once daily.
- Take at a similar time each day.
- May be taken without regard to meals, but take with food if stomach upset occurs.
- Take a missed dose as soon as possible. However, if it is almost time for the next dose, skip the

missed dose and return to your regular dosing
schedule.

Precautions:

Do not use if:

- you are allergic to bicalutamide.

Talk to your doctor if:

- you now have or ever had liver problems.

Side Effects:

Contact your health-care provider immediately if you experience:

- signs of a life-threatening reaction, which include
  fever; wheezing; chest tightness; and itching or
  swelling of face, lips, tongue, or throat.
- severe nausea or vomiting.
- dark and tarry stools, rectal bleeding, or vomiting
  of material that looks like coffee grounds.
- yellowing of the skin or eyes.

Commonly reported side effects:

- flushing
- nausea and/or vomiting
- breast tenderness or enlargement
- diarrhea
- dizziness or drowsiness

Time Required for Drug to Take Effect: May
take 2 to 3 months of treatment to have an effect.

Symptoms of Overdose:

- slow movement
- loss of appetite
- vomiting
- slow breathing

Special Notes:
- Do not change your dose or discontinue this medicine without consulting your health-care provider first.
- Liver function tests should be performed regularly during the first 4 months of treatment with this drug and periodically thereafter.
- If you have diabetes, monitor glucose closely and notify your health-care provider of changes, because this medication may alter glucose levels.

bimatoprost

Brand Name: Lumigan

Generic Available: no

Type of Drug: ophthalmologic prostaglandin analogue

Used for: Treatment of glaucoma.

How This Medication Works: Lowers pressure in the eye.

Dosage Form and Strength: ophthalmic solution (0.03%)

Storage:
- room temperature
- tightly closed

Administration:
- For use in the eye only.

- Usually used once daily in the evening.
- Wash your hands before and after administration.
- Review your health-care provider's instructions for administering eye medication, or read those provided under Taking Medications Correctly in the introduction of this book.
- Remove contact lenses before applying this drug.
- Do not touch the tip of the container to the eye or to anything else.
- After administering drug, keep eyes gently closed, and apply pressure to inside corner of treated eye for 2 to 3 minutes to keep drug from draining out through tear duct.
- Wait at least 15 minutes after using medicine to insert contact lenses.
- The eye can hold only one drop at a time; wait at least 5 minutes between drops if you have more than one drop or another medicine to apply.
- Administer a missed dose as soon as possible, but if it is almost time for the next dose, skip the missed dose and return to your regular dosing schedule.

Precautions:

Do not use if:
- you are allergic to bimatoprost.

Talk to your doctor if:
- you have or develop an eye infection, require eye surgery, or experience eye trauma.

Side Effects:

Contact your health-care provider immediately if you experience:
- sudden change in vision, eye pain, or irritation.

- signs of a life-threatening reaction, which include wheezing; chest tightness; and itching or swelling of face, lips, tongue, or throat.

Commonly reported side effects:
- headache
- eye irritation
- eye color change (increase in brown pigment) or darkening of eyelashes and skin around eye, which may be permanent

Time Required for Drug to Take Effect: Starts lowering eye pressure within 24 hours of administering the first dose.

Symptoms of Overdose: No information available.

Special Notes:
- Have your eye pressure checked regularly, as directed by your health-care provider.

brimonidine

Brand Names: Alphagan, Alphagan P

Generic Available:
- Alphagan: yes
- Alphagan P: no

Type of Drug: antiglaucoma agent (alpha$_2$ agonist)

Used for: Treating glaucoma or ocular hypertension.

How This Medication Works: Lowers pressure in the eye.

Dosage Form and Strength: ophthalmic solution
- Alphagan: 0.2% (5 mL, 10 mL, 15 mL)
- Alphagan P: 0.15% (5 mL, 10 mL, 15 mL)

Storage:
- room temperature
- tightly closed

Administration:
- For use in the eye only.
- Usually used 3 times daily.
- Wash your hands before and after use.
- Review your health-care provider's instructions for administering eye medication, or read those provided under Taking Medications Correctly in the introduction of this book.
- Remove contact lenses before using this drug.
- Do not touch the tip of the container to the eye or to anything else.
- After administering drug, keep eyes closed, and apply pressure to inside corner of treated eye for 2 to 3 minutes to keep drug from draining out through tear duct.
- Wait at least 15 minutes after using medicine to insert contact lenses.
- The eye can hold only one drop at a time; wait at least 5 minutes between drops if you have more than one drop or another medicine to apply.
- Administer a missed dose as soon as possible. However, if it is almost time for the next dose, skip the missed dose and return to your regular dosing schedule.

Precautions:

Do not use if:
- you have a hypersensitivity to brimonidine or preservatives.
- you are currently taking a monoamine oxidase (MAO) inhibitor (isocarboxazid, phenelzine, or tranylcypromine).

Talk to your doctor if:
- you have heart disease.
- you have Raynaud's phenomenon or low blood pressure.

Side Effects:

Contact your health-care provider immediately if you experience:
- signs of a life-threatening reaction, which include fever; wheezing; chest tightness; and itching or swelling of face, lips, tongue, or throat.
- severe dizziness.
- a sudden change in vision, eye pain, or irritation.
- a rash.

Commonly reported side effects:
- eye irritation
- blurred vision
- dry mouth
- light-headedness
- fatigue and/or drowsiness

Time Required for Drug to Take Effect: Starts lowering eye pressure within 2 hours of first dose.

Symptoms of Overdose: No information available (possible effects on blood pressure).

Special Notes:

- Have your eye pressure checked regularly.
- Check your blood pressure regularly if you have heart disease or high blood pressure.
- Avoid driving and other tasks that require alertness or clear vision until you see how this medicine affects you.
- Avoid drinking alcohol or taking other medicines or natural products that slow your actions and reactions.

bumetanide

Brand Name: Bumex

Generic Available: yes

Type of Drug: diuretic

Used for: Treatment of edema (extra fluid) and high blood pressure (hypertension).

How This Medication Works: Removes extra salt and water from the body through the kidneys. **This drug is very potent—excessive amounts can lead to dehydration, so be sure to follow your doctor's instructions.**

Dosage Form and Strength: tablets (0.5 mg, 1 mg, 2 mg)

Storage:

- room temperature
- tightly closed

- protect from moisture—do not store in bathroom or kitchen

Administration:
- Usually taken once daily in the morning.
- Take with food or milk if stomach upset occurs.
- Do not take more than instructed by your health-care provider.

Precautions:
Do not use if:
- you are allergic to bumetanide or to oral diabetes medication, such as glipizide or glyburide.

Talk to your doctor if:
- you have liver disease, coronary artery disease, kidney disease, or gout.
- you are taking digoxin, an angiotensin-converting enzyme (ACE) inhibitor (such as captopril, enalapril, or lisinopril), a thiazide diuretic (such as hydrochlorothiazide, chlorthalidone, or metolazone), warfarin, lithium, theophylline, propranolol, chloral hydrate, phenytoin, aspirin, a nonsteroidal anti-inflammatory drug (such as ibuprofen, piroxicam, diclofenac, naproxen, or oxaprozin), or oral diabetes medication (such as chlorpropamide, tolazamide, glipizide, or glyburide).

Side Effects:
Contact your health-care provider immediately if you experience:
- confusion.

- extreme water loss, or dehydration (thirst, rapid heartbeat, weakness, fatigue, drowsiness, and dizziness).
- difficulty breathing.
- muscle pain or cramps.
- fainting.
- chest pain or palpitations.
- significant weight gain.

Commonly reported side effects:
- dizziness
- dry mouth
- upset stomach or diarrhea
- headache

Time Required for Drug to Take Effect:

Begins to work in 30 to 60 minutes, and its effects last about 6 hours.

Symptoms of Overdose:

- sudden and extreme water loss, or dehydration (thirst, rapid heartbeat, weakness, fatigue, drowsiness, and dizziness)
- loss of appetite
- vomiting
- confusion

Special Notes:

- Take with orange juice or a banana to help replace lost potassium.
- Unless otherwise instructed by your doctor, drink 6 to 8 eight-ounce glasses of water daily to avoid dehydration while taking this drug.

- Use a sunblock with at least SPF 15 when outside because bumetanide may increase your sensitivity to the sun.
- To ease dry mouth symptoms, chew gum, suck on ice chips or hard candy, or try a saliva substitute.
- Weigh yourself daily. If you gain or lose more than 3 pounds in a day, call your doctor.
- Your doctor will check your calcium, magnesium, and potassium levels to determine if you need supplements.
- Changing positions slowly when sitting and/or standing up may help decrease dizziness caused by this medication.
- If you have diabetes, you may need to check your blood glucose more frequently.

bupropion

Brand Names:

Wellbutrin

Wellbutrin SR

Wellbutrin XL

Zyban

Generic Available: yes

Type of Drug: antidepressant

Used for: Treatment of depression. Also used to aid smoking cessation.

How This Medication Works: Has a mild effect on several brain chemicals.

Dosage Form and Strength:
- tablets (75 mg, 100 mg)
- extended-release (XL) tablets (150 mg, 300 mg)
- sustained-release (SR) tablets (100 mg, 150 mg, 200 mg)

Storage:
- room temperature
- tightly closed
- protect from light and moisture—do not store in bathroom or kitchen

Administration:
- Usually taken 1 to 3 times daily, depending on the formulation.
- Swallow the long-acting forms (SR and XL) whole; do not chew, break, or crush.
- May be taken with food to reduce stomach upset.

Precautions:
Do not use if:
- you are allergic to bupropion.
- you have taken a monoamine oxidase (MAO) inhibitor within the past 14 days.

Talk to your doctor if:
- you have ever had seizures, taken medicine for seizures, had a serious head injury or brain tumor, had hepatitis or other liver problems, or had serious problems with your kidneys.
- you are currently taking other medicine for insomnia, depression, or other mental conditions.
- you have an eating disorder.
- you use alcohol or illegal drugs.

Side Effects:

Contact your health-care provider immediately if you experience:
- **a desire to harm yourself.**
- seizures.
- unusual agitation or restlessness.
- hallucinations or severe confusion.
- rapid heartbeat or chest pain.
- difficulty breathing.
- extreme drowsiness.
- skin rash, hives, or itching.
- severe headache.

Commonly reported side effects:
- drowsiness
- insomnia
- tremor
- nausea and/or vomiting
- change in appetite or weight
- constipation
- dry mouth
- sweating
- blurred vision
- ringing in the ears

Time Required for Drug to Take Effect: For
depression, it may take 4 to 8 weeks of treatment to reach maximum effectiveness. For smoking cessation, it may take up to 2 weeks.

Symptoms of Overdose:
- seizures
- difficulty breathing
- chest pains

- hallucinations
- loss of consciousness

Special Notes:

- The desire to harm yourself is a serious symptom of depression. If you are planning to harm yourself, call 911 immediately.
- Do not use Zyban and Wellbutrin together.
- Know which "target symptoms" (restlessness, worry, fear, or changes in sleep or appetite) you are being treated for and be prepared to tell your doctor if they are improving, worsening, or unchanged.
- Do not drink alcohol while taking this drug.
- Do not stop taking this drug without consulting your doctor first.
- Never increase your dose without the advice of your doctor.

buspirone

Brand Name: BuSpar

Generic Available: yes

Type of Drug: antianxiety

Used for: Treatment of anxiety disorders and depression with anxiety.

How This Medication Works: Exact mechanism is unknown, but may act by increasing levels of the brain chemicals dopamine and norepinephrine.

Dosage Form and Strength: tablets (5 mg, 7.5 mg, 10 mg, 15 mg, 30 mg)

Storage:
- room temperature
- tightly closed

Administration:
- Usually taken 2 to 3 times daily.
- May be taken with food if stomach upset occurs.
- Take a missed dose as soon as possible. However, if it is almost time for the next dose, skip the missed dose and return to your regular dosing schedule.

Precautions:
Do not use if:
- you have ever had an allergic reaction to buspirone.

Talk to your doctor if:
- you have kidney or liver disease.
- you are taking haloperidol or trazodone or have taken a monoamine oxidase (MAO) inhibitor within the past 14 days.

Side Effects:
Contact your health-care provider immediately if you experience:
- confusion or hostility.
- muscle weakness.
- sore throat with fever.

Commonly reported side effects:
- dizziness or restlessness
- headache
- nausea

Time Required for Drug to Take Effect: May take 1 to 2 weeks of treatment before any effect on anxiety is seen and 3 to 4 weeks to reach maximum effectiveness.

Symptoms of Overdose:
- severe dizziness or drowsiness
- nausea and/or vomiting
- pinpoint pupils

Special Notes:
- Do not stop taking this drug without consulting your doctor first.
- Do not consume large amounts of grapefruit juice while taking this drug.
- Avoid driving and other tasks that require alertness until you see how this drug affects you.

calcitonin

Brand Names: Fortical, Miacalcin

Generic Available: no

Type of Drug: hormone

Used for: Treatment of Paget's disease and high blood calcium levels (hypercalcemia), and prevention of bone loss in osteoporosis.

How This Medication Works: Lowers blood calcium levels by preventing loss of calcium from bone and increasing calcium removal through the kidneys.

Dosage Form and Strength: nasal spray
(200 IU/0.09 mL)

Storage:
- store unopened nasal spray in refrigerator until ready to use; do not freeze
- store opened nasal spray upright at room temperature, and discard after 30 days
- protect from light

Administration:
- Usually taken as a single spray in one nostril daily.
- Alternate daily the nostril into which you spray the drug.
- Carefully read the package instructions, including those for priming the nasal spray pump.
- If you take this drug once a day and forget a dose but remember later the same day, take the dose at once and return to your regular dosing schedule. However, if you do not remember until the next day, skip the missed dose and resume your regular dosing schedule; do not double the dose.

Precautions:
Do not use if:
- you have had a severe allergic or unusual reaction to calcitonin.

Talk to your doctor if:
- you have any allergies or have had any unusual reactions to foods, preservatives, dyes, proteins, gelatin, or vitamin D.
- you are taking any other prescription or over-the-counter medications.

Side Effects:
Contact your health-care provider immediately if you experience:
- difficulty breathing.
- skin rash, irritation, swelling, or hives.
- severe nasal irritation.

Commonly reported side effects:
- loss of appetite
- diarrhea
- flushing, redness, or tingling of the face, ears, hands, or feet
- nausea and/or vomiting
- nasal irritation
- back pain
- increased urination

Time Required for Drug to Take Effect:
Usually starts working in the first month or so of treatment but may take up to 6 months to reach maximum effectiveness.

Symptoms of Overdose: nausea and/or vomiting

Special Notes:
- Do not use the medicine if there are particles floating in the nasal spray solution; use only if it is clear and colorless.
- Consult your health-care provider about the need to take calcium or vitamin D supplements while you are taking this drug.

candesartan

Brand Name: Atacand

Generic Available: no

Type of Drug: angiotensin II receptor blocker

Used for: Treatment of high blood pressure (hypertension).

How This Medication Works: Lowers blood pressure by decreasing the amount of angiotensin, a strong chemical in the body that constricts blood vessels.

Dosage Form and Strength: tablets (4 mg, 8 mg, 16 mg, 32 mg)

Storage:
- room temperature
- protect from light and moisture—do not store in bathroom or kitchen

Administration:
- Usually taken once or twice daily.
- May be taken without regard to meals, but take with food if stomach upset occurs.
- Take a missed dose as soon as possible. However, if it is almost time for the next dose, skip the missed dose and return to your regular dosing schedule.

Precautions:
Do not use if:
- **you are pregnant or may become pregnant.**

- you have a hypersensitivity to candesartan.
- you have bilateral renal artery stenosis.

Talk to your doctor if:

- you use a potassium-containing salt substitute, potassium-sparing diuretic, or potassium supplement.
- you have or had angioedema (swelling of the face or mouth).
- you have liver or kidney problems.
- you have heart problems, including cardio-myopathy or stenosis.
- you have a history of high blood-potassium levels.

Side Effects:

Contact your health-care provider immediately if you experience:

- signs of a life-threatening reaction, which include fever; wheezing; chest tightness; and itching or swelling of face, lips, tongue, or throat.
- severe dizziness or fainting.
- severe headache.
- chest pain or tightness.

Commonly reported side effects:

- dizziness
- headache
- drowsiness
- flushing
- symptoms like those of the common cold

Time Required for Drug to Take Effect: Starts
lowering blood pressure within 24 hours of first dose, but it may take 2 to 4 weeks of treatment to reach maximum effectiveness.

Symptoms of Overdose:
- low blood pressure
- fast heartbeat

Special Notes:
- Follow a diet plan and exercise program recommended by your health-care provider.
- While taking this drug, consult your health-care provider or pharmacist before using any over-the-counter medications; some may increase blood pressure.
- Avoid driving and other tasks that require alertness or clear vision until you see how this medicine affects you.
- Limit alcohol consumption while you are taking this medication.
- Be careful in hot weather: Drink plenty of fluids to prevent dehydration.
- To avoid dizziness, rise slowly over several minutes from a sitting or lying position.

captopril

Brand Name: Capoten

Generic Available: yes

Type of Drug: antihypertensive (angiotensin-converting enzyme [ACE] inhibitor)

Used for: Treatment of high blood pressure (hypertension), congestive heart failure, and kidney disease caused by diabetes (diabetic nephropathy), and preservation of heart function after a heart attack.

How This Medication Works: Inhibits enzyme necessary for the formation of angiotensin, a substance that causes powerful constriction of blood vessels.

Dosage Form and Strength: tablets (12.5 mg, 25 mg, 50 mg, 100 mg)

Storage:
- room temperature
- tightly closed
- protect from moisture—do not store in bathroom or kitchen

Administration:
- Usually taken 2 to 3 times daily.
- Best taken on an empty stomach.
- Take at least 1 hour before or 2 hours after taking an antacid.
- Take a missed dose as soon as possible. However, if it is almost time for the next dose, skip the missed dose and return to your regular dosing schedule.

Precautions:
Do not use if:
- **you are pregnant or could become pregnant.**
- you are allergic to captopril or other ACE inhibitors, such as enalapril or lisinopril.
- you have renal artery stenosis.

Talk to your doctor if:
- you are taking a diuretic (such as hydrochloro-thiazide or furosemide), a potassium supplement, allopurinol, digoxin, or lithium.
- you have kidney or liver disease.

Side Effects:

Contact your health-care provider immediately if you experience:
- swelling of the mouth, lips, or tongue.
- fainting or falling.
- a rash or hives.
- chest pain.
- irregular heartbeat.

Commonly reported side effects:
- cough
- taste disturbances
- headache
- dizziness
- fatigue
- impotence or decreased sexual desire

Time Required for Drug to Take Effect: Starts to work within 1 hour after taking the first dose, but it may take several weeks of treatment to reach maximum effectiveness.

Symptoms of Overdose:
- very low blood pressure or slow pulse
- extreme muscle weakness
- nausea, vomiting, diarrhea

Special Notes:
- Avoid salt substitutes containing potassium while taking this drug.
- You will need tests to monitor kidney function and electrolyte (sodium, potassium) levels in your blood while taking this drug.
- Consult your health-care provider before using any over-the-counter drugs or natural remedies while you are taking this drug.
- This medication may cause a dry cough. Talk to your doctor if you develop a particularly bothersome cough.
- Use a sunblock with at least SPF 15 when outside because captopril may increase your sensitivity to the sun.

carbamazepine

Brand Names:
Carbatrol

Epitol

Tegretol

Tegretol-XR

Generic Available: yes

Type of Drug: anticonvulsant

Used for: Treatment of seizures, epilepsy, and trigeminal neuralgia.

How This Medication Works: Interferes with abnormal electrical activity in the brain to reduce the frequency of seizures.

Dosage Form and Strength:
- tablets (200 mg)
- chewable tablets (100 mg)
- extended-release tablets (100 mg, 200 mg, 400 mg)
- extended-release capsules (100 mg, 200 mg, 300 mg)
- liquid/oral suspension (100 mg/5 mL)

Storage:
Tablets/Capsules:
- room temperature
- tightly closed
- protect from light and moisture—do not store in bathroom or kitchen

Liquid:
- room temperature
- tightly closed

Administration:
- Dose is based on measurement of how much medication is in the blood.
- Take with food if stomach upset occurs.
- Shake liquid forms well before use.
- Chewable tablets may be chewed or swallowed whole.
- Swallow extended-release forms whole; do not crush, break, or chew.
- Take a missed dose as soon as possible. However, if it is almost time for the next dose, skip the missed dose and return to your regular dosing schedule.

Precautions:

Do not use if:

- you have bone marrow disease.
- you are allergic to carbamazepine or tricyclic antidepressants (such as amitriptyline, amoxapine, or desipramine).
- you have taken a monoamine oxidase (MAO) inhibitor in the past 14 days.

Talk to your doctor if:

- you have angina, coronary artery disease, liver disease, glaucoma, or severe kidney disease.
- you have ever had a heart attack, cirrhosis of the liver, or hepatitis.
- you are currently taking any other seizure medication (such as phenytoin, phenobarbital, primidone, or valproic acid), cimetidine, diltiazem, erythromycin, propoxyphene, verapamil, haloperidol, lithium, or theophylline.

Side Effects:

Contact your health-care provider immediately if you experience:

- **fever, sore throat, or mouth sores.**
- **easy bruising or skin splotches.**
- yellowing of the skin or eyes.
- blurred or double vision.
- a rash or itchy skin.
- confusion, nervousness, or agitation.
- severe nausea.
- severe drowsiness.

Commonly reported side effects:
- mild light-headedness
- mild nausea
- constipation or diarrhea
- sensitivity of skin to sunlight

Time Required for Drug to Take Effect: Starts
working within hours of first dose, and decreases the number and frequency of seizures as long as treatment is continued.

Symptoms of Overdose:
- decrease in amount of urine
- severe nausea and vomiting
- agitation
- dizziness or drowsiness
- irregular breathing
- tremor

Special Notes:
- Do not stop taking this drug or change your dose without contacting your doctor first.
- Contact your physician or pharmacist before using any over-the-counter medication while taking this drug.
- Talk to your doctor about the need for bloodwork while you take this drug.
- Use a sunblock with at least SPF 15 when outside, because carbamazepine may increase your sensitivity to the sun.
- Do not consume grapefruit or grapefruit juice while taking this drug.

carvedilol

Brand Names: Coreg, Coreg CR

Generic Available: no

Type of Drug: beta-blocker with alpha-blocking activity

Used for: Treatment of heart failure or high blood pressure (hypertension).

How This Medication Works: Blocks chemicals that stimulate the heart and increase blood pressure.

Dosage Form and Strength:
- tablets (3.125 mg, 6.25 mg, 12.5 mg, 25 mg)
- extended-release capsules (10 mg, 20 mg, 40 mg, 80 mg)

Storage:
- room temperature
- protect from light and moisture—do not store in bathroom or kitchen

Administration:
- Usually taken twice daily.
- Take at a similar time each day.
- Take with food.
- Swallow extended-release capsules whole; do not break, crush, or chew.
- Take a missed dose as soon as possible. However, if it is almost time for the next dose, skip the missed dose and return to your regular dosing schedule.

- Do not change the dose or stop taking this medicine without first consulting your health-care provider. **Suddenly stopping the use of this drug can cause serious side effects.**

Precautions:
Do not use if:
- you are allergic to carvedilol.
- you have severe liver problems.

Talk to your doctor if:
- you have asthma, liver disease, a slow heartbeat without a working pacemaker, or wheezing.
- you have a history of arrhythmia or heart block.

Side Effects:
Contact your health-care provider immediately if you experience:
- signs of a life-threatening reaction, which include fever; wheezing; chest tightness; and itching or swelling of face, lips, tongue, or throat.
- severe dizziness or fainting.
- chest pain.
- difficulty breathing.
- significant weight gain.
- extreme tiredness or weakness.

Commonly reported side effects:
- dizziness
- fatigue
- headache
- diarrhea
- nausea and/or vomiting
- change in sexual ability or desire

Time Required for Drug to Take Effect: Begins lowering blood pressure within 24 hours of first dose.

Symptoms of Overdose:

- low blood pressure
- heart arrhythmias, including heart stoppage
- difficulty breathing
- convulsions
- coma

Special Notes:

- Avoid stopping this medication suddenly. Contact your health-care provider before stopping this medication or if you run out of pills.
- While taking this drug, consult your health-care provider or pharmacist before using any over-the-counter medications; some may increase blood pressure.
- To avoid dizziness, rise slowly over several minutes from a sitting or lying position.
- Follow a diet plan and exercise program recommended by your health-care provider.
- If you have diabetes, monitor glucose closely and notify your health-care provider of changes, because this medication may alter glucose levels.
- Patients with contact lenses may have decreased tear production while taking this drug; artificial tears may be helpful.

celecoxib

Brand Name: Celebrex

Generic Available: no

Type of Drug: nonsteroidal anti-inflammatory drug (selective COX–2 inhibitor)

Used for: Relief of pain and inflammation, and reduction of colon polyps.

How This Medication Works: Blocks body's production and release of chemicals that cause pain and inflammation.

Dosage Form and Strength: capsules (100 mg, 200 mg, 400 mg)

Storage:
- room temperature
- protect from light and moisture—do not store in bathroom or kitchen

Administration:
- Usually taken once or twice daily.
- May be taken without regard to meals, but take with food if stomach upset occurs.
- Take a missed dose as soon as possible. However, if it is almost time for the next dose, skip the missed dose and return to your regular dosing schedule.
- Do not double the dose or take extra doses.
- If you are taking this drug on an "as-needed" basis, do not take it more often than every 12 hours unless instructed to by your health-care provider.

Precautions:

Do not use if:
- **you've recently had coronary bypass surgery.**
- you are allergic to celecoxib.
- you are allergic to sulfonamides.
- you are allergic to aspirin or other nonsteroidal anti-inflammatory drugs.

Talk to your doctor if:
- you have heart disease, heart failure, or other heart problems.
- you have a history of stomach problems.
- you have kidney or liver disease.
- you have high blood pressure.
- you have asthma.
- you use aspirin-containing products; other pain medicines; blood thinners; or garlic, ginseng, ginkgo, or vitamin E supplements.

Side Effects:

Contact your health-care provider immediately if you experience:
- signs of a life-threatening reaction, which include fever; wheezing; chest tightness; and itching or swelling of face, lips, tongue, or throat.
- severe stomach pain.
- severe nausea or vomiting.
- severe diarrhea.
- unusual bruising or bleeding.
- a rash.
- excessive swelling in your feet or hands.
- dark and tarry stools or vomiting of material that looks like coffee grounds.

Commonly reported side effects:
- headache
- stomach pain or heartburn
- nausea and/or vomiting
- diarrhea
- slight swelling of the hands and feet
- dizziness or confusion

Time Required for Drug to Take Effect: Starts relieving pain within 1 hour of first dose, but may take up to 2 weeks of treatment to reach maximum effectiveness. If used for colorectal polyps, it may take 6 months of treatment to work.

Symptoms of Overdose:
- stomach pain
- drowsiness
- nausea and/or vomiting
- slow breathing
- coma

Special Notes:
- **Due to safety concerns, COX–2 inhibitors may not be appropriate for patients with heart disease or for patients with significant risk factors for heart disease; discuss these risks with your health-care provider.**
- **This type of drug may increase your risk for heart attack, stroke, stomach ulcer, and stomach bleeds. Discuss the risks vs. benefits with your physician.**
- Avoid driving or other tasks requiring alertness until you see how this medicine affects you.

- Tell your dentist, surgeon, and other health-care providers that you use this medicine.
- If you take a blood thinner, you may need more frequent monitoring while using celecoxib.
- Talk with your health-care provider or pharmacist before starting any new medicine.

cephalexin

Brand Names: Biocef, Keflex

Generic Available: yes

Type of Drug: antibiotic (cephalosporin)

Used for: Treatment of bacterial infections.

How This Medication Works: Kills bacteria by inhibiting the growth of their cell walls.

Dosage Form and Strength:
- tablets (250 mg, 500 mg)
- capsules (250 mg, 500 mg)
- suspension (125 mg/5 mL, 250 mg/5 mL)

Storage:
Tablets and capsules:
- room temperature
- tightly closed
- protect from moisture—do not store in bathroom or kitchen

Suspension:
- refrigerate; do not freeze
- tightly closed

Administration:
- Take at even intervals, as prescribed.
- May be taken without regard to meals.
- Shake suspension well before you measure the dose.
- Take until completely gone, even if symptoms have improved.
- Take a missed dose as soon as possible. However, if it is almost time for the next dose, skip the missed dose and return to your regular dosing schedule.

Precautions:
Do not use if:
- you are allergic to cephalexin or other cephalosporins, such as cefuroxime, cefaclor, or cefadroxil.

Talk to your doctor if:
- you are allergic to penicillin or drugs in the penicillin class (such as ampicillin and amoxicillin).
- you are taking probenecid.

Side Effects:
Contact your health-care provider immediately if you experience:
- a rash or hives.
- vaginal itching or discharge.
- severe diarrhea.
- shortness of breath or wheezing.
- unusual bleeding or bruising.

Commonly reported side effects:
- diarrhea

- abnormal taste
- nausea
- headache

Time Required for Drug to Take Effect: Begins
to kill bacteria within hours after first dose, but you must finish the prescribed amount of medicine, even if symptoms disappear.

Symptoms of Overdose:
- seizures
- stomach upset
- diarrhea

Special Notes:
- Do not use for infections other than the one for which it was prescribed.
- Discard liquid after 14 days.
- Long-term treatment may lead to bacterial resistance to cephalexin.
- Eating yogurt with active cultures may help relieve mild diarrhea, but contact your doctor if diarrhea persists.

cetirizine

Brand Name: Zyrtec

Generic Available: no

Type of Drug: nonsedating antihistamine

Used for: Relief of allergy symptoms and hives.

How This Medication Works: Stops allergic reaction by blocking histamine and preventing body's response to whatever is causing the allergy.

Dosage Form and Strength:
- syrup (5 mg/5 mL in 120 mL or 480 mL bottles)
- tablets (5 mg, 10 mg)
- chewable tablets (5 mg, 10 mg)

Storage:
- room temperature
- protect from moisture—do not store in bathroom or kitchen

Administration:
- Usually taken once daily.
- This medicine is most effective if started before symptoms occur. Take it several hours before expected contact with the cause of your allergic reactions.
- Take at a similar time each day.
- May be taken without regard to meals, but take with food if stomach upset occurs.
- Take a missed dose as soon as possible. However, if it is almost time for the next dose, skip the missed dose and return to your regular dosing schedule.
- Chewable tablets may be taken with or without water, but they must be chewed or crushed well; do not swallow them whole.
- A syrup form of the medicine is available if you have difficulty with pills.

Precautions:

Do not use if:
- you are allergic to cetirizine or hydroxyzine.

Talk to your doctor if:
- you take other medications that make you drowsy, such as sedatives, tranquilizers, mood stabilizers, other antihistamines, or pain medicines.
- you have an enlarged prostate or urinary retention.
- you have closed-angle glaucoma.
- you have liver or kidney problems.

Side Effects:

Contact your health-care provider immediately if you experience:
- signs of a life-threatening reaction, which include fever; wheezing; chest tightness; and itching or swelling of face, lips, tongue, or throat.
- extreme weakness or tiredness.
- extreme sedation or confusion.
- severe agitation.
- changes in urinary pattern.
- chest pain or palpitations.
- a rash.

Commonly reported side effects:
- light-headedness
- dry mouth
- drowsiness
- blurred vision
- confusion
- insomnia

Time Required for Drug to Take Effect: Starts
working within 1 hour of taking a dose.

Symptoms of Overdose:
- drowsiness
- restlessness
- irritability

Special Notes:
- While taking this drug, avoid use of other antihistamines (such as diphenhydramine and chlorpheniramine), alcohol, or sleep-inducing medications unless approved by your health-care provider.
- Avoid driving or other tasks that require alertness or clear vision until you see how this medicine affects you.
- Chewing gum, sucking hard candy, or brushing your teeth may help to relieve dry mouth.
- To avoid duplication while taking this drug, consult your health-care provider or pharmacist before taking any over-the-counter medication.
- Sound-alike warning: Zyrtec may be confused with Serax, Xanax, or Zantac.

cilostazol

Brand Name: Pletal

Generic Available: yes

Type of Drug: antiplatelet agent

Used for: Relief of the pain, numbness, and tingling in the legs of peripheral vascular disease.

How This Medication Works: Improves blood flow by making platelets less sticky.

Dosage Form and Strength: tablets (50 mg, 100 mg)

Storage:
- room temperature
- protect from light and moisture—do not store in bathroom or kitchen

Administration:
- Usually taken twice daily.
- Take this medicine on an empty stomach, 1 hour before or 2 hours after a meal.
- Take a missed dose as soon as possible. However, if it is almost time for the next dose, skip the missed dose and return to your regular dosing schedule.

Precautions:
Do not use if:
- **you have a weakened heart or heart failure.**
- you are allergic to cilostazol.

Talk to your doctor if:
- you use aspirin-containing products; other pain medicines; blood thinners; or garlic, ginseng, ginkgo, or vitamin E supplements.
- you have severe heart disease.
- you are taking ketoconazole or erythromycin.

Side Effects:
Contact your health-care provider immediately if you experience:
- confusion.

- unusual bruising or bleeding.
- chest pain or trouble breathing.
- fast heartbeat or palpitations.
- severe headache.
- any rash or swelling.

Commonly reported side effects:
- sleepiness or light-headedness
- blurred vision
- headache
- nervousness
- diarrhea

Time Required for Drug to Take Effect: Starts
working within 2 to 4 weeks of beginning treatment, but it may take up to 3 months to reach maximum effectiveness.

Symptoms of Overdose:
- headache
- diarrhea
- low blood pressure
- fast heartbeat or heart arrhythmias

Special Notes:
- Tell your dentist, surgeon, and other health-care providers that you use this medicine.
- Do not consume grapefruit or grapefruit juice while taking this drug.
- Do not consume alcohol while taking this drug.
- Avoid driving or other tasks that require alertness or clear vision until you see how this medicine affects you.

cimetidine

Brand Names: Tagamet, Tagamet HB

Generic Available: yes

Type of Drug: gastrointestinal (histamine H_2 antagonist)

Used for: Treatment of excess acid production in the stomach, ulcers, and heartburn (gastroesophageal reflux disease [GERD]).

How This Medication Works: Blocks histamine from binding to sites in the stomach that cause acid secretion, so less stomach acid is produced.

Dosage Form and Strength:
- tablets (200 mg, 300 mg, 400 mg, 800 mg)
- liquid (300 mg/5 mL)

Storage:
- room temperature
- protect from light and moisture—do not store in bathroom or kitchen

Administration:
- For prevention of heartburn, take this drug 30 minutes prior to eating.
- Take with meals for maximum effect.
- If you take only 1 dose daily, take it at bedtime, unless your doctor directs otherwise.
- Take a missed dose as soon as possible. However, if it is almost time for the next dose, skip the

missed dose and return to your regular dosing schedule.
- If also taking an antacid, separate doses of cimetidine and the antacid by 2 hours.

Precautions:

Do not use if:
- you are allergic to cimetidine or other histamine H_2 antagonists, such as ranitidine, famotidine, or nizatidine.

Talk to your doctor if:
- you have kidney or liver disease.
- you are taking any other medication, especially amiodarone, theophylline, or phenytoin; an anticoagulant (such as warfarin), antianxiety drug, antidepressant (such as amitriptyline or fluoxetine), or antibiotic; or any medication for heart disease or high blood pressure (hypertension).

Side Effects:

Contact your health-care provider immediately if you experience:
- skin rash, hives, or itching.
- confusion or agitation.
- irregular heartbeat.
- fever or sore throat.
- chest tightness.
- unusual bleeding or bruising.
- dark, tarry stools or vomit that resembles coffee grounds.

Commonly reported side effects:
- constipation or diarrhea

- decreased sexual ability or desire
- dizziness or drowsiness
- headache
- dry mouth
- joint or muscle pain
- nausea and/or vomiting
- swelling of breasts (in men and women)
- hair loss

Time Required for Drug to Take Effect: Starts to work within 1 to 2 hours of beginning treatment, but ulcer healing may require 4 to 12 weeks of therapy with this drug.

Symptoms of Overdose:
- difficulty breathing
- irregular heartbeat
- tremors
- vomiting or diarrhea

Special Notes:
- Consult your physician or pharmacist before using any over-the-counter medications while taking this drug.
- Avoid medications that may make your condition worse, including nonsteroidal anti-inflammatory drugs (aspirin, ibuprofen, naproxen, ketoprofen).
- This medication may cause drowsiness. Use caution when driving or operating machinery.
- Tell your doctor you are taking cimetidine if you are going to have a skin test for allergies.

ciprofloxacin

Brand Names: Cipro, Cipro XR

Generic Available: yes

Type of Drug: antibiotic

Used for: Treatment of bacterial infections.

How This Medication Works: Interferes with bacterial DNA gyrase, an enzyme vital for bacterial cell growth and reproduction.

Dosage Form and Strength:
- tablets (250 mg, 500 mg, 750 mg)
- extended-release tablets (500 mg, 1,000 mg)
- oral suspension (250 mg/5mL, 500 mg/5 mL)

Storage:
- room temperature; suspension may also be refrigerated, but not frozen
- tightly closed
- protect from heat, light, and moisture—do not store in bathroom or kitchen
- discard suspension after 7 days (14 days if it has been refrigerated)

Administration:
- Tablets and suspension usually taken twice daily; extended-release tablets, once every 24 hours.
- Take until completely gone, even if symptoms have improved.
- Take at even intervals.
- May be taken without regard to meals.

- Take each dose with 6 to 8 ounces of water.
- Swallow extended-release tablets whole; do not crush, break, or chew.
- Take a missed dose as soon as possible. However, if it is almost time for the next dose, skip the missed dose and return to your regular dosing schedule.
- Do not take a calcium-containing product, antacid, ferrous sulfate, zinc sulfate, or sucralfate within 2 hours of a ciprofloxacin dose.

Precautions:

Do not use if:

- you are allergic to ciprofloxacin or other drugs in the fluoroquinolone family, such as nalidixic acid or norfloxacin.

Talk to your doctor if:

- you are taking probenecid, cimetidine, phenytoin, warfarin, theophylline, or cyclosporine.
- you have a seizure disorder.
- you are younger than 18 years of age.
- you have a history of a heart condition called QT prolongation.
- you have liver or kidney problems.

Side Effects:

Contact your health-care provider immediately if you experience:

- hallucinations or tremors.
- swelling of the tongue or lips.
- a rash.
- eye pain or a sudden change in vision.
- pain in the back or ankles.

- vaginal itching or discharge.
- tingling or numbness.
- shortness of breath.
- severe diarrhea.
- chest pain.

Commonly reported side effects:
- restlessness or nervousness
- nausea or stomach upset
- diarrhea
- dizziness

Time Required for Drug to Take Effect: Begins to kill bacteria within hours of first dose. However, you must take the full course of treatment, even if symptoms disappear.

Symptoms of Overdose:
- seizures
- renal failure

Special Notes:
- Avoid the use of caffeine while taking this drug.
- Do not use for infections other than the one for which it was prescribed.
- Long-term treatment may lead to bacterial resistance to ciprofloxacin.
- Avoid excessive sunlight. Drugs in this class have caused extreme sensitivity to the sun.

citalopram

Brand Name: Celexa

Generic Available: yes

Type of Drug: antidepressant (selective serotonin reuptake inhibitor)

Used for: Treatment of depression.

How This Medication Works: Prolongs the effects of the brain chemical serotonin.

Dosage Form and Strength:
- oral solution, alcohol-free, sugar-free (10 mg/5 mL)
- tablets (10 mg, 20 mg, 40 mg)

Storage:
- room temperature
- protect from light and moisture—do not store in bathroom or kitchen

Administration:
- Usually taken once daily.
- May be taken without regard to meals, but take with food if stomach upset occurs.
- Take a missed dose as soon as possible. However, if it is almost time for the next dose, skip the missed dose and return to your regular dosing schedule.

Precautions:
Do not use if:
- you are allergic to citalopram.
- you are taking medication for migraine headaches.
- you are currently taking a monoamine oxidase (MAO) inhibitor, such as phenelzine or tranylcypromine. You should stop taking an MAO

inhibitor 2 weeks before starting Celexa, and you should be off Celexa for 2 weeks before starting on an MAO inhibitor.

Talk to your doctor if:
- you have a history of mania/hypomania.
- you have a history of seizure disorders.
- you had an allergy or other adverse effect from another antidepressant.
- you have severe kidney or liver disease.

Side Effects:

Contact your health-care provider immediately if you experience:
- **a desire to harm yourself.**
- signs of a life-threatening reaction, which include fever; wheezing; chest tightness; and itching or swelling of face, lips, tongue, or throat.
- extreme nervousness, excitability, confusion, or hallucinations.
- a rash.

Commonly reported side effects:
- light-headedness, fatigue, or drowsiness
- nervousness
- headache
- nausea or vomiting
- change in sexual ability or desire
- insomnia
- blurred vision
- dry mouth

Time Required for Drug to Take Effect: May

take 3 to 6 weeks of treatment to have an effect.

Symptoms of Overdose:
- dizziness
- sleepiness
- nausea and/or vomiting
- sweating
- tremor
- confusion or amnesia
- seizures
- coma

Special Notes:
- The desire to kill yourself is a serious symptom of depression. If you are planning suicide, dial 911 immediately.
- With antidepressant therapy, sleep and appetite may improve quickly. Other depression symptoms may take up to 4 to 6 weeks to improve.
- Avoid driving or other tasks that require alertness or clear vision until you see how this medicine affects you.
- Do not consume alcohol while you are being treated with this medication.
- If you have been taking this medication for several weeks, consult your health-care provider before stopping. You may need to gradually withdraw from this medicine.

clonazepam

Brand Name: Klonopin

Generic Available: yes

Type of Drug: anticonvulsant (benzodiazepine)

Used for: Treatment of seizures and panic disorder.

How This Medication Works: Enhances the activity of the brain chemical gamma-aminobutyric acid (GABA) to calm the brain.

Dosage Form and Strength:
- tablets (0.5 mg, 1 mg, 2 mg)
- disintegrating wafer (0.125 mg, 0.25 mg, 0.5 mg, 1 mg, 2 mg)

Storage:
- room temperature
- tightly closed

Administration:
- Usually taken 2 to 3 times daily.
- Take with food if stomach upset occurs.
- Use the disintegrating wafer immediately after opening packaging.
- Take a missed dose as soon as possible. However, if it is almost time for the next dose, skip the missed dose and return to your regular dosing schedule.

Precautions:
Do not use if:
- you are allergic to clonazepam or other drugs in the benzodiazepine family, such as diazepam, lorazepam, and oxazepam.
- you have narrow-angle glaucoma.

Talk to your doctor if:
- you are taking any other substance that depresses the central nervous system, including alcohol, phenobarbital, or a narcotic (such as codeine, meperidine, or morphine).
- you have asthma or other lung problems, kidney disease, or liver disease.
- you have difficulty swallowing or have been told that you snore.

Side Effects:
Contact your health-care provider immediately if you experience:
- confusion or difficulty concentrating.
- a change in balance or falls.
- seizures.
- hallucinations.
- a rash.
- trouble breathing.

Commonly reported side effects:
- unsteadiness
- drowsiness
- blurred vision

Time Required for Drug to Take Effect:
Controls seizures within 20 to 60 minutes of dose, but treatment must be continued to maintain desired effect.

Symptoms of Overdose:
- continuing confusion or slurred speech
- severe weakness or drowsiness
- coma

Special Notes:
- This drug may cause drowsiness. Use caution when driving or operating dangerous machinery.
- Do not drink alcohol while taking this medication.
- This drug may be habit-forming; do not discontinue without first talking with your doctor.

clonidine

Brand Names: Catapres, Catapres-TTS

Generic Available:
- tablets: yes
- topical patch: no

Type of Drug: antihypertensive

Used for: Treatment of high blood pressure (hypertension).

How This Medication Works: Decreases the body's release of chemicals that increase blood pressure and anxiety.

Dosage Form and Strength:
- tablets (0.1 mg, 0.2 mg, 0.3 mg)
- topical patch (0.1 mg released every 24 hours, 0.2 mg released every 24 hours, 0.3 mg released every 24 hours)

Storage:
- room temperature
- tightly closed

- protect from moisture—do not store in bathroom or kitchen

Administration:
- Tablets are usually taken once or twice daily; patches are applied once weekly.
- Take a missed dose of the tablet form as soon as possible. However, if it is almost time for the next dose, skip the missed dose and return to your regular dosing schedule.
- Do not abruptly stop taking this medication.
- Tablets may be taken with food if stomach upset occurs.
- Apply the patch to a hairless area of unbroken skin on the upper arm or torso, rotating sites with each patch.
- If you forget a patch, apply it as soon as you remember, and try to maintain the same patch-replacement schedule. Do not wear more than one patch at a time.

Precautions:
Do not use if:
- you are allergic to clonidine or any of the components in the patch (such as the adhesive).

Talk to your doctor if:
- you have arrhythmia or have recently had a heart attack.
- you are taking a beta-blocker (such as atenolol, metoprolol, or propranolol) or a tricyclic anti-depressant (such as nortriptyline, amitriptyline, imipramine, or desipramine).
- you have heart or kidney disease.

Side Effects:

Contact your health-care provider immediately if you experience:
- severe dizziness or fainting.
- a generalized rash.
- swelling of the mouth, lips, or tongue.
- hallucinations or confusion.

Commonly reported side effects:
- drowsiness or dizziness
- dry mouth
- constipation
- impotence or lack of sexual desire
- localized rash at site of patch application

Time Required for Drug to Take Effect:

Tablets lower pressure within 30 to 60 minutes of the first dose; patches lower pressure within 2 to 3 days of starting treatment.

Symptoms of Overdose:
- severe sedation
- difficulty breathing
- seizures
- low body temperature
- diarrhea

Special Notes:
- This drug may be habit-forming; do not stop taking it without first consulting your doctor, as serious side effects may occur.
- Constipation, dizziness, headache, and fatigue will generally diminish after about 1 month of therapy.

- Taking clonidine at bedtime (if prescribed once a day) will make the side effects of dizziness and sedation more tolerable.
- Use caution if you consume alcohol, because clonidine may increase its effects.
- To ease dry mouth symptoms, chew gum, suck on hard candy or ice chips, or try a saliva substitute.
- Tell your dentist, surgeon, and other health-care providers you are taking this drug.

clopidogrel

Brand Name: Plavix

Generic Available: no

Type of Drug: antiplatelet agent

Used for: Prevention of heart attacks and strokes; protection of arteries after heart procedures; and prevention of future heart attacks in patients with a history of unstable angina or mild heart attacks.

How This Medication Works: Prevents blood platelets from becoming sticky and clumping together to form clots.

Dosage Form and Strength: tablets (75 mg)

Storage:
- room temperature
- protect from moisture—do not store in bathroom or kitchen

Administration:
- Usually taken once daily.
- Take at a similar time each day.
- Take with food if stomach upset occurs.
- Take a missed dose as soon as possible. However, if it is almost time for the next dose, skip the missed dose and return to your regular dosing schedule.

Precautions:
Do not use if:
- you are allergic to clopidogrel.
- you have bleeding problems.

Talk to your doctor if:
- you have kidney or liver problems, have peptic ulcer disease, or had a recent trauma or surgery.
- you take aspirin-containing products; pain medicines; blood thinners; or garlic, ginseng, ginkgo, or vitamin E supplements.

Side Effects:
Contact your health-care provider immediately if you experience:
- a change in strength on one side of your body greater than on the other side, difficulty speaking or thinking, or a change in balance.
- unusual bruising or bleeding.
- chest pain or pressure.
- a sudden change in vision.
- severe headache.
- severe nausea, vomiting, or diarrhea.
- a rash.

Commonly reported side effects:
- flulike symptoms
- stomach pain or heartburn
- nausea and/or vomiting
- diarrhea or constipation
- dizziness

Time Required for Drug to Take Effect:

Starts working within 2 to 5 hours of the first dose, and reaches maximum effectiveness after about 7 days of treatment.

Symptoms of Overdose:
- vomiting
- weakness
- difficulty breathing
- stomach bleeding

Special Notes:
- Do not stop taking this medication before talking with your health-care provider.
- Tell your dentist, surgeon, and other health-care providers that you use this medicine.
- You may bleed more easily while taking this medicine. Consider switching to a soft toothbrush and an electric shaver.
- Do not consume alcohol while taking this drug.
- Avoid over-the-counter products that contain aspirin while taking this drug.
- Consult your health-care provider or pharmacist before taking any over-the-counter medication while you are taking this drug.
- Sound-alike/look-alike warning: Plavix may be confused with Paxil or Elavil.

codeine and acetaminophen combination

Brand Names: Capital with Codeine, Tylenol with Codeine

Generic Available: yes

Type of Drug: narcotic analgesic

Used for: Relief of mild to moderately severe pain.

How This Medication Works: Codeine acts in the brain to decrease the recognition of pain impulses. Acetaminophen blocks pain impulses to the brain.

Dosage Form and Strength:
- oral elixir (12 mg codeine/120 mg acetaminophen per 5 mL)
- tablets (7.5 mg codeine/300 mg acetaminophen, 15 mg/300 mg, 30 mg/300 mg, 60 mg/300 mg)

Storage:
- room temperature
- protect from moisture—do not store in bathroom or kitchen

Administration:
- Do not exceed the maximum number of doses per day. Never take a larger dose or more doses per day than your doctor has prescribed.
- Take with milk or food if stomach upset occurs.
- Take a missed dose as soon as possible. However, if it is almost time for the next dose, skip the missed dose and return to your regular dosing schedule.

Precautions:

Do not use if:
- you are allergic to codeine or other narcotics, such as morphine or hydrocodone.
- you are allergic to acetaminophen.

Talk to your doctor if:
- you have alcoholism or other substance abuse problems; brain disease or a head injury; colitis; seizures; emotional problems or mental illness; emphysema, asthma, or other lung disease; kidney, liver, or thyroid disease; prostate problems or problems with urination; or gallbladder disease or gallstones.
- you are taking other pain medications.
- you are taking any other medication, especially a medication that can cause drowsiness, such as an antihistamine, barbiturate (such as phenobarbital), benzodiazepine (such as diazepam, alprazolam, or lorazepam), muscle relaxant, or antidepressant.

Side Effects:

Contact your health-care provider immediately if you experience:
- skin rash or hives.
- difficulty breathing.
- fainting or falling.
- uncontrolled pain.
- stomach pain.
- hallucinations or confusion.
- severe constipation.
- unusual bruising or bleeding.
- trembling or uncontrolled muscle movements.
- yellowing of the skin or eyes.

Commonly reported side effects:
- nausea
- constipation
- drowsiness
- dry mouth
- loss of appetite
- nervousness or restlessness

Time Required for Drug to Take Effect: Starts
to work within 30 to 60 minutes of taking a dose.

Symptoms of Overdose:
- cold, clammy skin
- severe confusion
- seizures
- diarrhea, stomach cramps or pain
- extreme dizziness or drowsiness
- low blood pressure, slowed heartbeat
- severe nausea or vomiting
- severe nervousness or restlessness
- pinpoint pupils of eyes
- shortness of breath or difficulty breathing

(Symptoms associated with acetaminophen overdose may not occur until 2 to 4 days after it is taken, but treatment should begin as soon as possible after the overdose to prevent liver damage or death.)

Special Notes:
- This medication may cause drowsiness. Do not drive or operate dangerous machinery while you are taking this medication.
- Codeine, morphine, and other narcotics (oxycodone, hydrocodone) cause constipation. This side effect may be diminished by drinking

6 to 8 eight-ounce glasses of water each day. If using this medication for chronic pain, taking a stool softener/laxative combination may be necessary.

- Check with your physician or pharmacist before using any over-the-counter medication while you are taking this drug.
- If you use codeine for a long time, your body may become tolerant and require larger doses.
- Do not stop taking this medication abruptly, because you may experience unpleasant symptoms of withdrawal.
- Nausea and vomiting may occur, especially after you take the first few doses. This effect may go away with time.
- Do not take more than 4,000 mg of acetaminophen in a day.
- Do not drink alcohol while you are taking this medication.

colchicine

Brand Name: Colchicine

Generic Available: yes

Type of Drug: antigout

Used for: Prevention and treatment of gout.

How This Medication Works: Reduces the deposition of uric acid crystals in joints.

Dosage Form and Strength: tablets (0.5 mg, 0.6 mg)

Storage:
- room temperature
- protect from moisture—do not store in bathroom or kitchen

Administration:
- Colchicine can be used during an acute attack, or it may be taken on a long-term basis to prevent gout attacks. The instructions for use during an acute attack are different from the instructions for long-term therapy.
- May be taken with food or water if stomach upset occurs.
- Do not use more than the prescribed dose.
- Take a missed dose as soon as possible. However, if it is almost time for the next dose, skip the missed dose and return to your regular dosing schedule.

Precautions:
Do not use if:
- you are allergic to colchicine.

Talk to your doctor if:
- you drink alcohol or take other medication, especially an antibiotic or drug for diabetes, heart or thyroid disease, cancer, depression, or seizures.
- you have heart disease, blood disease, diarrhea or other stomach or intestinal disease, or kidney or liver disease.

Side Effects:

Contact your health-care provider immediately if you experience:
- skin rash, hives, or itching.
- fever or sore throat.
- muscle or stomach aches.
- tingling in the hands or feet.
- unusual bleeding or bruising.
- severe diarrhea.
- nausea and/or vomiting.

Commonly reported side effects:
- drowsiness
- loss of appetite, upset stomach
- hair loss

Time Required for Drug to Take Effect: Starts
to work within 12 to 24 hours of the first dose.

Symptoms of Overdose:
- blood in urine or stool
- burning feeling in throat or stomach
- nausea, vomiting, or diarrhea
- fever
- convulsions or delirium
- muscle weakness
- difficulty breathing

Special Notes:
- Ask your physician or pharmacist before using any over-the-counter medications while on this drug.
- Colchicine may cause drowsiness. Use caution when operating a motor vehicle or dangerous machinery.
- Do not drink alcohol while taking colchicine.

darifenacin

Brand Name: Enablex

Generic Available: no

Type of Drug: cholinergic antagonist

Used for: Treatment of overactive bladder symptoms.

How This Medication Works: Blocks the action of a chemical that causes spasms of the bladder, which triggers symptoms of urgency, increased trips to the bathroom, and incontinence.

Dosage Form and Strength: 24-hour tablets (7.5 mg, 15 mg)

Storage:
- room temperature
- protect from heat, light, and moisture—do not store in bathroom or kitchen

Administration:
- Usually taken once daily.
- May be taken without regard to meals, but take with food if stomach upset occurs.
- Swallow tablet whole; do not break, crush, or chew.
- Take a missed dose as soon as possible. However, if it is almost time for the next dose, skip the missed dose and return to your regular dosing schedule.

Precautions:

Do not use if:
- you are allergic to darifenacin.
- you have uncontrolled narrow-angle glaucoma, urinary retention, or myasthenia gravis.

Talk to your doctor if:
- you have a bladder disorder or gastric obstructive disorder.
- you are being treated for narrow-angle glaucoma.
- you have kidney disease or liver disease.
- you take fluoxetine (Sarafem); mirtazapine (Remeron); nefazodone; paroxetine (Paxil); risperidone (Risperdal); ritonavir (Norvir); tricyclic antidepressants, such as nortriptyline (Pamelor) or amitriptyline (Elavil); or venlafaxine (Effexor).
- you are or may be pregnant or are breast-feeding.

Side Effects:

Contact your health-care provider immediately if you experience:
- signs of a life-threatening reaction, which include fever; wheezing; chest tightness; and itching or swelling of face, lips, tongue, or throat.
- the inability to start urinating.
- a racing heartbeat.
- confusion or become unable to think clearly.

Commonly reported side effects:
- dry mouth
- headache
- dizziness
- blurred vision
- dry eyes

- constipation
- upset stomach

Time Required for Drug to Take Effect: May take 1 to 2 weeks to reach maximum effectiveness.

Symptoms of Overdose:
- blurred vision
- hallucinations
- racing heartbeat
- chest pain

Special Notes:
- This medication can cause dizziness, so avoid driving or engaging in tasks that require alertness until you know how your body responds to this drug.
- Chewing gum, sucking on hard candy, or brushing your teeth may help with the side effect of dry mouth.
- Drink plenty of noncaffeinated liquids, unless told otherwise by your health-care provider.
- Do not consume grapefruit or grapefruit juice while you are taking this medication.

desloratadine

Brand Name: Clarinex

Generic Available: no

Type of Drug: nonsedating antihistamine

Used for: Relief of allergy symptoms and itching.

How This Medication Works: Stops allergic reaction by blocking histamine and preventing the body's response to whatever is causing the allergy.

Dosage Form and Strength:
- tablets (5 mg)
- syrup (0.5 mg/mL)
- orally disintegrating tablets (2.5 mg, 5 mg)

Storage:
- room temperature
- protect from light, heat, and moisture—do not store in bathroom or kitchen

Administration:
- Usually taken once daily.
- Take at a similar time each day.
- May be taken without regard to meals, but take with food if stomach upset occurs.
- Take a missed dose as soon as possible. However, if it is almost time for the next dose, skip the missed dose and return to your regular dosing schedule.
- A syrup form of the medicine is available if you have difficulty with pills.

Precautions:
Do not use if:
- you are allergic to desloratadine or loratadine.

Talk to your doctor if:
- you have kidney or liver disease.
- you have phenylketonuria (PKU); some desloratadine products contain phenylalanine.

Side Effects:

Contact your health-care provider immediately if you experience:
- signs of a life-threatening reaction, which include fever; wheezing; chest tightness; and itching or swelling of face, lips, tongue, or throat.
- extreme weakness or sedation.
- a rash.

Commonly reported side effects:
- dizziness
- dry mouth
- sleepiness
- sore throat
- blurred vision
- headache

Time Required for Drug to Take Effect:

Begins working within 24 hours of first dose.

Symptoms of Overdose:

- sedation
- possible slight increase in pulse

Special Notes:

- To avoid duplication while on this drug, contact your health-care provider or pharmacist before taking any over-the-counter medications.
- Avoid driving or other tasks that require alertness or clear vision until you see how this medicine affects you.
- Chewing gum, sucking hard candy, or using a saliva substitute may help relieve dry mouth.

- While taking this drug, do not use other antihistamines (such as diphenhydramine and chlorpheneramine), alcohol, or sleep-inducing medications unless approved by your health-care provider.

diazepam

Brand Names:
Diastat
Diazepam Intensol
Valium

Generic Available: yes

Type of Drug: antianxiety, antiseizure

Used for: Treatment of anxiety, seizures, muscle spasms, and alcohol withdrawal.

How This Medication Works: Enhances the activity of the brain chemical gamma-aminobutyric acid (GABA) to calm the brain.

Dosage Form and Strength:
- tablets (2 mg, 5 mg, 10 mg)
- oral solution (5 mg/mL, 5 mg/5 mL)
- rectal gel (2.5 mg, 5 mg, 15 mg, 20 mg)

Storage:
- room temperature
- tightly closed
- protect tablets from moisture—do not store in bathroom or kitchen

Administration:

- Usually taken 2 to 4 times daily.
- Do not use the rectal gel form of this medication more than 5 times in a month or more than once every 5 days.
- If an oral form of this medication (tablets or oral solution) has been prescribed for you, take the medication with food.
- Do not stop taking this medication abruptly; consult your doctor before discontinuing this medication.
- Take a missed dose as soon as possible. However, if it is almost time for the next dose, skip the missed dose and return to your regular dosing schedule.

Precautions:

Do not use if:

- you have ever had an allergic reaction to diazepam or any other drug in the benzodiazepine family, such as alprazolam, clonazepam, or oxazepam.

Talk to your doctor if:

- you are taking any other medication, especially any that depress the central nervous system, such as alcohol, phenobarbital, or narcotics (such as codeine, meperidine, and morphine).
- you have asthma or other lung problems, kidney disease, liver disease, or glaucoma.
- you have trouble walking or problems keeping your balance.
- you have difficulty swallowing or have been told that you snore.

Side Effects:

Contact your health-care provider immediately if you experience:
- confusion or difficulty concentrating.
- seizures.
- hallucinations.
- a rash.
- falls or a change in balance.

Commonly reported side effects:
- unsteadiness
- drowsiness or light-headedness
- dry mouth
- blurred vision

Time Required for Drug to Take Effect:

Tablets and oral solution begin to work within 30 to 60 minutes; rectal gel reaches peak efficacy in 90 minutes.

Symptoms of Overdose:

- continuing or worsening confusion and/or slurred speech
- shortness of breath
- severe weakness or drowsiness, coma

Special Notes:

- This medication may cause drowsiness. Use caution when driving a motor vehicle or operating dangerous machinery.
- This medication may be habit-forming; do not stop using it without first consulting your doctor.
- Do not drink alcohol while taking this medication.
- Do not consume grapefruit, grapefruit juice, or Saint John's wort while you are taking this medication.

diclofenac

Brand Names:
Cataflam
Voltaren
Voltaren-XR

Generic Available: yes

Type of Drug: nonsteroidal anti-inflammatory drug (NSAID)

Used for: Relief of pain associated with rheumatoid arthritis, osteoarthritis, surgery, headache, dental problems, muscle aches, orthopedic procedures, backache, athletic injuries, and other aches and pains.

How This Medication Works: Blocks chemicals called prostaglandins that cause pain and inflammation in the body.

Dosage Form and Strength:
- tablets (50 mg)
- delayed-release tablets (25 mg, 50 mg, 75 mg)
- extended-release tablets (100 mg)

Storage:
- room temperature
- tightly closed
- protect from light and moisture—do not store in bathroom or kitchen

Administration:
- Usually taken 2 to 3 times daily.
- Take with a full glass of water (6 to 8 ounces).

- Take with meals or milk to reduce stomach upset.
- Do not lie down for at least 30 minutes after taking this medicine.
- Swallow delayed- or extended-release tablets whole; do not break, crush, or chew.
- Take a missed dose as soon as possible. However, if it is almost time for the next dose, skip the missed dose and return to your regular dosing schedule.

Precautions:

Do not use if:

- **you've recently had coronary artery bypass surgery.**
- you have ever had an allergic reaction to diclofenac or any other nonsteroidal anti-inflammatory drug, such as ibuprofen, indomethacin, piroxicam, or aspirin.
- you have porphyria.

Talk to your doctor if:

- you are taking aspirin, another nonsteroidal anti-inflammatory drug (such as ibuprofen, indomethacin, or piroxicam), an anticoagulant (such as warfarin), a steroid (such as prednisone), lithium, methotrexate, garlic, ginseng, ginkgo, or a supplement containing vitamin E.
- you have peptic ulcer disease, bleeding from your stomach or intestines, bleeding abnormalities, ulcerative colitis, high blood pressure (hypertension), kidney disease, liver disease, heart disease, asthma, or nasal polyps.
- you smoke tobacco or drink alcohol.

Side Effects:

Contact your health-care provider immediately if you experience:
- blood in your stool or dark, tarry stools.
- persistent or severe stomach or abdominal pain or bloody vomit.
- weakness on one side of your body.
- blood in your urine or dark, smoky-looking urine.
- a rash or skin irritation.
- difficulty breathing.
- swelling of the eyelids, throat, lips, or face.
- vision or hearing changes.
- unexplained sore throat or fever.
- unusual bleeding or bruising.
- irregular heartbeat, heart palpitations, or chest pain.

Commonly reported side effects:
- stomach upset
- gas
- heartburn
- diarrhea or constipation
- swelling of the hands or feet
- dizziness or drowsiness
- headache

Time Required for Drug to Take Effect: Starts
to relieve pain within 1 to 3 hours of taking a dose. However, for arthritis, it may take 2 to 4 weeks of treatment to reach maximum effectiveness.

Symptoms of Overdose:
- severe stomach pain or nausea
- heartburn

- vomiting
- drowsiness or confusion
- headache
- loss of consciousness

Special Notes:

- **This type of drug may increase you risk for heart attack, stroke, stomach ulcer, and stomach bleeds. Discuss the risks vs. benefits with your physician.**
- Contact your physician if pain or fever worsens during treatment.
- Consult your health-care provider before using any over-the-counter medication or pain reliever while taking this drug.
- Drinking alcohol and/or smoking tobacco while taking diclofenac may increase your risk of bleeding from the stomach or intestines.
- Diclofenac contains sodium, which may worsen heart failure, high blood pressure (hypertension), or ankle edema (fluid retention).
- Use a sunblock with at least SPF 15 when outside because diclofenac may increase your sensitivity to the sun.
- Tell the doctor or dentist you are taking diclofenac if you are going to have surgery or emergency treatment.

dicyclomine

Brand Name: Bentyl

Generic Available: yes

Type of Drug: gastrointestinal (anticholinergic)

Used for: Treatment of disorders of the stomach and intestines, such as irritable bowel syndrome and cramps.

How This Medication Works: Decreases the contraction of the muscles of the stomach and intestine, slowing the movement of stomach and intestinal contents.

Dosage Form and Strength:
- tablets (20 mg)
- capsules (10 mg)
- syrup (10 mg/5 mL)

Storage:
- room temperature
- protect from moisture—do not store in bathroom or kitchen

Administration:
- Take it 30 minutes to 1 hour before meals.
- Do not take antacids within 1 hour of taking dicyclomine.
- To measure the correct amount of syrup to take, use a dosing device that indicates amounts in milliliters (mL or ml). An ordinary kitchen teaspoon is not accurate enough.

- Take a missed dose as soon as possible. However, if it is almost time for the next dose, skip the missed dose and return to your regular dosing schedule.

Precautions:

Do not use if:

- you are allergic to dicyclomine or other anticholinergic medications, such as atropine or clidinium.
- you have uncontrolled glaucoma, myasthenia gravis, intestinal blockage, or urinary tract blockage.

Talk to your doctor if:

- you have glaucoma, heart disease, high blood pressure, a hernia, kidney disease, liver disease, thyroid disease, bladder disease, prostate disease, or ulcerative colitis.
- you drink alcohol or are taking an antidepressant, antacid, antidiarrheal, antifungal, potassium supplement, or another anticholinergic (such as atropine or clidinium).

Side Effects:

Contact your health-care provider immediately if you experience:

- skin rash, hives, or itching.
- confusion or hallucinations.
- dizziness or fainting.
- eye pain or blurred vision.
- difficulty urinating.
- difficulty swallowing or breathing.

Commonly reported side effects:
- drowsiness or dizziness
- constipation or bloated feeling
- dry mouth
- headache
- increased sensitivity to bright light
- nausea and/or vomiting
- decreased sweating

Time Required for Drug to Take Effect: Starts
to work within 1 to 2 hours of taking a dose.

Symptoms of Overdose:
- blurred vision
- drowsiness, dizziness, or confusion
- dryness of mouth, throat, or nose
- irregular heartbeat
- hallucinations
- fever or skin flushing
- excitement

Special Notes:
- This medication may cause drowsiness. Use caution when driving or operating potentially dangerous machinery.
- Consult your physician or pharmacist before using any over-the-counter medications while taking this drug.
- Do not drink alcohol while taking this medication.
- If you experience dryness of the mouth, chew gum, suck on ice chips or hard candy, or try a saliva substitute.
- Dicyclomine decreases your body's ability to sweat. Avoid getting overheated during outdoor

activities in hot weather or in saunas, hot baths, or hot showers.
- Tell your dentist, surgeon, or other health-care professional you are taking dicyclomine prior to surgery or other treatment.

digoxin

Brand Names:
Digitek
Lanoxicaps
Lanoxin

Generic Available: yes

Type of Drug: antiarrhythmic (cardiac glycoside)

Used for: Treatment of congestive heart failure and abnormal heart rhythms such as atrial fibrillation.

How This Medication Works: Increases the ability of the heart muscle to pump blood and prevents part of the heart from beating abnormally.

Dosage Form and Strength:
- tablets (0.125 mg, 0.25 mg)
- capsules (0.05 mg, 0.1 mg, 0.2 mg)
- elixir (0.05 mg/mL)

Storage:
- room temperature
- protect from moisture—do not store in bathroom or kitchen

Administration:
- Take with water or food (excluding foods high in fiber) to minimize stomach upset.
- Take at the same time every day.
- Do not take an antacid or fiber supplement, cholestyramine, or sucralfate within 2 hours of a dose of digoxin.
- Take a missed dose as soon as possible. However, if it is almost time for the next dose, skip the missed dose and return to your regular dosing schedule.

Precautions:
Do not use if:
- you have ever had an allergic or unusual reaction to digoxin.
- you have pericarditis, poor electrical activity in the heart, or Wolff-Parkinson-White syndrome.

Talk to your doctor if:
- you have kidney disease or thyroid disease.
- you are taking any other medicine, especially an antacid, diuretic, antibiotic, or other medicine for the heart or blood pressure.

Side Effects:
Contact your health-care provider immediately if you experience:
- loss of appetite or weight loss.
- nausea and/or vomiting.
- diarrhea.
- change in vision.
- dizziness or disorientation.
- palpitations.
- hallucinations or irritability.

Commonly reported side effects:
- drowsiness
- headache
- muscle weakness
- slower heart rate
- enlarged breasts (in men and women)

Time Required for Drug to Take Effect: Starts to work within 1 to 2 hours of first dose. However, the drug must be taken on a regular basis to achieve constant levels in the blood.

Symptoms of Overdose:
- nausea, vomiting, and diarrhea
- blurred vision or seeing yellow/green halos
- headache
- drowsiness, dizziness, disorientation
- weakness
- hallucinations

Special Notes:
- Digoxin does not cure your condition, and you may have to take this medication for a long time.
- Ask your doctor to tell you the safe range for your heart rate, but generally it is important to call your physician if your heart rate falls below 50 beats per minute.
- Check with your physician or pharmacist before using any over-the-counter medication or any new prescription drug while taking digoxin.
- You will need to have certain blood tests while you are taking digoxin.

diltiazem

Brand Names:

Cardizem
Cardizem CD
Cardizem LA
Cardizem SR

Cartia
Dilacor XR
Taztia XT
Tiazac

Generic Available: yes

Type of Drug: cardiovascular (calcium channel blocker)

Used for: Treatment of angina, high blood pressure (hypertension), and heart rhythm problems.

How This Medication Works: Inhibits smooth-muscle contraction and causes dilation of the blood vessels.

Dosage Form and Strength:

- tablets (30 mg, 60 mg, 90 mg, 120 mg)
- extended-release capsules (120 mg, 180 mg, 240 mg, 300 mg, 360 mg, 420 mg)
- sustained-release capsules (60 mg, 90 mg, 120 mg)

Storage:

- room temperature
- protect from moisture—do not store in bathroom or kitchen

Administration:

- Swallow the sustained-release capsules whole; do not crush or chew.

- The contents of the extended-release capsules may be sprinkled into soft food or liquid and swallowed immediately.
- Take at the same time every day.
- Take a missed dose as soon as possible. However, if it is almost time for the next dose, skip the missed dose and return to your regular dosing schedule.

Precautions:

Do not use if:

- you have ever had an allergic reaction to diltiazem or another calcium channel blocker, such as nifedipine or verapamil.
- you have heart-conduction problems or Wolff-Parkinson-White syndrome.

Talk to your doctor if:

- you have heart, kidney, or liver disease; low blood pressure; or problems with your blood vessels or circulation.
- you are taking any other medications, especially carbamazepine, cyclosporin, or warfarin.

Side Effects:

Contact your health-care provider immediately if you experience:

- severe headache.
- skin rash or itching.
- bleeding from your gums or a thickening of your gums.
- difficulty breathing.
- slow heartbeat (fewer than 50 beats per minute).
- chest pressure or discomfort.

- fainting or feeling extremely weak.
- swelling of the feet or lower legs.

Commonly reported side effects:
- low blood pressure (marked by light-headedness or dizziness)
- headache
- sexual dysfunction
- flushing
- drowsiness or tiredness
- nausea
- constipation

Time Required for Drug to Take Effect: Starts
to work within 30 to 60 minutes of taking the first dose but requires at least 2 to 4 weeks of treatment to reach maximum effectiveness.

Symptoms of Overdose:
- nausea and/or vomiting
- weakness
- dizziness or drowsiness
- confusion or slurred speech
- palpitations
- loss of consciousness

Special Notes:
- Changing positions slowly when sitting and/or standing up may help decrease dizziness caused by this medication.
- Check with your physician or pharmacist before using any over-the-counter medications while taking this drug.
- Diltiazem does not cure your condition, and you may have to take it for a long time.

- Ask your doctor to tell you the safe range for your heart rate, but generally it is important to contact your physician if your heart rate falls below 50 beats per minute.
- Be careful to avoid becoming dehydrated or overheated. Avoid saunas and strenuous exercise in hot weather, and drink plenty of fluids.
- Do not drink alcohol while taking this medication.

donepezil

Brand Names: Aricept, Aricept ODT

Generic Available: no

Type of Drug: acetylcholinesterase inhibitor

Used for: Treatment of mild to moderate Alzheimer's disease.

How This Medication Works: Increases the amount of the brain chemical acetylcholine; lack of acetylcholine in the brain is thought to contribute to Alzheimer's disease.

Dosage Form and Strength: tablets (5 mg, 10 mg)

Storage:
- room temperature
- protect from moisture—do not store in bathroom or kitchen

Administration:
- Usually taken once daily.

- Take this medicine at bedtime.
- May be taken without regard to meals, but take with food if stomach upset occurs.
- Take a missed dose as soon as possible. However, if it is almost time for the next dose, skip the missed dose and return to your regular dosing schedule.

Precautions:
Do not use if:
- you have a hypersensitivity to donepezil or piperidine derivatives.

Talk to your doctor if:
- you have lung disease.
- you have stomach disease or a history of ulcers.
- you have a seizure disorder.
- you have heart conduction problems or a slow heartbeat.
- you experience weight loss after starting this medication.

Side Effects:
Contact your health-care provider immediately if you experience:
- signs of a life-threatening reaction, which include fever; wheezing; chest tightness; and itching or swelling of face, lips, tongue, or throat.
- severe dizziness.
- severe nausea or vomiting.
- severe diarrhea.
- a rash.

Commonly reported side effects:
- nausea and/or vomiting
- loss of appetite

- diarrhea
- fatigue
- insomnia
- muscle cramps

Time Required for Drug to Take Effect: Takes up to 1 month of treatment with the medication to have an effect.

Symptoms of Overdose:
- severe nausea and vomiting
- weakness
- salivation
- sweating
- slow heartbeat
- low blood pressure
- convulsions

Special Notes:
- This drug is not a cure for Alzheimer's disease, but it may temporarily reduce some of the symptoms of the disease.
- Eating small, frequent meals; chewing gum; frequently brushing the teeth; or sucking hard candy may help relieve nausea.
- This medicine is normally started at a low dose that is gradually increased.
- Sound-alike warning: Aricept may be confused with Aciphex.

dorzolamide and timolol combination

Brand Name: Cosopt

Generic Available: no

Type of Drug: beta-blocker and carbonic anhydrase inhibitor

Used for: Treatment of glaucoma.

How This Medication Works: Dorzolamide and timolol work together to lower pressure in the eye.

Dosage Form and Strength: ophthalmic solution, with benzalkonium chloride (2% dorzolamide and 0.5% timolol in 5 mL, 10 mL)

Storage:
- room temperature
- with cap on
- protect from light

Administration:
- For use in the eye only.
- Usually used twice daily.
- Wash hands before and after applying drops.
- Review your health-care provider's instructions for administering eye medication, or read those provided under Taking Medications Correctly in the introduction of this book.
- Take out contact lenses before applying drops.
- Do not touch the tip of the container to the eye or to anything else.

- After administering the medication, keep your eyes closed, and apply pressure to the inside corner of the treated eye (next to the nose) for 3 to 5 minutes; this keeps the medicine from draining out through the tear duct.
- Wait at least 5 minutes before inserting additional drops of the same medication (if prescribed) or a different eye medication into the eye; the eye can only hold one drop at a time.
- Wait at least 15 minutes after using this medicine to insert contact lenses.
- Administer a missed dose as soon as possible, but if it is almost time for the next dose, skip the missed dose and return to your regular dosing schedule.

Precautions:

Do not use if:
- you are allergic to dorzolamide, timolol, or preservatives.
- you have certain severe heart rhythm problems (ask your physician if you are unsure).

Talk to your doctor if:
- you take oral timolol.
- you have lung disease.
- you have an allergy to sulfonamides, sulfonyl-ureas, carbonic anhydrase inhibitors, thiazides, or loop diuretics.

Side Effects:

Contact your health-care provider immediately if you experience:
- a sudden change in your vision, eye pain, or eye irritation.

- signs of a life-threatening reaction, which include fever; wheezing; chest tightness; and itching or swelling of face, lips, tongue, or throat.
- a rash.

Commonly reported side effects:
- mild eye irritation or mild stinging
- temporary blurred vision
- abnormal taste in mouth
- changes in blood pressure or heart rate
- dry mouth
- headache

Time Required for Drug to Take Effect: Starts lowering eye pressure within 2 hours of first dose, but it takes 2 to 4 weeks of treatment to reach maximum effectiveness.

Symptoms of Overdose:
- low blood pressure and slow pulse
- convulsions, coma, cardiac arrest (in severe cases)

Special Notes:
- Do not wash the tip of the dropper with water, soap, or any other cleaner.
- Avoid driving or other tasks that require alertness or clear vision until you see how this medicine affects you.
- Have your eye pressure checked regularly, as directed by your health-care provider.
- Check your blood pressure regularly if you have heart disease or high blood pressure (hypertension).

doxycycline

Brand Names:

Adoxa	Periostat
Doryx	Vibramycin
Monodox	Vibra-Tabs

Generic Available: yes

Type of Drug: antibiotic

Used for: Treatment of bacterial infections and peri-odontitis (gum disease).

How This Medication Works: Inhibits protein synthesis in invading bacteria, damaging the bacteria.

Dosage Form and Strength:
- tablets (20 mg, 50 mg, 75 mg, 100 mg)
- capsules (50 mg, 75 mg, 100 mg)
- syrup (50 mg/5 mL)

Storage:
- room temperature
- tightly closed
- protect from light and moisture—do not store in bathroom or kitchen

Administration:
- Usually taken once or twice daily.
- Take at even intervals.
- May be taken with food or milk.
- Avoid taking within 2 hours of taking an antacid or iron preparation.
- Take a missed dose as soon as possible. However, if it is almost time for the next dose, skip the

missed dose and return to your regular dosing schedule.
- Take until gone, even if symptoms disappear.

Precautions:

Do not use if:
- you are allergic to doxycycline or drugs in the tetracycline family.

Talk to your doctor if:
- you are taking warfarin, carbamazepine, phenobarbital, phenytoin, cimetidine, digoxin, insulin, iron, lithium, or another antibiotic.
- you have liver disease.

Side Effects:

Contact your health-care provider immediately if you experience:
- severe headache.
- severe nausea and/or vomiting.
- a rash.
- swelling of the tongue or lips.
- unexplained muscle aches or back pain.
- severe, persistent diarrhea.
- vaginal itching or discharge.

Commonly reported side effects:
- nausea or stomach upset
- diarrhea

Time Required for Drug to Take Effect:

Begins to kill infecting bacteria within hours after taking the first dose. However, take the full course of doxycycline, even if symptoms disappear.

Symptoms of Overdose:
- loss of appetite

- severe nausea and vomiting
- diarrhea

Special Notes:

- Use a sunblock with at least SPF 15 when outside because doxycycline may increase your sensitivity to the sun.
- Do not use for infections other than the one for which it was prescribed.
- Long-term treatment may lead to bacterial resistance to doxycycline.
- Doxycycline may decrease your need for insulin. Monitor blood glucose levels carefully while you are taking doxycycline.
- Eating yogurt with active cultures may help relieve mild diarrhea, but contact your health-care provider if diarrhea persists.

duloxetine

Brand Name: Cymbalta

Generic Available: no

Type of Drug: serotonin/norepinephrine reuptake inhibitor

Used for: Treatment of depression, painful nerve disorders, and anxiety.

How This Medication Works: Increases levels of the chemicals serotonin and norepinephrine in the brain.

Dosage Form and Strength: capsules (20 mg, 30 mg, 60 mg)

Storage:
- room temperature
- protect from light and moisture—do not store in bathroom or kitchen

Administration:
- Usually taken once or twice daily.
- Swallow capsule whole; do not break, crush, or chew.
- Take with food to avoid an upset stomach.
- Take a missed dose as soon as possible. However, if it is almost time for the next dose, skip the missed dose and return to your regular dosing schedule.

Precautions:
Do not use if:
- you are allergic to duloxetine.
- you have taken a monoamine oxidase (MAO) inhibitor, such as isocarboxazid (Marplan), phenelzine (Nardil), or tranylcypromine (Parnate), in the past 14 days.
- you have uncontrolled narrow-angle glaucoma.

Talk to your doctor if:
- you have high blood pressure.
- you have a history of liver disease.
- you have a history of seizures.
- you have a history of bipolar disorder.
- you take medication for migraine headaches.

Side Effects:

Contact your health-care provider immediately if you experience:

- **the desire to harm yourself or you have suicidal thoughts.**
- signs of a life-threatening reaction, which include wheezing; chest tightness; itching; or swelling of face, lips, tongue, or throat.
- agitation, diarrhea, fast heartbeat, hallucinations, nausea or vomiting, significant change in balance, or a change in thinking clearly and logically.

Commonly reported side effects:

- light-headedness
- sleepiness or drowsiness
- nervousness or feeling excitable
- constipation
- dry mouth
- change in sexual ability or desire (usually reversible)
- sleeping problems
- increased blood pressure

Time Required for Drug to Take Effect: May require 4 to 8 weeks of treatment for symptoms to improve.

Symptoms of Overdose:

- vomiting
- seizures
- sedation
- agitation
- fast heartbeat
- hallucinations

- change in balance
- illogical thinking

Special Notes:
- You can get sunburned more easily while taking this drug; wear protective clothing and eyewear when outside.
- Avoid driving or engaging in tasks that require alertness until you know how your body responds to this drug.
- Avoid other medicines and herbal products that slow your actions and reactions.
- Do not take more of this medication than is prescribed for you; contact your health-care provider immediately if you take more than the prescribed amount.

dutasteride

Brand Name: Avodart

Generic Available: no

Type of Drug: antitestosterone

Used for: Treatment of an enlarged prostate.

How This Medication Works: Reduces prostate growth by lowering testosterone levels.

Dosage Form and Strength: capsules (0.5 mg)

Storage:
- room temperature

- protect from moisture—do not store in bathroom or kitchen

Administration:
- Usually taken once daily.
- Take at a similar time each day.
- May be taken without regard to meals, but take with food if stomach upset occurs.
- Swallow capsule whole; do not break, crush, or chew.
- Take a missed dose as soon as possible. However, if it is almost time for the next dose, skip the missed dose and return to your regular dosing schedule.

Precautions:
Do not use if:
- you are allergic to dutasteride.
- you are a woman.
- you are or may be pregnant or are breast-feeding.

Talk to your doctor if:
- you have liver disease.
- you are taking saw palmetto or Saint John's wort.

Side Effects:
Contact your health-care provider immediately if you experience:
- signs of a life-threatening reaction, which include wheezing; chest tightness; itching; or swelling of face, lips, tongue, or throat.
- a lump in the breast or breast tenderness.
- a rash.
- significant changes in urine volume or voiding patterns.
- a change in mood or sadness.

Commonly reported side effects:
- dizziness or weakness
- change in sexual ability or desire (usually reversible)
- drowsiness

Time Required for Drug to Take Effect: May take 3 to 6 months of treatment to reach maximum effectiveness.

Symptoms of Overdose: No information currently available; contact local poison control center.

Special Notes:
- Do not donate blood while taking this drug, and do not donate blood for 6 months after discontinuing it.
- Children and pregnant women should not handle crushed or broken tablets.
- If you are a sexually active man, you and/or your partner should use birth control methods while you are taking this drug.
- You may need to use this drug for a minimum of 6 months to determine if it will work for you.
- If you are tested for prostate cancer using the prostate-specific antigen (PSA) blood test, tell your doctor that you are taking this drug because it can affect the test results.

enalapril

Brand Name: Vasotec

Generic Available: yes

Type of Drug: antihypertensive (angiotensin-converting enzyme [ACE] inhibitor)

Used for: Treatment of high blood pressure (hypertension), congestive heart failure, kidney disease caused by diabetes (diabetic nephropathy), and preservation of heart function after a heart attack.

How This Medication Works: Inhibits an enzyme needed to make angiotensin. Angiotensin causes powerful constriction of blood vessels.

Dosage Form and Strength: tablets (2.5 mg, 5 mg, 10 mg, 20 mg)

Storage:
- room temperature
- tightly closed
- protect from moisture—do not store in bathroom or kitchen

Administration:
- Usually taken once or twice daily.
- May be taken without regard to food.
- Take a missed dose as soon as possible. However, if it is almost time for the next dose, skip the missed dose and return to your regular dosing schedule.

Precautions:
Do not use if:
- **you are pregnant or could become pregnant.**
- you are allergic to enalapril or another ACE inhibitor, such as captopril or lisinopril.

- you have kidney disease (bilateral renal artery stenosis).

Talk to your doctor if:
- you are taking a diuretic (such as hydrochlorothiazide or furosemide) or a potassium supplement.
- you are taking indomethacin, any nonsteroidal anti-inflammatory drug (such as aspirin, ibuprofen, naproxen, piroxicam, or ketoprofen), allopurinol, digoxin, lithium, or rifampin.

Side Effects:
Contact your health-care provider immediately if you experience:
- swelling of the mouth, lips, or tongue.
- severe dizziness or fainting.
- generalized rash.
- chest pain or irregular heartbeat.
- severe headache.

Commonly reported side effects:
- cough
- headache
- dizziness or fatigue
- abnormal taste

Time Required for Drug to Take Effect:
Usually starts to work 1 to 4 hours after first dose, but sometimes several weeks of treatment are needed for enalapril to reach maximum effectiveness.

Symptoms of Overdose:
- very low blood pressure (marked by dizziness or fainting)
- extreme muscle weakness
- nausea, vomiting, and diarrhea

Special Notes:
- You will need laboratory bloodwork to monitor kidney function and electrolytes (sodium, potassium) in the blood while on enalapril.
- Do not use any salt substitutes containing potassium while you are taking this medication.
- Enalapril may cause a dry cough. Consult your doctor if the cough is particularly bothersome.
- Consult your health-care provider or pharmacist before using any over-the-counter drugs or herbal products while taking this medication.
- Use a sunblock with at least SPF 15 when outside because enalapril may increase your sensitivity to the sun.

escitalopram

Brand Name: Lexapro

Generic Available: no

Type of Drug: antidepressant (selective serotonin reuptake inhibitor)

Used for: Treatment of depression and anxiety.

How This Medication Works: Prolongs the effects of the brain chemical serotonin.

Dosage Form and Strength:
- tablets (5 mg, 10 mg, 20 mg)
- oral solution (1 mg/mL)

Storage:
- room temperature
- protect from moisture—do not store in bathroom or kitchen

Administration:
- Usually taken once daily.
- May be taken without regard to meals, but take with food if stomach upset occurs.
- Take a missed dose as soon as possible. However, if it is almost time for the next dose, skip the missed dose and return to your regular dosing schedule.

Precautions:
Do not use if:
- you are allergic to escitalopram.
- you are currently taking a monoamine oxidase (MAO) inhibitor, such as phenelzine or tranylcypromine. You should stop taking an MAO inhibitor 2 weeks before starting Lexapro, and you should be off Lexapro for 2 weeks before starting an MAO inhibitor.
- you are currently taking linezolid.

Talk to your doctor if:
- you have a history of mania/hypomania.
- you have a history of seizure disorders.
- you have had an allergic reaction to, or other adverse effect from, another antidepressant.
- you have severe kidney or liver disease.
- you are also taking medication for migraine headaches.

Side Effects:

Contact your health-care provider immediately if you experience:

- **thoughts of harming yourself, of if the desire to harm yourself increases.**
- signs of a life-threatening reaction, which include fever; wheezing; chest tightness; and itching or swelling of face, lips, tongue, or throat.
- extreme nervousness, excitability, or confusion.
- a rash.

Commonly reported side effects:

- light-headedness
- fatigue and/or drowsiness
- nervousness
- headache
- nausea and/or vomiting
- change in sexual ability or desire
- insomnia
- blurred vision
- dry mouth

Time Required for Drug to Take Effect: It may take 2 to 4 weeks of treatment to have an effect.

Symptoms of Overdose:

- dizziness
- sleepiness
- nausea and/or vomiting
- sweating
- tremor
- amnesia or confusion
- seizures
- coma

Special Notes:

- The desire to kill yourself is a serious symptom of depression. If you are planning suicide, dial 911 immediately.
- When treating depression, sleep and appetite may improve quickly. Other depressive symptoms may take up to 4 to 6 weeks to improve.
- Avoid driving or other tasks that require alertness until you see how this medicine affects you.
- Do not consume alcohol while taking this drug.
- If you have been taking this medicine for several weeks, consult your health-care provider before stopping. You may need to gradually withdraw from this medicine.

esomeprazole

Brand Name: Nexium

Generic Available: no

Type of Drug: proton pump inhibitor

Used for: Prevention or treatment of heartburn, stomach ulcers, or ulcers of the esophagus (food tube).

How This Medication Works: Prevents symptoms of heartburn, and prevents acid-induced damage to the gastrointestinal tract by reducing stomach acid.

Dosage Form and Strength: capsules (20 mg, 40 mg)

Storage:
- room temperature
- protect from moisture—do not store in bathroom or kitchen

Administration:
- Usually taken once daily.
- Take at a similar time each day.
- Take this medicine 1 hour before your first meal of the day.
- Swallow the capsules whole; do not chew, break, or crush.
- Take a missed dose as soon as possible. However, if it is almost time for the next dose, skip the missed dose and return to your regular dosing schedule.
- You may sprinkle the contents of the capsule on soft food or into liquid, but swallow the mixture immediately; do not store it for future use, and do not chew it or warm it. Acceptable food and liquids include applesauce, yogurt, tap water, orange juice, and apple juice.

Precautions:
Do not use if:
- you have had an allergic reaction to esomeprazole or similar medicines, such as omeprazole (Prilosec), lansoprazole (Prevacid), pantoprazole (Protonix), or rabeprazole (Aciphex).

Talk to your doctor if:
- you are taking iron, ketoconazole, or ampicillin.
- you are taking a protease inhibitor (medication for the treatment of HIV).

Side Effects:

Contact your health-care provider immediately if you experience:

- signs of a life-threatening reaction, which include fever; wheezing; chest tightness; and itching or swelling of face, lips, tongue, or throat.
- unusual bruising or bleeding.
- persistent diarrhea or constipation.
- dark, tarry stools or vomit that resembles coffee grounds.
- a rash.

Commonly reported side effects:

- abdominal pain
- diarrhea, constipation, or flatulence
- dry mouth
- headache
- nausea

Time Required for Drug to Take Effect: Starts working within 1 to 2 hours of first dose, but it may take a week of treatment to reach maximum effectiveness.

Symptoms of Overdose:

- confusion
- drowsiness
- blurred vision
- racing heartbeat
- nausea
- sweating
- headache
- dry mouth

Special Notes:
- While taking this medication, consult your health-care provider or pharmacist before taking any other drugs, including over-the-counter medications.
- Do not smoke or consume alcohol; both can aggravate your condition.

estrogens, conjugated (synthetic)

Brand Name: Premarin

Generic Available: yes

Type of Drug: estrogen hormone

Used for: Controlling menopausal symptoms and abnormal uterine bleeding and preventing osteoporosis in women; controlling prostate cancer in men.

How This Medication Works: Replaces estrogen losses that occur after menopause or ovary removal. In men with prostate cancer, it causes a decrease in blood testosterone levels.

Dosage Form and Strength:
- tablets (0.3 mg, 0.45 mg, 0.625 mg, 0.9 mg, 1.25 mg, 2.5 mg)
- cream (0.625 mg/g)

Storage:
- room temperature
- tightly closed
- protect from light

Administration:
- Usually 0.3 mg to 1.25 mg daily for menopausal symptoms and estrogen replacement.
- Usually 1.25 mg to 2.5 mg 3 times daily for prostate cancer.
- Cream usually inserted once daily at bedtime.
- Take a missed dose as soon as possible. However, if it is almost time for the next dose, skip the missed dose and return to your regular dosing schedule.

Precautions:
Do not use if:
- you are allergic to estradiol, chlorotrianisene, conjugated estrogens, diethylstilbestrol, esterified estrogens, estrone estropipate, ethinyl estradiol, or quinestrol.
- you have breast cancer or experience abnormal vaginal bleeding.
- you are or may be pregnant.

Talk to your doctor if:
- you have endometriosis, gallbladder disease, liver disease, thrombophlebitis (blood clots), heart disease, an estrogen-dependent tumor, or high blood calcium levels from metastatic breast cancer.
- you are taking any other medication, especially bromocriptine, cyclosporine, dantrolene, or tamoxifen.

Side Effects:
Contact your health-care provider immediately if you experience:
- breast pain or a breast lump.

- severe nausea or vomiting.
- chest pain or tightness.
- shortness of breath.
- weakness on one side of the body greater than on the other side, difficulty walking, change in vision, or slurred speech.
- swelling, pain, or redness of the arms, legs, or feet.
- menstrual changes or vaginal bleeding.
- yellowing of the eyes or skin.

Commonly reported side effects:
- breast tenderness or enlargement (in women and men)
- contact lens problems
- dizziness
- increased libido in women; decreased in men
- migraine headaches
- hair loss or unusual hair growth
- stomach cramping, bloating, nausea, or diarrhea

Time Required for Drug to Take Effect: Varies depending on the type of condition treated.

Symptoms of Overdose:
- headache
- nausea and/or vomiting
- vaginal bleeding

Special Notes:
- **Estrogens should not be used for the prevention of heart disease. Use of estrogens may increase your risk for heart attack, stroke, certain cancers, and blood clots. Discuss the risks and benefits with your physician.**

- A woman with an intact uterus should not use estrogens alone and should consult her doctor about adding progestins to prevent endometrial cancer.
- Discuss the risks and benefits of estrogen therapy with your health-care provider.
- If you are taking this medication to prevent osteoporosis, you need to get adequate amounts of calcium and vitamin D; consult your health-care provider or pharmacist for advice.

eszopiclone

Brand Name: Lunesta

Generic Available: no

Type of Drug: sedative/hypnotic (sleeping pill)

Used for: Treatment of insomnia.

How This Medication Works: Calms the brain by interacting with gamma-aminobutyric acid (GABA) receptors, enabling you to fall asleep.

Dosage Form and Strength: tablets (1 mg, 2 mg, 3 mg)

Storage:
- room temperature
- protect from light and moisture—do not store in bathroom or kitchen

Administration:
- Usually one tablet is taken when you are having trouble falling asleep.
- This drug may be taken with or without food, but avoid taking it with a very high-fat meal.
- Take with food to avoid an upset stomach.
- Do not take more often than every 24 hours, unless instructed by your health-care provider.

Precautions:
Do not use if:
- you are allergic to eszopiclone.

Talk to your doctor if:
- you have any type of mental illness or depressive condition.
- you have liver disease or lung disease.
- you drink alcohol or take other sedating medications or herbal products.
- you take antifungals, clarithromycin (Biaxin Filmtab), erythromycin (PCE), nefazodone, protease inhibitors, or verapamil (Calan).

Side Effects:
Contact your health-care provider immediately if you experience:
- signs of a life-threatening reaction, which include wheezing; chest tightness; itching; or swelling of face, lips, tongue, or throat.
- feelings of depression, anxiety, nervousness, or suicidal thoughts.
- a change in ability to think clearly and logically.

Commonly reported side effects:
- feeling light-headed, sleepy, tired, or weak

- altered taste sensations
- blurred vision
- change in balance
- headache

Time Required for Drug to Take Effect: Starts working 10 to 30 minutes after dosing.

Symptoms of Overdose:
- excessive sleepiness
- coma

Special Notes:
- Do not take this medicine unless you can get at least 4 hours of sleep.
- Avoid driving or engaging in tasks that require alertness until you know how your body responds to this drug.
- Avoid alcohol and other sedating medications.
- Talk to your health-care provider before taking any new medicine, including over-the-counter, natural products or vitamins, in conjunction with this drug.
- An increased risk for hazardous sleep-related activities, such as sleep-driving, eating/cooking while asleep, and making phone calls while asleep have been observed.
- Keep good sleep habits by avoiding naps during the day; getting up and going to bed at the same time every day; only using your bed for sleeping; making sure your bed and bedroom are quiet and comfortable; and avoiding alcohol, heavy meals, and caffeine in the evenings.

ezetimibe

Brand Name: Zetia

Generic Available: no

Type of Drug: cholesterol-lowering agent

Used for: Lowering cholesterol levels in the body.

How This Medication Works: Reduces the amount of cholesterol absorbed by the body.

Dosage Form and Strength: tablets (10 mg)

Storage:
- room temperature
- protect from moisture—do not store in bathroom or kitchen

Administration:
- Usually taken once daily.
- May be taken without regard to meals, but take with food if stomach upset occurs.
- Take a missed dose as soon as possible. However, if it is almost time for the next dose, skip the missed dose and return to your regular dosing schedule.

Precautions:
Do not use if:
- you are allergic to ezetimibe.
Talk to your doctor if:
- you have liver disease.
- you drink more than 3 alcoholic beverages per day.

Side Effects:

Contact your health-care provider immediately if you experience:
- signs of a life-threatening reaction, which include fever; wheezing; chest tightness; and itching or swelling of face, lips, tongue, or throat.

Commonly reported side effects:
- headache
- stomach pain
- tiredness or weakness
- cough

Time Required for Drug to Take Effect: Starts
lowering cholesterol within 1 week of first dose, but it may take up to 4 weeks of treatment to reach maximum effectiveness.

Symptoms of Overdose: None seen in overdoses
of up to 50 mg. Contact local poison control center.

Special Notes:
- Zetia may be taken at the same time as other cholesterol medications, such as atorvastatin, lovastatin, or simvastatin. However, take Zetia 2 hours before or 4 hours after taking a bile-acid binding agent, such as cholestyramine or colestipol.
- Follow a diet plan and exercise program recommended by your health-care provider.

famotidine

Brand Names: Pepcid, Pepcid AC

Generic Available: yes

Type of Drug: gastrointestinal (histamine H_2 blocker)

Used for: Treatment of excess acid production in the stomach, ulcers, and heartburn, or gastroesophageal reflux disease (GERD).

How This Medication Works: Blocks histamine from binding to sites in the stomach that would cause acid secretion.

Dosage Form and Strength:
- tablets (10 mg, 20 mg, 40 mg)
- suspension (40 mg/5 mL)

Storage:
Tablets:
- room temperature
- tightly closed
- protect from moisture—do not store in bathroom or kitchen

Suspension:
- room temperature
- tightly closed
- discard unused portion after 30 days

Administration:
- If you are taking multiple doses daily, take with or immediately after meals unless your doctor directs you to do otherwise.

- If you are only taking 1 dose daily, take it before bedtime unless your doctor directs you to do otherwise.
- If you also take an antacid, separate doses of famotidine and the antacid by 2 hours.
- Take a missed dose as soon as possible. However, if it is almost time for the next dose, skip the missed dose and return to your regular dosing schedule.
- Shake the suspension form of this drug well before measuring each dose.
- Do not swallow chewable tablets whole; chew or crush them well.

Precautions:
Do not use if:
- you are allergic to famotidine or other histamine H_2 blockers, such as cimetidine or ranitidine.

Talk to your doctor if:
- you have kidney or liver disease.
- you are taking any other medications, especially an anticoagulant (such as warfarin), an antibiotic, theophylline, itraconazole, or ketoconazole.

Side Effects:
Contact your health-care provider immediately if you experience:
- signs of a life-threatening reaction, which include fever; wheezing; chest tightness; and itching or swelling of face, lips, tongue, or throat.
- confusion or anxiety.
- fast heartbeat.
- dark, tarry stools or vomit that looks like coffee grounds.
- unusual bleeding or bruising.

Commonly reported side effects:
- constipation or diarrhea
- decreased sexual ability or desire
- dizziness or drowsiness
- headache
- dry mouth
- loss of appetite or stomach upset
- nausea and/or vomiting
- swelling of breasts (in men and women)
- hair loss

Time Required for Drug to Take Effect: Starts to work within 1 hour of taking the first dose. However, ulcer healing may require 4 to 12 weeks of treatment.

Symptoms of Overdose:
- difficulty breathing
- irregular heartbeat
- tremors
- vomiting or diarrhea
- light-headedness

Special Notes:
- Check with your physician or pharmacist before taking any over-the-counter medications while using this drug.
- Avoid medications that may make your condition worse, including nonsteroidal anti-inflammatory drugs (aspirin, ibuprofen, naproxen, ketoprofen).
- This medication may cause drowsiness. Use caution when driving or operating dangerous machinery.
- If you self-medicate with Pepcid AC for more than 2 weeks, contact your health-care provider.

- Avoid consuming alcohol and smoking; these activities can aggravate your condition.

felodipine

Brand Name: Plendil

Generic Available: no

Type of Drug: calcium channel blocker

Used for: Treatment of high blood pressure (hypertension).

How This Medication Works: Relaxes smooth muscles and causes blood vessels to dilate.

Dosage Form and Strength: tablets (2.5 mg, 5 mg, 10 mg)

Storage:
- room temperature
- protect from light and moisture—do not store in bathroom or kitchen

Administration:
- Usually taken once daily.
- Take at the same time every day.
- Take with or without food.
- Swallow the tablets whole; do not crush or chew.
- Take a missed dose as soon as possible. However, if it is almost time for the next dose, skip the missed dose and return to your regular dosing schedule.

Precautions:

Do not use if:

- You have ever had an allergic reaction to felodipine or another calcium channel blocker, such as amlodipine.

Talk to your doctor if:

- you have heart disease, kidney disease, liver disease, or problems with your blood vessels or circulation.
- you are taking any other medications, especially medications for the heart or blood pressure, carbamazepine, cyclosporine, warfarin, cimetidine, erythromycin, or antifungal medication.

Side Effects:

Contact your health-care provider immediately if you experience:

- bleeding or bruising, especially in the gum area.
- skin rash or itching.
- difficulty breathing.
- chest pressure or discomfort.
- severe dizziness or fainting.
- swelling of the lower legs, ankles, or feet.

Commonly reported side effects:

- low blood pressure (marked by light-headedness or dizziness)
- headache
- sexual dysfunction
- flushing
- drowsiness or fatigue
- nausea or constipation

Time Required for Drug to Take Effect: Starts
to work within 2 to 5 hours of the first dose, but it takes
at least 2 to 4 weeks of treatment to reach maximum
effectiveness.

Symptoms of Overdose:
- nausea and/or vomiting
- weakness
- dizziness or drowsiness
- confusion
- low blood pressure and slow pulse
- loss of consciousness

Special Notes:
- Felodipine does not cure high blood pressure, and
  you may have to take it for a long time.
- To decrease dizziness caused by this drug, stand
  up slowly from a sitting or lying position.
- If this drug makes you dizzy, avoid driving and
  other tasks that require alertness.
- Check with your physician or pharmacist before
  using any over-the-counter medications while
  taking this drug.
- Avoid becoming dehydrated or overheated while
  taking this drug. Drink plenty of fluids.
- Do not drink alcohol while taking this medication.
- Do not consume grapefruit or grapefruit juice
  while taking this medication.
- Look-alike/sound-alike warning: Plendil may be
  confused with Prinivil or Pletal.

fenofibrate

Brand Names: Lofibra, TriCor

Generic Available: no

Type of Drug: antihyperlipidemic (fibric acid)

Used for: Reduction of triglyceride and cholesterol levels in the blood.

How This Medication Works: Decreases body's production of LDL (bad) cholesterol and triglycerides.

Dosage Form and Strength:
- tablets (48 mg, 145 mg)
- micronized capsules (67 mg, 134 mg, 200 mg)

Storage:
- room temperature
- protect from moisture—do not store in bathroom or kitchen

Administration:
- Usually taken once daily.
- May be taken without regard to meals, but take with food if stomach upset occurs.
- Take a missed dose as soon as possible. However, if it is almost time for the next dose, skip the missed dose and return to your regular dosing schedule.

Precautions:
Do not use if:
- you are allergic to fenofibrate.

- you have gallbladder disease or severe liver or kidney disease.

Talk to your doctor if:
- you are taking the blood thinner warfarin or a cholesterol medication other than fenofibrate, such as atorvastatin, simvastatin, lovastatin, or fluvastatin.

Side Effects:

Contact your health-care provider immediately if you experience:
- signs of a life-threatening reaction, which include fever; wheezing; chest tightness; and itching or swelling of face, lips, tongue, or throat.
- severe stomach pain.
- severe nausea or vomiting.
- a rash.
- yellowing of the skin or eyes.
- severe muscle pain or weakness.

Commonly reported side effects:
- stomach upset or heartburn
- nausea and/or vomiting
- flatulence

Time Required for Drug to Take Effect: Starts
lowering blood cholesterol within 2 weeks of first dose, but it takes 6 to 8 weeks of treatment to reach maximum effectiveness.

Symptoms of Overdose:
- nausea and/or vomiting
- diarrhea

Special Notes:
- Follow a diet plan and exercise program recommended by your health-care provider.
- Do not consume alcohol while taking this drug.
- Talk to your health-care provider about having your cholesterol and liver enzymes measured while you are on this medication.

fentanyl

Brand Names: Actiq, Duragesic

Generic Available: yes (patch only)

Type of Drug: narcotic analgesic

Used for: These drugs should only be used for lasting, chronic pain that is not managed by other medications. These products contain a very potent narcotic and have a high potential for abuse, overdose, and criminal diversion.

How This Medication Works: Decreases the brain's recognition of pain signals.

Dosage Form and Strength:
- patch (25 mcg/hr, 50 mcg/hr, 75 mcg/hr, 100 mcg/hr)
- oral lozenge (200 mcg, 400 mcg, 600 mcg, 800 mcg, 1,200 mcg, 1,600 mcg)

Storage:
- room temperature; do not freeze

- protect from heat and moisture—do not store in bathroom or kitchen

Administration:

- Patch form: Generally prescribed as 1 patch every 3 days (72 hours).
- Lozenge/lollipop form usually prescribed on an "as-needed" basis.
- Read directions for application of the patch closely; they may vary among products.
- Wash and dry hands thoroughly before and after applying patch.
- Never cut the patch or the wrapper with scissors. Do not use any patch that has been cut or torn.
- Apply patch to a clean, dry, nonoily area of the chest, upper back, or upper arm that is free of hair. If necessary, clip hair; do not shave.
- Do not apply on cuts or abrasions.
- Do not put the patch on the same spot each time; rotate patch placement so that at least 1 week passes between applications to the same spot.
- Remove the old (used) patch before applying the new one.
- Do not use soap, lotions, oils, or alcohol before applying a patch.
- Apply the patch to a prepared site immediately after removing it from its sealed package.
- If you forget to change a patch, do so as soon as you can. However, if it is almost time to apply the next patch, wait until then to apply a new one. Do not apply an extra patch to make up for a missed one.

- The lozenge or lollipop should be placed between your cheek and lower gum. Do not crush, break, or chew it.
- If you are taking the lozenge on a routine basis, take a missed lozenge as soon as possible. However, if it is almost time for the next lozenge, skip the missed one and return to your regular dosing schedule. Do not use more than 1 lozenge at a time.
- The lozenge in lollipop form may appear especially appealing to children; extra caution should therefore be taken to keep this medicine out of the reach of children.
- Do not take this medication more often than prescribed.

Precautions:

Do not use if:

- you are allergic to fentanyl or any related medications, such as meperidine, diphenoxylate, or loperamide.

Talk to your doctor if:

- you have a substance-abuse problem or alcoholism; brain disease or a head injury; colitis; seizures; emotional problems or mental illness; emphysema, asthma, or other lung disease; kidney, liver, or thyroid disease; prostate or urination problems; gallstones; or gallbladder disease.
- you have ever had an abnormal heartbeat.
- you are taking any other medications, especially naltrexone, zidovudine, or a medication that can cause drowsiness, such as an antihistamine,

barbiturate (phenobarbital), benzodiazepine (diazepam, alprazolam, lorazepam), muscle relaxant, or antidepressant.
- you weigh less than 110 pounds.
- you have a fever above 102 degrees Fahrenheit.

Side Effects:
Contact your health-care provider immediately if you experience:
- skin rash or hives.
- severe confusion, hallucinations, or seizures.
- fainting or extreme weakness.
- painful or difficult urination.
- severe nausea, vomiting, or constipation.
- fast, slow, or pounding heartbeat.
- irregular breathing or difficulty breathing.
- uncontrolled pain.

Commonly reported side effects:
- constipation
- drowsiness or sedation
- nausea and/or vomiting
- nervousness or restlessness

Time Required for Drug to Take Effect: Starts
to work within several hours of first dose. However, it takes at least 24 hours of treatment to achieve maximum pain relief. It may take up to 6 days after a dosage increase to feel the full pain-relieving effect of the higher dose.

Symptoms of Overdose:
- cold, clammy skin
- severe confusion
- seizures

- severe dizziness or drowsiness
- continued nausea and/or vomiting
- severe nervousness or restlessness
- difficulty breathing
- slowed heartbeat

Special Notes:

- Do not allow the patch to become too hot; avoid exposing it to direct sunlight, electric blankets or heating pads, or saunas or hot tubs.
- This drug may cause dizziness or drowsiness. Use caution when driving or performing other tasks that require alertness until you see how this medication affects you.
- Fentanyl may cause constipation. This side effect may be diminished by drinking 6 to 8 eight-ounce glasses of water per day. If using this medication for chronic pain, ask your doctor about adding a stool softener-laxative combination.
- Check with your physician or pharmacist before using any over-the-counter medications while taking this drug.
- When fentanyl is used over a long period, your body may become tolerant and require larger doses. If your pain is no longer relieved by the current dose, talk to your doctor or pharmacist.
- Do not stop taking this medication abruptly.
- Nausea and vomiting may occur, especially after the first few doses; this effect will usually diminish with time.
- Do not drink alcohol while taking this drug.
- If you think you or anyone else may have taken an overdose, get emergency help immediately.

- Use this medication as prescribed; do not exceed the dose or frequency prescribed by your doctor.
- Keep away from children and pets. Dispose of used patches or lozenges in such a way that pets or other people cannot handle them. Consult your pharmacist for advice if you are unsure how to dispose of them safely.

ferrous sulfate

Brand Names:

Feosol

Feratab

Fer-In-Sol Syrup

Fer-Iron

Slow FE

Generic Available: yes

Type of Drug: iron supplement

Used for: Treatment of anemia caused by low iron stores in the body.

How This Medication Works: Replaces iron that is needed to make the oxygen-carrying hemoglobin in red blood cells.

Dosage Form and Strength:

- tablets (200 mg, 300 mg, 325 mg)
- extended-release tablets (160 mg)
- elixir (220 mg/5 mL)
- solution (75 mg/0.6 mL)

Storage:

- room temperature

- protect from light and moisture—do not store in bathroom or kitchen

Administration:
- This medication can be taken with food to avoid stomach upset.
- Swallow extended-release tablets whole; do not break, crush, or chew.
- Do not take a multivitamin or a supplement of calcium, zinc, or copper within 2 hours of a dose of this medication.
- Do not take an antacid within 2 hours of a dose of this medication.
- Take a missed dose as soon as possible. However, if it is almost time for the next dose, skip the missed dose and return to your regular dosing schedule.

Precautions:
Do not use if:
- you are receiving iron shots or injections.
- you are allergic to ferrous sulfate.
- you suffer from either thalassemia or hemochromatosis.

Talk to your doctor if:
- you have rheumatoid arthritis, other blood diseases or anemias, colitis or other intestine problems, stomach ulcers, liver problems, or kidney problems.
- you are taking any other medication, especially an antacid or calcium supplement, etidronate, tetracycline, levofloxacin, ciprofloxacin, moxifloxacin, or gatifloxacin.

Side Effects:

Contact your health-care provider immediately if you
experience:
- signs of a life-threatening reaction, which include fever; wheezing; chest tightness; and itching or swelling of face, lips, tongue, or throat.
- bluish-colored lips, fingernails, and palms.
- severe nausea, vomiting, or diarrhea.
- severe constipation.
- weak and fast heartbeat.

Commonly reported side effects:
- stomach pain or cramping
- constipation
- dark stools or urine
- nausea and/or vomiting
- heartburn

Time Required for Drug to Take Effect:

Usually takes 3 to 6 months of treatment to replace the iron that has been lost.

Symptoms of Overdose:

- bloody vomit and diarrhea
- stomach pain
- bluish-colored lips, fingernails, and palms
- seizures
- drowsiness
- coma

Call 911 or poison control center immediately if overdose occurs or is suspected.

Special Notes:

- Do not take iron for more than 6 months without discussing it with your doctor.

- Do not consume dairy products, spinach, whole-grain breads, cereals, bran, tea, or coffee with your dose of iron; these foods can decrease the amount of iron absorbed by the body. Separate your dose of iron from consumption of these foods and drinks by at least 1 to 2 hours.
- If your teeth become stained from treatment, brush with baking soda and peroxide.
- Increasing fluid and fiber intake and getting regular exercise can help relieve constipation. If constipation continues, talk to your health-care provider about adding a stool softener or laxative.
- Store this drug out of the reach of children; iron is a leading cause of fatal poisoning in children younger than 6.

fexofenadine

Brand Name: Allegra

Generic Available: yes

Type of Drug: nonsedating antihistamine

Used for: Relief of allergy symptoms and treatment of hives.

How This Medication Works: Stops allergic reaction by blocking histamine and preventing the body's response to whatever is causing the allergy.

Dosage Form and Strength:
- tablets (30 mg, 60 mg, 180 mg)
- oral suspension (6 mg/mL)

Storage:
- room temperature
- protect from moisture—do not store in bathroom or kitchen

Administration:
- Usually taken once or twice daily. Many times, this medicine is prescribed for use on an "as-needed" basis.
- This medicine is most effective if started before symptoms occur. Take it several hours before expected contact with the cause of your allergic reactions.
- Swallow the 180 mg tablet whole; do not chew, break, or crush.
- Shake oral suspension well before each use.
- Do not take this medicine with fruit juice.
- May be taken without regard to meals, but take with food if stomach upset occurs.
- Take a missed dose as soon as possible. However, if it is almost time for the next dose, skip the missed dose and return to your regular dosing schedule.

Precautions:
Do not use if:
- you are allergic to fexofenadine or to terfenadine.

Talk to your doctor if:
- you take any other medication that makes you drowsy, such as a sedative, tranquilizer, mood stabilizer, another antihistamine, or pain medicine.

Side Effects:

Contact your health-care provider immediately if you experience:
- signs of a life-threatening reaction, which include fever; wheezing; chest tightness; and itching or swelling of face, lips, tongue, or throat.
- extreme weakness or fatigue.
- extreme sedation or confusion.
- a rash.
- chest pain or heart palpitations.

Commonly reported side effects:
- headache
- dry mouth
- drowsiness or dizziness
- nausea or stomach upset

Time Required for Drug to Take Effect: Starts working within 1 to 3 hours of taking a dose.

Symptoms of Overdose:
- drowsiness
- dizziness
- dry mouth

Special Notes:
- Avoid use of other antihistamines (such as diphenhydramine or chlorpheniramine), alcohol, or sleep-inducing medications while taking this medication unless approved by your health-care provider.
- Fexofenadine should not be taken at the same time as an antacid; separate doses by at least 1 hour.
- Avoid driving and other tasks that require alertness until you see how this medicine affects you.

- Consult your health-care provider or pharmacist before taking any over-the-counter medications while taking this drug.

finasteride

Brand Names: Propecia, Proscar

Generic Available: yes

Type of Drug: antitestosterone

Used for: Treatment of symptoms of an enlarged prostate or of hair loss in male pattern baldness.

How This Medication Works: Reduces prostate growth by lowering testosterone levels. Also increases hair regrowth and slows hair loss.

Dosage Form and Strength: tablets (1 mg, 5 mg)

Storage:
- room temperature
- protect from moisture—do not store in bathroom or kitchen

Administration:
- Usually taken once daily.
- Take at a similar time each day.
- May be taken without regard to meals, but take with food if stomach upset occurs.
- Take a missed dose as soon as possible. However, if it is almost time for the next dose, skip the missed dose and return to your regular dosing schedule.

Precautions:

Do not use if:

- you are allergic to finasteride.
- you are or may be pregnant.

Talk to your doctor if:

- you take saw palmetto or Saint John's wort.
- you have liver disease.

Side Effects:

Contact your health-care provider immediately if you experience:

- signs of a life-threatening reaction, which include fever; wheezing; chest tightness; and itching or swelling of face, lips, tongue, or throat.
- a lump in the breast or breast tenderness.
- a rash.
- a change in amount of urine or frequency of urination.
- unexplained sadness or change in mood.

Commonly reported side effects:

- dizziness or weakness
- change in sexual ability or desire
- drowsiness

Time Required for Drug to Take Effect: May take 3 to 6 months of treatment to reach maximum effectiveness.

Symptoms of Overdose: No data currently available. Contact your local poison control center for instructions.

Special Notes:

- Do not donate blood while you are taking finasteride and for 1 month after stopping treatment with it.
- Children and pregnant women should not handle crushed or broken tablets.
- If you are a sexually active male, protect your partner from pregnancy while you are being treated with this medication.
- A minimum of 6 months of treatment may be necessary to determine if this medication will work for you.
- If you are tested for prostate cancer using a blood test called PSA (prostate-specific antigen), tell the doctor you are taking finasteride; the drug can affect the test results.

fluoxetine

Brand Names:
Prozac
Prozac Weekly
Sarafem

Generic Available: yes

Type of Drug: antidepressant (selective serotonin reuptake inhibitor)

Used for: Treatment of depression, obsessive-compulsive disorder, eating disorders, panic attacks, and premenstrual dysphoric disorder (PMDD).

How This Medication Works: Increases the brain chemical serotonin.

Dosage Form and Strength:
- daily capsules (10 mg, 20 mg, 40 mg)
- weekly capsules (90 mg)
- liquid (20 mg/5 mL)
- tablets (10 mg, 20 mg)

Storage:
- room temperature
- protect from light and moisture—do not store in bathroom or kitchen

Administration:
- Usually taken once daily in the morning, except for Prozac Weekly, which is taken once every 7 days.
- May be taken with food if medicine causes an upset stomach.
- Swallow Prozac Weekly whole; do not crush, break, or chew.
- Take a missed dose as soon as possible. However, if it is almost time for the next dose, skip the missed dose and return to your regular dosing schedule.

Precautions:
Do not use if:
- you have ever had an allergic reaction to fluoxetine or another selective serotonin reuptake inhibitor antidepressant, such as paroxetine or citalopram.
- you have taken a monoamine oxidase (MAO) inhibitor, such as phenelzine or tranylcypromine, within the past 14 days.
- you are taking thioridazine or mesoridazine.

Talk to your doctor if:
- you have ever had liver or kidney problems.
- you have seizures (or take medicines to control seizures), diabetes, heart disease, or bipolar disorder.
- you are taking medication for migraine headaches.
- you are taking any other type of antidepressant medicine, lithium, a cough suppressant (dextromethorphan), selegiline, warfarin, or tryptophan.

Side Effects:

Contact your health-care provider immediately if you experience:
- **suicidal thoughts or feelings of harming yourself.**
- seizures.
- unusual agitation or restlessness.
- severe nausea or vomiting.
- chest pains or palpitations.
- skin rash, hives, itching, or swelling.
- unusual movements of the mouth, face, arms, or legs.

Commonly reported side effects:
- difficulty sleeping
- anxiety, nervousness
- drowsiness or dizziness
- vivid dreams
- headache
- tremor
- nausea, stomach upset
- diarrhea
- loss of appetite and weight loss

- increased appetite and weight gain
- dry mouth
- decreased sexual function or desire

Time Required for Drug to Take Effect:

Appetite or sleep may begin to improve within the first few weeks of treatment, but it may take 4 to 8 weeks to reach maximum effectiveness.

Symptoms of Overdose:

- seizures
- severe nausea and vomiting
- agitation or increased excitement
- difficulty breathing
- sedation or coma

Special Notes:

- The desire to harm yourself is a serious symptom of depression. If you are planning suicide, call 911 immediately.
- Know which "target symptoms" (sadness, worry, fear, or changes in sleep or appetite) you are being treated for and note whether they are improving, worsening, or unchanged.
- Fluoxetine may interact with several other medicines commonly used by older adults. Show your doctor and pharmacist a complete list of all your medicines, including nonprescription drugs.
- Do not drink alcohol while taking this medication.
- Never change your dose of this medication without your doctor's consent.
- If you have diabetes, you may need to check your blood glucose more frequently.

- Do not drive or operate machinery until you see how this medication affects you.

fluticasone

Brand Names: Flonase Nasal Spray, Flovent HFA Oral Inhaler

Generic Available: yes (nasal inhaler only)

Type of Drug: corticosteroid

Used for: As oral inhalation, prevention of asthma symptoms. As nasal inhalation, treatment of nasal congestion.

How This Medication Works: Reduces irritation and swelling by minimizing or preventing the body's response to whatever is causing the reaction.

Dosage Form and Strength:
- oral inhaler (44 mcg/inhalation, 110 mcg/inhalation, 220 mcg/inhalation)
- nasal inhaler (50 mcg/inhalation)

Storage:
- room temperature; do not freeze
- always store with cap on

Administration:
- Take a missed dose as soon as possible. However, if it is almost time for the next dose, skip the missed dose and return to your regular dosing schedule.

Oral inhalation:
- Follow all instructions provided with inhaler.
- Shake well before use.
- Test spray in air before using for first time or if inhaler has not been used for a while.
- Rinse out mouth after each use.

Nasal spray:
- Use in nose only.
- Shake well before use.
- Blow nose to clear nostrils before use.
- Before using spray the first time, prime it by pumping or squeezing bottle until some of the medicine sprays out; it is then ready to use.
- Prime the spray again after each pump cleaning or if it has not been used for 5 or more days.
- After use, wipe off tip of bottle and put cap back on.

Precautions:

Do not use if:
- you are allergic to fluticasone.
- you have a severe allergy to milk proteins (applies to oral inhalation powder only).

Talk to your doctor if:
- you are switching from oral steroids to inhaled steroids.
- you are having surgery or you have an infection.

Side Effects:

Contact your health-care provider immediately if you experience:
- signs of a life-threatening reaction, which include wheezing; chest tightness; and itching or swelling of face, lips, tongue, or throat.

- signs of infection, which may include fever, chills, severe sore throat, ear or sinus pain, or cough.
- extreme fatigue, weakness, or irritability.
- trembling or a fast heartbeat.
- confusion or dizziness.
- any sores or white patches in your mouth, throat, or nose.
- a worsening of your asthma or allergy symptoms.

Commonly reported side effects:
- headache
- nasal congestion
- nasal irritation

Time Required for Drug to Take Effect: This
medication starts working within 24 hours of taking the first dose, but it often takes as long as 2 weeks of treatment to reach maximum effectiveness and provide relief.

Symptoms of Overdose: Symptoms may include
stomach pain, muscle weakness, chest pain, or sei-zures. If you have been regularly taking more than the prescribed amount, it is very important that you don't stop the medication abruptly; contact your health-care provider or local poison control center for instructions.

Special Notes:
- Flovent should not be used for emergency relief of an asthma attack.

- Do not keep this medicine inside a car or anywhere else it can be exposed to extreme heat or extreme cold.
- Avoid exposure to chicken pox or measles while you are taking this drug. If exposed, inform your doctor as soon as possible.

fluvastatin

Brand Names: Lescol, Lescol XL

Generic Available: no

Type of Drug: antihyperlipidemic (HMG-CoA reductase inhibitor)

Used for: Treatment of high blood cholesterol levels and heart disease.

How This Medication Works: Decreases the amount of cholesterol produced in the liver by inhibiting an enzyme.

Dosage Form and Strength:
- capsules (20 mg, 40 mg)
- extended-release tablets (80 mg)

Storage:
- room temperature
- protect from light and moisture—do not store in bathroom or kitchen

Administration:
- Usually taken once daily in the evening.
- Take at the same time every day.

- May be taken without regard to meals, but take with food if stomach upset occurs.
- Swallow the extended-release tablets whole; do not break, chew, or crush.
- Do not take cholestyramine or colestipol within 4 hours of a dose of fluvastatin.
- Take a missed dose as soon as possible. However, if it is almost time for the next dose, skip the missed dose and return to your regular dosing schedule.

Precautions:
Do not use if:
- you are allergic to fluvastatin or similar drugs, such as simvastatin, lovastatin, or pravastatin.
- you have severe liver disease.
- you are or may be pregnant.

Talk to your doctor if:
- you have liver disease.
- you drink more than 3 alcoholic beverages per day.
- you are taking any other medication, especially cyclosporine, erythromycin, warfarin, niacin, or gemfibrozil.

Side Effects:
Contact your health-care provider immediately if you experience:
- a rash.
- unexplained muscle aches or weakness.
- breathing difficulty.
- swelling of the face, throat, lips, or tongue.
- yellowing of the eyes or skin.

Commonly reported side effects:
- abdominal pain

- diarrhea
- headache
- dizziness
- taste disturbances

Time Required for Drug to Take Effect: Starts lowering blood cholesterol levels within 1 to 2 weeks of first dose, but it may take 4 to 6 weeks of treatment to reach maximum effectiveness.

Symptoms of Overdose: stomach upset

Special Notes:

- Use a sunblock with at least SPF 15 when outside because fluvastatin may increase your sensitivity to the sun.
- Do not drink alcohol while taking this medication.
- Reduce cholesterol by adhering to a cholesterol-lowering diet and getting regular exercise. Contact your health-care provider for direction.
- Fluvastatin is not a cure and must be taken on a long-term basis to have an effect.
- Your doctor will monitor your liver function with laboratory blood tests while you are taking this medicine.

fosinopril sodium

Brand Name: Monopril

Generic Available: yes

Type of Drug: antihypertensive (angiotensin-converting enzyme [ACE] inhibitor)

Used for: Treatment of high blood pressure (hypertension), heart failure, or kidney problems due to diabetes. Also used to strengthen the heart muscle after heart attack.

How This Medication Works: Lowers blood pressure by decreasing production of angiotensin, a strong chemical that causes blood vessels to constrict.

Dosage Form and Strength: tablets (10 mg, 20 mg, 40 mg)

Storage:
- room temperature
- protect from moisture—do not store in bathroom or kitchen

Administration:
- Usually taken once or twice daily.
- Take at a similar time each day.
- May be taken without regard to meals, but take with food if stomach upset occurs.
- Take a missed dose as soon as possible. However, if it is almost time for the next dose, skip the missed dose and return to your regular dosing schedule.

Precautions:
Do not use if:
- **you are pregnant or could become pregnant.**
- you are allergic to fosinopril or other ACE inhibitor, such as lisinopril, enalapril, benazepril, or ramipril.
- you have bilateral renal artery stenosis (blockage of the kidney's blood vessels).

Talk to your doctor if:
- you have severe aortic stenosis.
- you have severe liver or kidney disease.
- you have low blood pressure.
- you become dehydrated.
- you are taking allopurinol, lithium, potassium supplements, or spironolactone.

Side Effects:

Contact your health-care provider immediately if you experience:
- signs of a life-threatening reaction, which include fever; wheezing; chest tightness; and itching or swelling of face, lips, tongue, or throat.
- severe dizziness or fainting.
- chest pain or palpitations.
- severe headache.
- a rash.

Commonly reported side effects:
- dizziness or light-headedness
- headache
- abnormal taste in mouth
- cough

Time Required for Drug to Take Effect: Starts
working within 24 hours of taking the first dose, but it may take up to 2 weeks of treatment to reach maximum effectiveness.

Symptoms of Overdose:
- low blood pressure
- slow pulse
- nausea and/or vomiting
- confusion

Special Notes:

- Do not use potassium-containing salt substitutes while taking this drug.
- Follow a diet plan and exercise program recommended by your health-care provider.
- To avoid dizziness while you are taking this medication, rise slowly over several minutes from a sitting or lying position.
- Notify your health-care provider if you develop a persistent cough that becomes bothersome while taking this drug.

furosemide

Brand Name: Lasix

Generic Available: yes

Type of Drug: diuretic

Used for: Treatment of fluid retention (edema) and high blood pressure (hypertension).

How This Medication Works: Removes excess salt and water from the body through the kidneys, resulting in loss of water through urine. **This medication is very potent and can cause severe dehydration if used incorrectly.**

Dosage Form and Strength:

- tablets (20 mg, 40 mg, 80 mg)
- liquid (10 mg/mL)

Storage:
- room temperature
- protect from light and moisture—do not store in bathroom or kitchen

Administration:
- Usually taken once or twice daily.
- Take furosemide in the morning to avoid sleep disruption.
- Take this medication with food or milk if stomach upset occurs.
- Take a missed dose as soon as possible. However, if it is almost time for the next dose, skip the missed dose and return to your regular dosing schedule.

Precautions:
Do not use if:
- you are allergic to furosemide or any oral antidiabetic medication, such as tolazamide, glipizide, or glyburide.

Talk to your doctor if:
- you have liver or kidney disease, coronary artery disease, or gout.
- you are taking digoxin, an angiotensin-converting enzyme (ACE) inhibitor (such as captopril, enalapril, or lisinopril), a thiazide diuretic (such as hydrochlorothiazide or metolazone), warfarin, lithium, theophylline, propranolol, phenytoin, a salicylate (such as aspirin), or a nonsteroidal anti-inflammatory drug (such as ibuprofen, diclofenac, naproxen, and oxaprozin).

- you have diabetes or are taking an oral diabetic medication, such as chlorpropamide, tolazamide, glipizide, or glyburide.
- you are or become dehydrated.

Side Effects:

Contact your health-care provider immediately if you experience:

- severe dehydration (thirst, rapid heartbeat, weakness, and dizziness).
- a rash.
- difficulty breathing.
- muscle pain or cramps.
- severe dizziness or fainting.
- chest pain.
- prolonged vomiting or diarrhea.

Commonly reported side effects:

- ringing in the ears
- nausea and/or vomiting
- dizziness
- dry mouth
- headache
- constipation or diarrhea

Time Required for Drug to Take Effect:

Begins to work within about 45 minutes after dosing.

Symptoms of Overdose:

- large urine loss
- loss of appetite
- weakness or dizziness
- vomiting
- mental confusion
- low blood pressure

Special Notes:
- Take this drug with orange juice or a banana to help replace lost potassium.
- Unless otherwise instructed by your doctor, be sure to drink 6 to 8 eight-ounce glasses of water daily to avoid dehydration.
- Use a sunblock with at least SPF 15 when outside because furosemide may increase your sensitivity to the sun.
- Weigh yourself daily. If you gain significant weight, contact your doctor.
- Your doctor will check calcium, magnesium, and potassium levels in your blood and determine if supplementation is necessary.
- Changing positions slowly when sitting and/or standing up may help decrease dizziness caused by this medication.
- Do not take more of this drug than directed by your health-care provider.

gabapentin

Brand Name: Neurontin

Generic Available: yes

Type of Drug: anticonvulsant

Used for: Prevention of seizures and management of postherpetic neuralgia.

How This Medication Works: Exact mechanism is unknown.

Dosage Form and Strength:
- capsules (100 mg, 300 mg, 400 mg)
- tablets (600 mg, 800 mg)
- oral solution (250 mg/5mL)

Storage:
- room temperature
- protect from light and moisture—do not store in bathroom or kitchen

Administration:
- Usually taken 3 times daily.
- May be taken without regard to meals, but take with food to reduce nausea and vomiting.
- If capsules are difficult to take, they may be opened and the contents mixed in juice or applesauce, but only do so immediately before you take the medication.
- If using an antacid, separate doses of gabapentin and the antacid by 2 hours.
- Take a missed dose as soon as possible. However, if it is almost time for the next dose, skip the missed dose and return to your regular dosing schedule.

Precautions:
Do not use if:
- you have had an allergic reaction to gabapentin.

Talk to your doctor if:
- you have kidney disease.
- you are taking any other medication, especially cimetidine, another seizure medication, or an antacid, antihistamine, sedative, or muscle relaxant.

Side Effects:

Contact your health-care provider immediately if you experience:
- a rash, difficulty breathing, or swelling of the face or throat.
- severe dizziness or fainting.
- clumsiness or weakness.
- mood changes (depression, irritability).

Commonly reported side effects:
- double vision or blurred vision
- dizziness or drowsiness
- diarrhea
- nausea and/or vomiting

Time Required for Drug to Take Effect:

Decreases the number and/or frequency of seizures or treats pain as long as the drug is continued.

Symptoms of Overdose:
- double vision
- severe diarrhea, dizziness, or drowsiness

Special Notes:
- Talk to your doctor before stopping this drug.
- Tell your doctor, dentist, or surgeon you take this drug before undergoing treatment or surgery.
- Do not drink alcohol while taking this drug.
- Do not take valerian, Saint John's wort, kava, or gotu kola while you are taking this medication.

galantamine

Brand Names: Razadyne, Razadyne ER

Generic Available: no

Type of Drug: acetylcholinesterase inhibitor

Used for: Treatment of mild to moderate dementia of Alzheimer's disease.

How This Medication Works: Increases the amount of acetylcholine, a chemical in the brain; lack of acetylcholine in the brain is thought to contribute to Alzheimer's disease.

Dosage Form and Strength:
- tablets (4 mg, 8 mg, 12 mg)
- extended-release capsules (8 mg, 16 mg, 24 mg)
- oral solution (4 mg/mL)

Storage:
- room temperature; do not freeze
- protect from moisture—do not store in bathroom or kitchen

Administration:
- Immediate-release forms usually taken twice daily; extended-release form, once daily.
- Take medicine with breakfast and dinner.
- Treatment is usually begun at a lower dose. The doctor may increase it every 4 weeks or so.
- Take a missed dose with a meal as soon as possible. However, if it is almost time for the next dose, skip the missed dose and return to your regular dosing schedule. If you miss more than 3 days of this medicine, contact your health-care provider; the dose may need to be changed.
- Mix solution with ½ cup liquid before drinking.

Precautions:

Do not use if:

- you are allergic to galantamine.
- you have severe kidney disease.

Talk to your doctor if:

- you have lung or heart disease, since you may be more sensitive to this medicine.
- you have kidney or liver disease.
- you have seizures.
- you have a slow heartbeat.
- you have stomach ulcers or stomach problems.
- you lose weight after starting this medication.
- you have mild cognitive impairment
- you take any of the following: atropine, benztropine, dicyclomine, glycopyrrolate, hyoscyamine, oxybutynin, scopolamine, tolterodine, trihexyphenidyl, or trimethobenzamide.

Side Effects:

Contact your health-care provider immediately if you experience:

- signs of a life-threatening reaction, which include fever; wheezing; chest tightness; and itching or swelling of face, lips, tongue, or throat.
- a rash.
- severe headache.
- severe nausea, vomiting, or diarrhea.
- difficulty breathing.
- signs or symptoms of depression, nervousness, abnormal thinking, anxiety, or a lack of interest in life.
- severe dizziness or fainting.

Commonly reported side effects:
- nausea and/or vomiting
- loss of appetite
- dizziness or headache
- increased salivation and/or urination (report to health-care provider if either continues)
- diarrhea

Time Required for Drug to Take Effect: May take up to 3 months of treatment to reach maximum effectiveness.

Symptoms of Overdose:
- severe nausea and/or vomiting
- increased salivation
- sweating
- low blood pressure, slow pulse, and slow breathing
- convulsions

Special Notes:
- This drug does not cure Alzheimer's disease, but it may reduce some symptoms.
- Eating small, frequent meals; brushing the teeth often; and sucking hard candy or chewing gum may help minimize nausea and vomiting.
- Nausea and vomiting often improve once the dose of this medicine has been stabilized.
- Drink plenty of caffeine-free liquid unless directed otherwise by your health-care provider.
- To avoid dizziness, rise slowly over several minutes from a sitting or lying position.

gemfibrozil

Brand Name: Lopid

Generic Available: yes

Type of Drug: antihyperlipidemic (fibric acid)

Used for: Treatment of high blood cholesterol levels, high blood triglyceride levels, and heart disease.

How This Medication Works: Decreases production of cholesterol and triglycerides in the body.

Dosage Form and Strength:
- tablets (600 mg)

Storage:
- room temperature
- protect from moisture—do not store in bathroom or kitchen

Administration:
- Usually taken twice daily.
- Take 30 minutes before meals (breakfast and dinner).
- Take a missed dose as soon as possible. However, if it is almost time for the next dose, skip the missed dose and return to your regular dosing schedule.

Precautions:
Do not use if:
- you are allergic to gemfibrozil or clofibrate.
- you have severe liver, kidney, or gallbladder disease.

Talk to your doctor if:
- you have liver disease, kidney disease, or gallbladder disease (gallstones).
- you are taking fluvoxamine, theophylline, diazepam, glyburide, warfarin, or another cholesterol medication.

Side Effects:
Contact your health-care provider immediately if you experience:
- signs of a life-threatening reaction, which include fever; wheezing; chest tightness; and itching or swelling of face, lips, tongue, or throat.
- unexplained muscle aches, especially if accompanied by fatigue.
- severe stomach pain, nausea, or vomiting.
- yellowing of the eyes or skin.

Commonly reported side effects:
- heartburn
- feeling of fullness or bloating
- diarrhea
- dry mouth
- dizziness

Time Required for Drug to Take Effect: May take 1 to 3 months of treatment to reach maximum effectiveness.

Symptoms of Overdose:
- stomach pain, nausea, and/or vomiting
- diarrhea

Special Notes:
- Reduce cholesterol by adhering to a cholesterol-lowering diet and getting regular exercise. Contact your health-care provider for direction.
- Your doctor will monitor your liver function and cholesterol and triglyceride levels with blood tests while you are on this drug.
- Do not drink alcohol while taking this medication.
- Gemfibrozil is not a cure, and you may have to take this medication for a long time.

glimepiride

Brand Name: Amaryl

Generic Available: yes

Type of Drug: antidiabetic (sulfonylurea)

Used for: Lowering of blood glucose (sugar) levels in people with type 2 (non–insulin-dependent) diabetes.

How This Medication Works: Increases insulin release from the pancreas to lower blood sugar levels.

Dosage Form and Strength: tablets (1 mg, 2 mg, 4 mg)

Storage:
- room temperature
- protect from light and moisture—do not store in bathroom or kitchen

Administration:
- Usually taken once daily.

- Take with first meal of day.
- May be used alone or in combination with other diabetes medicines.
- Take a missed dose as soon as possible. However, if it has been longer than 12 hours since you missed the dose, skip the missed dose and return to your regular dosing schedule. Do not double the dose or take extra doses.

Precautions:

Do not use if:

- you have an allergy to glimepiride or other drugs in this category, such as glipizide, glyburide, or chlorpropamide.
- you have diabetic ketoacidosis (a diabetic emergency).
- you have type 1 (insulin-dependent or juvenile-onset) diabetes.

Talk to your doctor if:

- you have an allergy to sulfonamides, carbonic anhydrase inhibitors, thiazides, or loop diuretics.
- you have severe kidney disease, liver disease, heart disease, or an adrenal or pituitary gland disorder.
- you have symptoms of low blood sugar, which may include palpitations, headache, tremor, sweating, light-headedness, irritability, and blurred vision.
- your eating habits change suddenly, such as during illness or dieting or as a result of nausea.
- you take warfarin, carbamazepine, phenobarbital, phenytoin, rifampin, a beta-blocker (such as

propranolol, metoprolol, or atenolol),
fluconazole, gemfibrozil, or ketoconazole.

Side Effects:

Contact your health-care provider immediately if you experience:

- signs of a life-threatening reaction, which include fever; wheezing; chest tightness; and itching or swelling of face, lips, tongue, or throat.
- any unusual bleeding or bruising.
- yellowing of the skin or eyes.
- very low blood sugar or very high blood sugar (as defined by your health-care provider).
- a rash.

Commonly reported side effects:

- headache
- dizziness
- mild nausea or vomiting
- sensitivity of skin to sunlight
- low blood sugar (see Precautions for symptoms)

Time Required for Drug to Take Effect: Starts
lowering blood sugar within 2 to 3 hours of taking a dose, but it must be taken on a regular basis to control blood sugar.

Symptoms of Overdose:

- low blood sugar (see Precautions for symptoms)
- tingling of lips and tongue
- nausea
- confusion
- agitation
- fast heartbeat
- sweating

- convulsions
- coma

Special Notes:
- Follow a diet plan and exercise program recommended by your health-care provider.
- Always keep a fast-acting sugar source (such as hard candy, glucose tablets or gel, fruit juice, or nondiet soda) handy.
- Teach your family, friends, and coworkers how to help you if you have low blood sugar.
- Do not drive if you recently had low blood glucose—your risk of an accident is higher.
- Do not consume alcohol while taking this drug.
- Check your blood glucose as directed by your health-care provider.
- Have yearly eye and foot examinations performed by health-care professionals.
- Sound-alike/look-alike warning: Glimepiride may be confused with glipizide.

glipizide

Brand Names: Glucotrol, Glucotrol XL

Generic Available: yes

Type of Drug: antidiabetic (sulfonylurea)

Used for: Lowering of blood glucose (sugar) levels in people with type 2 (non–insulin-dependent) diabetes.

How This Medication Works: Increases insulin release from the pancreas to lower blood sugar levels.

Dosage Form and Strength:
- tablets (5 mg, 10 mg)
- extended-release tablets (2.5 mg, 5 mg, 10 mg)

Storage:
- room temperature
- protect from moisture—do not store in bathroom or kitchen

Administration:
- Usually taken once or twice daily.
- Take 30 minutes before a meal.
- It is best to take the extended-release tablets with breakfast unless instructed otherwise.
- Take at about the same time every day.
- Swallow extended-release tablets whole; do not break, crush, or chew.
- Take a missed dose as soon as possible. However, if it is almost time for the next dose, skip the missed dose and return to your dosing schedule.

Precautions:
Do not use if:
- you are allergic to glipizide or any drug in the sulfonylurea family, such as glyburide, chlorpropamide, tolazamide, or tolbutamide.
- you have ever had diabetic ketoacidosis.
- you have type 1 (insulin-dependent or juvenile-onset) diabetes.

Talk to your doctor if:
- you are taking warfarin, a histamine H_2 antagonist (such as ranitidine, famotidine, or cimetidine), gemfibrozil, a beta-blocker (such as propranolol, metoprolol, or atenolol), cholestyramine, phen-

ytoin, rifampin, a thiazide diuretic (such as hydrochlorothiazide), or digoxin.
- you have liver or kidney disease.
- you have an allergy to sulfonamides, carbonic anhydrase inhibitors, thiazides, or loop diuretics.
- you have symptoms of low blood sugar, which may include palpitations, headache, tremor, sweating, light-headedness, irritability, and blurred vision.
- your eating habits change suddenly, such as during illness or dieting or as a result of nausea.

Side Effects:
Contact your health-care provider immediately if you experience:
- signs of a life-threatening reaction, which include fever; wheezing; chest tightness; and itching or swelling of face, lips, tongue, or throat.
- unexplained bruising or bleeding.
- low blood sugar (see Precautions for symptoms).
- a rash or hives.

Commonly reported side effects:
- stomach upset or fullness
- nausea
- headache
- diarrhea

Time Required for Drug to Take Effect:
Begins to work within 1 to 2 hours of taking a dose. However, you must take this medication on a regular basis to control blood glucose levels.

Symptoms of Overdose:
- low blood sugar (see Precautions for symptoms)

- confusion or agitation
- seizures or coma

Special Notes:
- Do not drink alcohol while taking this medication.
- Do not discontinue without your doctor's consent.
- Talk to your doctor or diabetes educator about how to handle sick days.
- Use a sunblock with at least SPF 15 when outside because glipizide may increase sun sensitivity.
- Sometimes, the ghost, or shell, of the extended-release tablet may show up in the stool; this is normal and does not mean the drug's active ingredient was not absorbed.
- When you begin glipizide therapy, check your blood glucose level frequently.
- Look-alike/sound-alike warning: Glipizide may be confused with glimepiride or glyburide.

glyburide

Brand Names:
DiaBeta
Glynase Prestab
Micronase

Generic Available: yes

Type of Drug: antidiabetic (sulfonylurea)

Used for: Lowering of blood glucose (sugar) levels in people with type 2 (non–insulin-dependent) diabetes.

How This Medication Works: Increases insulin release from the pancreas to lower blood sugar levels.

Dosage Form and Strength:
- tablets (1.25 mg, 2.5 mg, 5 mg)
- micronized tablets (1.5 mg, 3 mg, 6 mg)

Storage:
- room temperature
- protect from moisture—do not store in bathroom or kitchen

Administration:
- Usually taken once or twice daily.
- Take with meals (breakfast if taking once daily; breakfast and dinner if taking twice daily).
- Take a missed dose as soon as possible. However, if it is almost time for the next dose, skip the missed dose and return to your regular dosing schedule.

Precautions:
Do not use if:
- you are allergic to glyburide or any drug in the sulfonylurea family, such as glipizide, chlorpropamide, tolazamide, or tolbutamide.
- you have ever had diabetic ketoacidosis.
- you have type 1 (insulin-dependent or juvenile-onset) diabetes.

Talk to your doctor if:
- you are taking warfarin, a histamine H_2 antagonist (such as ranitidine or cimetidine), methyldopa, gemfibrozil, a beta-blocker (such as propranolol, metoprolol, or atenolol), cholestyramine, phen-

ytoin, rifampin, a thiazide diuretic (such as hydro-chlorothiazide or chlorthalidone), or digoxin.
- you have liver or kidney disease.
- you are allergic to sulfonamides, carbonic anhydrase inhibitors, thiazide diuretics, or loop diuretics.
- you have symptoms of low blood sugar, which may include palpitations, headache, tremor, sweating, light-headedness, irritability, and blurred vision.
- you suddenly change your eating habits, such as during illness or dieting or as a result of nausea.

Side Effects:

Contact your health-care provider immediately if you experience:
- signs of a life-threatening reaction, which include fever; wheezing; chest tightness; and itching or swelling of face, lips, tongue, or throat.
- unexplained bruising or bleeding.
- low blood sugar (see Precautions for symptoms).
- a rash or hives.

Commonly reported side effects:
- stomach upset or fullness
- nausea
- headache

Time Required for Drug to Take Effect:

The nonmicronized tablets begin to work within 2 to 3 hours of taking a dose and continue to have an effect for about 24 hours. The micronized tablets begin to work within about 1 hour of taking a dose and continue to have an effect for about 24 hours.

Symptoms of Overdose:
- low blood sugar (see Precautions for symptoms)
- confusion or agitation
- seizures or coma

Special Notes:
- Do not drink alcohol while taking this medication.
- Do not discontinue this drug without first consulting your doctor.
- Talk to your doctor or diabetes educator about how to handle sick days.
- Sometimes, the ghost, or shell, of the extended-release tablet may show up in the stool; this is normal and does not mean the drug's active ingredient was not absorbed.
- Use a sunblock with at least SPF 15 when outside, because glyburide may increase your sensitivity to the sun.
- When you begin glyburide therapy, check your blood glucose level frequently.
- Look-alike/sound-alike warning: Glyburide may be confused with glipizide or glucotrol.

glyburide and metformin combination

Brand Name: Glucovance

Generic Available: yes

Type of Drug: antidiabetic combination (sulfonylurea and biguanide)

Used for: Lowering of blood glucose (sugar) levels in people with type 2 (non–insulin-dependent) diabetes.

How This Medication Works: Glyburide increases insulin release from the pancreas, and metformin reduces glucose production and helps insulin work better in the body—all to lower blood glucose.

Dosage Form and Strength: tablets (1.25 mg glyburide/250 mg metformin, 2.5 mg/500 mg, 5 mg/500 mg)

Storage:
- room temperature
- protect from moisture—do not store in bathroom or kitchen

Administration:
- Usually taken once or twice daily.
- This medicine can be used alone or in combination with other diabetes medicines.
- All doses should be taken with a meal.
- Take a missed dose as soon as possible. However, if it is almost time for the next dose, skip the missed dose and return to your regular dosing schedule.

Precautions:
Do not use if:
- you are allergic to glyburide; metformin; or drugs related to glyburide, such as glimepiride, glipizide, or chlorpropamide.
- you have an acidic blood condition, consume more than 2 alcoholic drinks daily, or are dehydrated.

- you have kidney, liver, or lung disease; have had a recent heart attack; or have a severely weakened heart.
- you are having an X-ray with dye (consult your doctor for exact instructions).
- you have type 1 (insulin-dependent or juvenile-onset) diabetes.

Talk to your doctor if:
- you have an allergy to sulfonamides, carbonic anhydrase inhibitors, thiazides, or loop diuretics.
- you have symptoms of low blood sugar, which may include palpitations, headache, tremor, sweating, light-headedness, irritability, and blurred vision.
- you suddenly change your eating habits, such as during illness or dieting or as a result of nausea.
- you take warfarin, carbamazepine, phenobarbital, phenytoin, rifampin, a beta-blocker (such as propranolol, metoprolol, or atenolol), fluconazole, gemfibrozil, or ketoconazole.
- you become dehydrated.

Side Effects:
Contact your health-care provider immediately if you experience:
- signs of a life-threatening reaction, which include fever; wheezing; chest tightness; and itching or swelling of face, lips, tongue, or throat.
- very low blood sugar or very high blood sugar (as defined by your health-care provider).
- severe dizziness.
- severe nausea, vomiting, or diarrhea.
- severe muscle pain or weakness.

- extreme fatigue, weakness, or feeling cold.
- a rash.

Commonly reported side effects:
- headache
- dizziness
- mild nausea, vomiting, or stomach upset
- low blood sugar (see Precautions for symptoms)
- change in taste

Time Required for Drug to Take Effect: Starts lowering blood sugar within several hours of taking a dose, but it may take up to 2 weeks of treatment to reach maximum effectiveness.

Symptoms of Overdose:
- low blood sugar (see Precautions for symptoms)
- tingling of lips and tongue
- nausea
- confusion or agitation
- rapid heartbeat
- seizures or coma

Special Notes:
- Follow a diet plan and exercise program recommended by your health-care provider.
- Always keep a fast-acting sugar source (such as hard candy, glucose tablets or gel, fruit juice, or nondiet soda) handy.
- Teach your family, friends, and coworkers how to help you if you have low blood sugar.
- Do not drive if you recently had low blood glucose—your risk of an accident is higher.
- Do not consume alcohol while taking this drug.

- Check your blood glucose as directed by your health-care provider.
- Have yearly eye and foot examinations performed by health-care professionals.
- Metformin can cause a vitamin-B_{12} deficiency and a rare but serious side effect called lactic acidosis. For these reasons, your health-care provider will do blood tests to monitor for these effects.

haloperidol

Brand Name: Haldol

Generic Available: yes

Type of Drug: antipsychotic

Used for: Treatment of psychotic disorders (schizophrenia, drug-induced psychosis), Tourette's syndrome, and severe agitation.

How This Medication Works: Blocks the brain chemical dopamine.

Dosage Form and Strength:
- tablets (0.5 mg, 1 mg, 2 mg, 5 mg, 10 mg, 20 mg)
- oral solution (2 mg/mL)

Storage:
- room temperature
- protect from light and moisture—do not store in bathroom or kitchen

Administration:
- Usually taken 2 to 3 times daily.

- Take the tablets with a full 8-ounce glass of water.
- Take with food or milk if stomach upset occurs.
- For the solution, dilute the dose in water, orange juice, or soda before consuming; do not dilute with coffee or tea.
- Take a missed dose as soon as possible. However, if it is almost time for the next dose, skip the missed dose and return to your regular dosing schedule.

Precautions:

Do not use if:
- you are allergic to haloperidol.

Talk to your doctor if:
- you are taking any other medications, especially antacids, phenobarbital, carbamazepine, lithium, methyldopa, phenytoin, or antidepressants.
- you have kidney or liver disease, seizures, heart disease, or Parkinson's disease.
- you have benign prostatic hyperplasia (BPH) or decreased stomach motility.

Side Effects:

Contact your health-care provider immediately if you experience:
- signs of a life-threatening reaction, which include fever; wheezing; chest tightness; and itching or swelling of face, lips, tongue, or throat.
- difficulty speaking or swallowing.
- muscle spasms, stiffness, or strange movements.
- severe dizziness or fainting.
- weakness or extreme fatigue.

Commonly reported side effects:
- dizziness or light-headedness

- constipation
- dry mouth
- weight gain
- nausea and/or vomiting

Time Required for Drug to Take Effect: Starts working within 1 hour of taking a dose, but it may take several days or weeks of treatment to reach maximum effectiveness.

Symptoms of Overdose:
- severe dizziness or drowsiness, deep sleep
- agitation and confusion
- severe weakness
- trembling or strange movements

Special Notes:
- If you experience dry mouth, chew gum, suck on ice chips or hard candy, or try a saliva substitute.
- Know which "target symptoms" you are being treated for so you can tell your doctor if they are improving, worsening, or unchanged.
- Direct skin contact with the oral solution may cause a rash.

hydralazine

Brand Names: Apresoline, Hydralazine

Generic Available: yes

Type of Drug: cardiovascular (vasodilator)

Used for: Treatment of high blood pressure (hypertension) and congestive heart failure.

How This Medication Works:
Acts directly on vascular smooth muscle to cause relaxation and widening of blood vessels.

Dosage Form and Strength:
tablets (10 mg, 25 mg, 50 mg, 100 mg)

Storage:
- room temperature
- protect from moisture—do not store in bathroom or kitchen

Administration:
- Usually taken 3 to 4 times daily.
- Take with food.
- If you forget to take this medication, take your missed dose as soon as possible. However, if it is almost time for the next dose, skip the missed dose and return to your regular dosing schedule.

Precautions:
Do not use if:
- you are allergic to the medications hydralazine and tartrazine.
- you have heart-valve disease.

Talk to your doctor if:
- you have coronary artery or rheumatic heart disease, obstructive lung disease, or kidney disease.
- you have ever had a heart attack or stroke.
- you are taking propranolol, metoprolol, or indomethacin.

Side Effects:

Contact your health-care provider immediately if you experience:

- signs of a life-threatening reaction, which include fever; wheezing; chest tightness; and itching or swelling of face, lips, tongue, or throat.
- muscle aches, blotchy rash, fever (lupus erythematosus).
- chest pain.
- severe dizziness or fainting.
- significant weight gain or loss.

Commonly reported side effects:

- dizziness
- numbness or tingling in the arms and legs
- headache
- nausea and/or vomiting

Time Required for Drug to Take Effect: Begins to lower blood pressure within about 45 minutes of the first dose.

Symptoms of Overdose:

- very rapid heartbeat
- skin flushing
- low blood pressure

Special Notes:

- Talk to your doctor if you develop numbness or tingling in your arms or legs.
- Changing positions slowly when sitting and/or standing up may help decrease dizziness caused by this medication.
- Look-alike/sound-alike warning: Hydralazine may be confused with hydroxyzine.

hydrochlorothiazide

Brand Names:

Aquazide   Microzide
Esidrix   Oretic
HydroDiuril

Generic Available: yes

Type of Drug: diuretic

Used for: Treatment of fluid retention (edema) and high blood pressure (hypertension).

How This Medication Works: Increases the amount of sodium and chloride excreted by the kidneys, resulting in loss of water through urine.

Dosage Form and Strength:
- tablets (25 mg, 50 mg, 100 mg)
- capsules (12.5 mg)

Storage:
- room temperature
- protect from moisture—do not store in bathroom or kitchen

Administration:
- Usually taken once daily in the morning.
- Take with food or milk if stomach upset occurs.
- Take a missed dose as soon as possible. However, if it is almost time for the next dose, skip the missed dose and return to your dosing schedule.

Precautions:

Do not use if:
- you are allergic to hydrochlorothiazide or other thiazide diuretics, such as chlorthalidone or metolazone.
- you are allergic to sulfa drugs, such as oral diabetes medication (including glipizide and glyburide); acetazolamide; loop diuretics (such as furosemide or bumetanide); or sulfa antibacterials (such as sulfamethoxazole or sulfasalazine).

Talk to your doctor if:
- you have liver or kidney disease, diabetes, or gout.
- you are taking allopurinol, warfarin, digoxin, lithium, a loop diuretic, methyldopa, oral diabetes medication (such as glipizide or glyburide), insulin, cholestyramine, or a nonsteroidal anti-inflammatory drug (such as ibuprofen, naproxen, or diclofenac).

Side Effects:

Contact your health-care provider immediately if you experience:
- severe dizziness or fainting.
- a rash.
- prolonged vomiting or diarrhea.
- unexplained muscle pain, muscle weakness, or muscle cramps.

Commonly reported side effects:
- headache
- dry mouth
- dizziness or drowsiness
- high blood sugar

Time Required for Drug to Take Effect:

Begins to lower blood pressure within several days of taking the first dose, but it may take 2 to 4 weeks of treatment to reach maximum effectiveness.

Symptoms of Overdose:

- confusion
- dizziness or fainting
- muscle weakness
- nausea and vomiting
- drowsiness
- lethargy
- coma

Special Notes:

- Take with orange juice or a banana to help replace lost potassium.
- Unless otherwise instructed by your doctor, it is important to drink 6 to 8 eight-ounce glasses of water daily to avoid dehydration.
- Use a sunblock with at least SPF 15 when outside, because hydrochlorothiazide may increase your sensitivity to the sun.
- If you experience dry mouth, chew gum, suck on ice chips or hard candy, or try a saliva substitute.
- Weigh yourself daily. If you gain or lose a significant amount of weight, call your doctor.
- Your doctor will check calcium, magnesium, and potassium levels in the blood and determine if supplementation is necessary.
- Changing positions slowly when sitting and/or standing up may help decrease dizziness caused by this medication.

- If you have diabetes, you may need to check your blood glucose more frequently.
- Consult your doctor or pharmacist before starting any new medication or herbal product while you are taking this drug.

hydrocodone and acetaminophen combination

Brand Names:

Anexsia

Bancap HC

Lorcet

Lortab

Norco

Vicodin

Vicodin ES

Zydone

Generic Available: yes

Type of Drug: narcotic analgesic combination

Used for: Relief of pain.

How This Medication Works: Hydrocodone acts in the brain to decrease the recognition of pain. Acetaminophen works in the peripheral nervous system to block pain signals.

Dosage Form and Strength:

- tablets and capsules (2.5 mg hydrocodone/500 mg acetaminophen, 5 mg/325 mg, 5 mg/500 mg, 7.5 mg/325 mg, 7.5 mg/500 mg, 7.5 mg/650 mg, 7.5 mg/750 mg, 10 mg/325 mg, 10 mg/500 mg, 10 mg/650 mg, 10 mg/660 mg)
- liquid (7.5 mg hydrocodone/167 mg acetaminophen per 5 mL)

Storage:

- room temperature
- protect from moisture—do not store in bathroom or kitchen

Administration:

- Do not exceed the maximum number of doses per day. Each drug in this combination can be harmful if used in excess. Never take a larger dose or more doses per day than prescribed.
- Take with food or milk if stomach upset occurs.

Precautions:

Do not use if:

- you are allergic to hydrocodone or another narcotic, such as morphine, codeine, hydromorphone, or oxycodone.
- you are allergic to acetaminophen.

Talk to your doctor if:

- you have alcoholism or other substance-abuse problems; brain disease or a head injury; colitis; seizures; emotional problems or mental illness; emphysema, asthma, or other lung disease; kidney, liver, or thyroid disease; prostate problems or problems with urination; or gallbladder disease or gallstones.
- you are taking naltrexone, zidovudine, or any other medication, especially any that can cause drowsiness, such as an antihistamine, barbiturate (phenobarbital), benzodiazepine (diazepam, alprazolam, lorazepam), muscle relaxant, or antidepressant.

Side Effects:
Contact your health-care provider immediately if you experience:
- skin rash, hives, or pinpoint red spots on the skin.
- difficulty breathing.
- fainting or severe dizziness.
- severe nausea, vomiting, or constipation.
- a change in urination patterns.
- hallucinations or confusion.
- poor pain control.
- trembling or uncontrolled muscle movements.
- yellowing of the eyes or skin.

Commonly reported side effects:
- nausea
- constipation
- drowsiness or light-headedness
- dry mouth
- loss of appetite
- nervousness or restlessness

Time Required for Drug to Take Effect: Starts
to work within 15 to 30 minutes after taking a dose of the medication.

Symptoms of Overdose:
- cold, clammy skin
- confusion
- severe dizziness or drowsiness
- extreme nausea, vomiting, or diarrhea
- severe nervousness or restlessness
- shortness of breath or difficulty breathing
- slowed heartbeat

(Symptoms associated with acetaminophen overdose may not occur until 2 to 4 days after the overdose is taken, but it is important to begin treatment as soon as possible after the overdose is discovered to prevent liver damage and even death.)

Special Notes:

- This medication may cause drowsiness. Do not drive or operate potentially dangerous machinery while you are taking this medication.
- Hydrocodone and other narcotics (such as morphine, oxycodone, and codeine) cause constipation. This side effect may be diminished by drinking 6 to 8 full glasses of water each day. If you are using this medication for chronic pain, consult your doctor about adding a stool softener–laxative combination.
- Check with your physician or pharmacist before using any over-the-counter medications while taking this drug.
- When this medication is used over a long period of time, your body may become tolerant and require larger doses to achieve the same level of pain relief.
- Do not stop taking this medication abruptly, because you may experience symptoms of withdrawal. Consult your doctor about gradually reducing your dose if you plan to stop taking this medication.
- Nausea and vomiting may occur, especially after the first few doses. These side effects may subside if you lie down for a while.

- If you experience dry mouth, chew gum, suck on ice chips or hard candy, or try a saliva substitute.
- Do not drink alcohol while you are taking this medication.

hydroxyzine

Brand Names: Atarax, Vistaril

Generic Available: yes

Type of Drug: antihistamine and antiemetic

Used for: Treatment of itching and anxiety.

How This Medication Works: Blocks histamine—a substance that causes sneezing, itching, and runny nose. Also causes drowsiness as a side effect, which is why it is prescribed to treat anxiety.

Dosage Form and Strength:
- tablets (10 mg, 25 mg, 50 mg, 100 mg)
- capsules (25 mg, 50 mg, 100 mg)
- suspension (25 mg/5 mL)
- syrup (10 mg/5 mL)

Storage:
- room temperature
- protect from moisture—do not store in bathroom or kitchen

Administration:
- Shake the suspension well before measuring each dose of the medication.

- For the liquid forms, use a measuring device that can measure in milliliters (mL or ml); an ordinary kitchen teaspoon is not accurate enough.
- Take with food or milk if stomach upset occurs.
- Take a missed dose as soon as possible. However, if it is almost time for the next dose, skip the missed dose and return to your regular dosing schedule.

Precautions:

Do not use if:

- you are allergic to hydroxyzine or any other antihistamine, such as diphenhydramine or cyproheptadine.

Talk to your doctor if:

- you have an enlarged prostate or difficulty urinating.
- you have lung disease or glaucoma.
- you are taking any other medication, especially any that makes you drowsy or tired.

Side Effects:

Contact your health-care provider immediately if you experience:

- skin rash, hives, or itching.
- sore throat or fever.
- hallucinations or agitation.
- feeling faint or weak.
- seizures or tremors.
- difficulty breathing.
- a change in urination patterns.

Commonly reported side effects:

- drowsiness, dizziness, or blurred vision
- thickening of mucus or dry mouth

- increased sweating
- increased appetite
- constipation

Time Required for Drug to Take Effect: Starts to work within 15 to 30 minutes of taking a dose.

Symptoms of Overdose:
- dry mouth, throat, or nose
- dilated pupils
- difficulty breathing
- severe dizziness, drowsiness, or sedation
- seizures
- low blood pressure

Special Notes:
- Do not drink alcohol or use other drugs that cause drowsiness or mental slowing while taking this drug.
- This medication may cause drowsiness. Do not drive or operate potentially dangerous machinery while you are taking this medication.
- If you experience dry mouth, chew gum, suck on ice chips or hard candy, or try a saliva substitute.
- Consult your doctor or pharmacist before using any over-the-counter drug while on hydroxyzine.
- Sound-alike/look-alike warning: Hydroxyzine can be confused with hydralazine.

ibandronate

Brand Name: Boniva

Generic Available: no

Type of Drug: bisphosphonate

Used for: Treatment or prevention of osteoporosis and treatment of Paget's disease.

How This Medication Works: Reduces the rate of bone loss (resorption), making bones stronger.

Dosage Form and Strength:
- daily dose tablets (2.5 mg)
- monthly dose tablets (150 mg)

Storage:
- room temperature
- protect from moisture—do not store in bathroom or kitchen

Administration:
- Can be taken once daily or once monthly, depending on dose.
- Take this drug in the morning on an empty stomach before breakfast.
- Take this drug with a full glass of water.
- Do not drink, eat, or take any other medicine for at least 60 minutes after taking this drug.
- To prevent irritation of the esophagus, do not lie down for at least 60 minutes after taking this drug.
- Swallow tablet whole; do not break, crush, or chew.
- If you miss a daily dose or forget to take your medicine in the morning, skip the missed dose and take the drug the next morning.
- If you are taking the medicine once a month and forget it, take it as soon as you remember. Do not take two 150 mg tablets within the same week.

Precautions:

Do not use if:
- you are allergic to ibandronate, risedronate (Actonel), or alendronate (Fosamax).
- you have low calcium levels, severe kidney disease, narrowing of the esophagus, or slow movement through the esophagus.
- you are unable to stand or sit for 60 minutes after taking this drug.

Talk to your doctor if:
- you have kidney disease.
- you currently have or have had a history of ulcers of the stomach or throat.

Side Effects:

Contact your health-care provider immediately if you experience:
- signs of a life-threatening reaction, which include wheezing; chest tightness; itching; or swelling of face, lips, tongue, or throat.
- severe nausea or vomiting.
- severe heartburn, stomach pain, or painful swallowing.
- dark, tarry stools or vomit that resembles coffee grounds.
- severe or persistent joint or jaw pain.

Commonly reported side effects:
- flulike symptoms (such as weakness, fever, aches, pains)
- headache
- nausea or vomiting
- diarrhea or constipation
- mild bone pain

Time Required for Drug to Take Effect: Takes 3 to 6 weeks for effects to begin for osteoporosis; 3 to 6 months for effects to begin for Paget's disease.

Symptoms of Overdose:
- upset stomach
- heartburn
- irritated throat
- stomach pain or ulcers

Special Notes:
- Talk to your health-care provider about taking calcium with vitamin D supplements and about weight-bearing exercises, such as walking.
- Wait at least 1 hour after you take ibandronate before taking calcium or mineral supplements, or before taking antacids that contain aluminum, magnesium, or calcium.

ibuprofen

Brand Names:

Advil	Midol
I-Prin	Motrin
Menadol	Ultrapin

Generic Available: yes

Type of Drug: nonsteroidal anti-inflammatory drug

Used for: Treatment of pain and inflammation, and reduction of fever.

How This Medication Works: Blocks the production and release of chemicals that cause pain and inflammation in the body.

Dosage Form and Strength:
- tablets (100 mg, 200 mg, 300 mg, 400 mg, 600 mg, 800 mg)
- tablets, chewable (50 mg, 100 mg)
- oral suspension/drops (100 mg/5 mL, 40 mg/mL)

Storage:
- room temperature
- protect from light and moisture—do not store in bathroom or kitchen

Administration:
- Usually taken 3 or 4 times daily as needed.
- For nonprescription use, you may take 200 to 400 mg every 4 to 6 hours, up to 1,200 mg per 24 hours.
- Take with a full glass of water (6 to 8 ounces).
- Take with meals or milk to avoid stomach upset.
- Shake suspension well before measuring dose.
- Take a missed dose as soon as possible. However, if it is almost time for the next dose, skip the missed dose and return to your regular dosing schedule.

Precautions:
Do not use if:
- **you have recently had "bypass" surgery, or a coronary artery bypass graft (CABG).**
- you are allergic to ibuprofen or to any of the other nonsteroidal anti-inflammatory drugs, such as

naproxen, meloxicam, celecoxib, etodolac, or aspirin.

Talk to your doctor if:

- you are taking aspirin; another nonsteroidal anti-inflammatory drug, such as naproxen or celecoxib; a blood thinner; a steroid; or lithium.
- you have peptic ulcer disease, bleeding from your stomach or intestines, or a bleeding abnormality.
- you have a history of stomach problems.
- you have high blood pressure (hypertension), kidney disease, liver disease, or heart disease.
- you take other pain medication or a supplement of garlic, ginseng, ginkgo, or vitamin E.

Side Effects:

Contact your health-care provider immediately if you experience:

- signs of a life-threatening reaction, which include fever; wheezing; chest tightness; and itching or swelling of face, lips, tongue, or throat.
- blood in the stool or dark, tarry stool.
- persistent or severe stomach or abdominal pain.
- excessive vomiting or vomiting of blood or material that resembles coffee grounds.
- severe diarrhea.
- difficulty urinating.
- a rash or unusual bleeding or bruising.
- excessive swelling of the hands or feet.

Commonly reported side effects:

- stomach upset
- slight swelling of hands or feet
- dizziness
- drowsiness

Time Required for Drug to Take Effect: Starts to relieve pain within 30 to 60 minutes after taking a dose. However, it may take 1 to 2 weeks of treatment to reach maximum effectiveness for the treatment of arthritis.

Symptoms of Overdose:
- stomach pain
- nausea and vomiting
- drowsiness
- difficulty breathing
- ringing in the ears
- seizures or coma

Special Notes:
- **This type of drug may increase your risk for heart attack, stroke, stomach ulcer, and stomach bleeds. Discuss the risks vs. benefits with your physician.**
- Alcohol consumption during treatment with ibuprofen may increase your risk of bleeding from the stomach or intestines.
- Contact your physician if pain or fever worsens during self-treatment.
- Self-medication with ibuprofen should not exceed 10 days unless otherwise directed by a physician or pharmacist. Self-medication of fever should not exceed 3 days unless otherwise directed by a physician or pharmacist.
- Tell your doctor, dentist, or surgeon you use this drug before having surgery or other treatment.
- Consult your health-care provider or pharmacist before using any other over-the-counter drugs.

imipramine

Brand Names: Tofranil, Tofranil-PM

Generic Available: yes

Type of Drug: antidepressant (tricyclic)

Used for: Treatment of depression, chronic pain, and urinary incontinence.

How This Medication Works: Increases the action of the brain chemicals norepinephrine and serotonin.

Dosage Form and Strength:
- tablets (10 mg, 25 mg, 50 mg)
- capsules (75 mg, 100 mg, 125 mg, 150 mg)

Storage:
- room temperature
- protect from moisture—do not store in bathroom or kitchen

Administration:
- Usually taken once daily at bedtime; may also be prescribed 2 to 3 times daily; capsules are only prescribed for use at bedtime.
- May be taken with or without food.
- Take a missed dose as soon as possible. However, if it is almost time for the next dose, skip the missed dose and return to your regular dosing schedule.
- If you take more tablets or capsules than prescribed, contact your health-care provider immediately.

Precautions:

Do not use if:

- you have had an allergic reaction to imipramine or any other tricyclic antidepressant, such as amitriptyline or desipramine.
- you have taken a monoamine oxidase (MAO) inhibitor, such as phenelzine or isocarboxazid, in the past 14 days.
- you have recently had a heart attack.

Talk to your doctor if:

- you have glaucoma (angle-closure type), heart disease, urinary or prostate problems, severe constipation, breathing problems, seizures, diabetes, or a thyroid problem.
- you take cimetidine, clonidine, methyldopa, reserpine, guanethidine, a sedative or muscle relaxant, an antihistamine or decongestant, or a stimulant.
- you drink alcohol occasionally or regularly.

Side Effects:

Contact your health-care provider immediately if you experience:

- **suicidal thoughts or a desire to harm yourself.**
- dizziness with falls or fainting.
- chest pain or rapid heartbeat.
- confusion or hallucinations.
- severe constipation.
- difficulty urinating.
- a rash.
- severe sedation.
- fever.
- agitation or restlessness.

Commonly reported side effects:
- drowsiness
- dry mouth
- mild constipation
- weight gain
- unpleasant taste in mouth
- stomach upset

Time Required for Drug to Take Effect: It
may take anywhere from 4 to 8 weeks of treatment
to reach maximum effectiveness as an antidepressant. However, improvement may occur within 1 to
2 weeks of starting treatment when used to relieve
certain types of pain.

Symptoms of Overdose:
- confusion and hallucinations
- seizures
- extreme sedation
- very slow or rapid heartbeat
- low blood pressure
- difficulty breathing
- inability to urinate
- severe constipation
- dilated pupils

Special Notes:
- The desire to harm yourself is a serious symptom
  of depression. If you are planning to harm
  yourself in any way, call 911 immediately.
- Know which "target symptoms" (restlessness,
  worry, fear, or changes in sleep or appetite) you
  are being treated for and be prepared to tell your

doctor if your target symptoms are improving, worsening, or unchanged.

- If you are taking this medicine for urinary incontinence, your doctor may suggest that you keep a record of incontinence episodes.
- Do not change your dose or discontinue this medication without your doctor's consent.
- Check with your physician or pharmacist before using any over-the-counter medications while taking this drug.
- Use a sunblock with at least SPF 15 when outside because imipramine may increase your sensitivity to the sun.

insulin

Brand Names:
Humulin
Iletin
Novolin

Generic Available: no

Type of Drug: antidiabetic (hormone)

Used for: Lowering blood glucose (sugar) levels in people with type 1 (insulin-dependent or juvenile-onset) diabetes or type 2 (non–insulin-dependent) diabetes.

How This Medication Works: Serves as a replacement for the body's own insulin, allowing glucose to enter cells from the bloodstream and lowering glucose levels in the blood.

Dosage Form and Strength: There are several different sources, types, and concentrations of insulin available; all are injections. (See Time Required for Drug to Take Effect and Special Notes pages 284–285.)

Storage:
- refrigerate (room temperature is okay for up to 28 days; never freeze insulin or use insulin that has been frozen)
- protect from light and heat

Administration:
- Inject your insulin at about the same times every day (relative to meals).
- Roll the bottle gently between your palms to mix long-acting insulin (NPH, lente, ultralente). Never shake your insulin vigorously.
- Inject into the same general area (for example, the abdomen), but change the exact site of the injection with each dose.
- Injection under the skin of the abdomen will give the most predictable rate of absorption; injection into the fleshy portion of the upper arms or into the legs will be affected by exercise of the extremities.
- Some people can control their diabetes with 1 injection daily, but many people require 2 or more shots every day.
- Ask your health-care provider to instruct you in the correct technique for injecting insulin.
- Take a missed dose as soon as possible. However, if it is almost time for the next dose, skip the missed dose and return to your regular dosing schedule.

Precautions:

Do not use if:

- you have had a previous allergic reaction to the same species of insulin. (Because of the sources and the way they are produced, it is possible to be allergic to one kind of insulin and not to another.)
- the insulin has an unusual appearance—if your regular insulin appears cloudy, thickened, or slightly colored or has any solid particles in it; or if your NPH, lente, ultralente, 70/30, or 50/50 insulin stays at the bottom of the bottle after gentle shaking or contains clumps or solid particles that stick to the bottom or sides of the bottle after gentle shaking.

Talk to your doctor if:

- you are taking a diuretic, such as furosemide or hydrochlorothiazide, or a beta-blocker, such as metoprolol or atenolol.
- your eating habits suddenly change, such as during illness or dieting or as a result of nausea.
- you have kidney or liver disease.

Side Effects:

Contact your health-care provider immediately if you experience:

- very low blood sugar (symptoms of low blood sugar include palpitations, headache, tremor, sweating, light-headedness, irritability, and blurred vision; untreated, the falling sugar level can lead to seizures and coma).
- difficulty breathing.
- a rash or hives.
- unexplained muscle aches or cramps.

Commonly reported side effects:
  • irritation at site of injection

Time Required for Drug to Take Effect: There
are several types of insulin, each with a different onset
and duration of action. The times given here are esti-
mates; each insulin may work a little differently in different people.

  • Regular insulin is short-acting insulin. It has a
    peak effect about 1 hour after it is injected and
    will last for 6 to 8 hours.
  • NPH and lente insulin are intermediate-acting
    insulin. They reach peak effect in about 6 to
    8 hours after being injected and will last 18 to
    24 hours.
  • Mixtures of regular and NPH insulins (either
    70/30 or 50/50) combine the actions of the two
    types. For example, in an injection of 70/30, 30%
    of the dose peaks 1 hour after being injected and
    lasts for 6 to 8 hours (as regular insulin alone
    does), and 70% of the dose peaks in 6 to 8 hours
    from the time of injection and lasts for 18 to
    24 hours (as NPH insulin alone does).
  • Ultralente is a long-acting insulin. It reaches peak
    effect 6 to 16 hours after being injected and lasts
    27 to 29 hours.

Symptoms of Overdose:
  • very low blood sugar (see Side Effects for
    symptoms)
  • seizures
  • coma

Special Notes:

- Dietary management and regular physical activity remain important methods of controlling blood glucose levels.
- Do not discontinue insulin use without first consulting your doctor.
- Talk to your doctor or diabetes educator about how to handle sick days.
- Do not drink alcohol while taking this medication.
- When you begin insulin therapy, check your blood glucose level frequently.
- Make sure you get exactly the kind of insulin your doctor has prescribed. Using the wrong insulin can seriously affect your glucose control.
- You must know the type of insulin that you take. There is a large letter or number on the insulin bottle that shows the type of insulin: regular insulin (R), NPH insulin (N), lente insulin (L), ultralente (U), 70% NPH and 30% regular (70/30), or 50% NPH and 50% regular (50/50).
- Be consistent with exercise; increased or decreased exercise frequency and/or intensity can change your insulin needs.
- Always keep a fast-acting sugar source (such as hard candy, glucose tablets or gel, fruit juice, or nondiet soda) handy.
- Teach your family, friends, and coworkers how to help you if you have low blood sugar.
- Do not drive if you recently had low blood sugar; your risk of an accident is higher.
- Have yearly eye and foot examinations performed by health-care professionals.

insulin glargine/ detemir (basal)

Brand Names: Lantus, Levemir

Generic Available: no

Type of Drug: antidiabetic (hormone)

Used for: Lowering of glucose levels in people with type 1 (insulin-dependent or juvenile-onset) or type 2 (non–insulin-dependent) diabetes.

How This Medication Works: Serves as a replacement for the body's own insulin, allowing glucose to enter cells from the bloodstream and lowering glucose levels in the blood.

Dosage Form and Strength: injection (100 units/mL)

Storage:
- store unopened vials in refrigerator; do not freeze
- opened vials can be stored at room temperature, protected from heat and light; throw away any unused portion after 28 days (glargine) or 42 days (detemir)

Administration:
- Do not use expired insulin.
- DO NOT dilute; DO NOT mix with any other insulin product or solution.
- If you are taking this medicine for type 2 diabetes, it can be used alone or in combination with other types of diabetes medicine.

- Usually injected once daily under the skin.
- Rotate injection sites within an injection area (abdomen, thigh, or deltoid).

Precautions:

Do not use if:

- you are allergic to insulin.
- the insulin has an unusual appearance or is discolored; insulin glargine should look clear and colorless.

Talk to your doctor if:

- you have symptoms of low blood sugar (palpitations, headache, tremor, sweaty palms, light-headedness, irritability, and blurred vision).
- your eating habits change suddenly (such as during illness or dieting or due to nausea, for example).
- you have kidney or liver disease.
- you are taking a beta-blocker (such as atenolol, propranolol, or metoprolol), since these drugs may block the symptoms of low blood sugar.

Side Effects:

Contact your health-care provider immediately if you experience:

- signs of a life-threatening reaction, which include fever; wheezing; chest tightness; and itching or swelling of face, lips, tongue, or throat.
- very low blood sugar or very high blood sugar (as defined by your health-care provider).
- severe dizziness.
- a rash or change in your skin around the injection site.

- extreme fatigue, weakness, or feeling cold.
- a seizure or fainting.

Commonly reported side effects:
- low blood sugar (see Precautions for symptoms)
- slight discomfort at injection site

Time Required for Drug to Take Effect: Starts
lowering blood sugar levels within 24 hours after
injecting a dose.

Symptoms of Overdose:
- very low blood sugar (symptoms of low blood
  sugar include palpitations, headache, tremor,
  sweating, light-headedness, irritability, and
  blurred vision; untreated, the falling sugar level
  can lead to seizures and coma).

Special Notes:
- Follow a diet plan and exercise program
  recommended by your health-care provider. And
  be aware that increased exercise may change
  your insulin needs.
- Always keep a fast-acting sugar source (such as
  hard candy, glucose tablets or gel, fruit juice, or
  nondiet soda) handy.
- Teach your family, friends, and coworkers how to
  help you if you have low blood sugar.
- Do not drive if you recently experienced low
  blood glucose—your risk of having an accident is
  higher.
- Do not consume alcohol while you are taking this
  medication.
- Check your blood glucose as directed by your
  health-care provider.

- Have yearly eye and foot examinations performed by health-care professionals.
- Look-alike/sound-alike warning: Lantus may be confused with Lente.

insulin lispro/aspart/glulisine (rapid acting)

Brand Names:
Apidra
Humalog
Novolog

Generic Available: no

Type of Drug: antidiabetic (hormone)

Used for: Lowering glucose levels in people with type 1 (insulin-dependent or juvenile-onset) diabetes or type 2 (non–insulin-dependent) diabetes.

How This Medication Works: Serves as a replacement for the body's own insulin, allowing glucose to enter cells from the bloodstream and lowering glucose levels in the blood.

Dosage Form and Strength:
- injection vial (100 units/cc)
- cartridges (1.5 cc) for use with insulin "pen"

Storage:
- refrigerate (Room temperature is okay for up to 28 days; never freeze insulin.)
- protect from light and heat

Administration:

- Lispro and aspart are injected subcutaneously (under the skin) 15 minutes before a meal.
- Lispro and aspart can be used twice daily or in multiple daily injections.
- The fast absorption of both lispro and aspart means patients can tailor their insulin dosing to meals rather than plan meals based on their insulin dosing.
- Lispro and aspart should look clear and colorless; discard if lispro or aspart looks cloudy or discolored or has particles in it.
- Take a missed dose as soon as possible. However, if it is almost time for the next dose, skip the missed dose and return to your regular dosing schedule.

Precautions:

Do not use if:

- you have had an allergic reaction to insulin, insulin lispro, insulin aspart, or insulin glulisine.

Talk to your doctor if:

- you are taking a diuretic, such as furosemide or hydrochlorothiazide, or a beta-blocker, such as atenolol or metoprolol.
- your eating habits change suddenly, such as during an illness, when you are dieting, or as a result of nausea.

Side Effects:

Contact your health-care provider immediately if you experience:

- very low blood sugar (symptoms of low blood sugar include palpitations, headache, tremor,

sweating, light-headedness, irritability, and blurred vision; untreated, the falling sugar level can lead to seizures and coma).
- difficulty breathing.
- a rash or hives.
- unexplained muscle aches or cramps.

Commonly reported side effects:
- irritation at site of injection

Time Required for Drug to Take Effect:

Begins to work 15 minutes after injection and reaches its peak action in 30 to 90 minutes, coinciding with the body's need for insulin after a meal. Duration of action is about 3 to 5 hours.

Symptoms of Overdose:
- very low blood sugar (see Side Effects)

Special Notes:
- Dietary management and regular physical activity remain important methods of controlling blood glucose levels.
- Talk to your doctor before you stop taking this drug.
- Talk to your doctor or diabetes educator about how to handle sick days.
- Do not drink alcohol while taking this drug.
- When you begin insulin therapy, check your blood glucose level frequently.
- Due to the short duration of action of lispro and aspart, patients with type 1 diabetes will also require a long-acting insulin.

- Lispro or aspart can be mixed in the same syringe with NPH, lente, or ultralente insulin. The mixture should be injected immediately after mixing.
- Be consistent with exercise; increased or decreased exercise frequency and/or intensity can change your insulin needs.
- Always keep a fast-acting sugar source (such as hard candy, glucose tablets or gel, fruit juice, or nondiet soda) handy.
- Teach your family, friends, and coworkers how to help you if you have low blood sugar.
- Do not drive if you recently had low blood sugar—your risk of an accident is higher.
- Have yearly eye and foot examinations performed by health-care professionals.

ipratropium

Brand Names: Atrovent, Atrovent HFA

Generic Available: yes

Type of Drug: respiratory (anticholinergic)

Used for: Treatment of emphysema, chronic bronchitis, and chronic obstructive pulmonary disease (COPD).

How This Medication Works: Causes the passageways in the lungs to dilate.

Dosage Form and Strength:
- inhaler (17 mcg/inhalation)
- nasal spray (0.03%, 0.06%)
- solution for nebulization (0.02%)

Storage:
- room temperature
- protect from light and heat—do not store in bathroom or kitchen

Administration:
- Have your doctor or pharmacist demonstrate the proper use of the inhaler or nasal spray, and make sure you practice your technique in front of them.
- Allow at least 2 minutes between inhalations (puffs).
- If you use more than one type of inhaled drug, it is important to administer them in the correct order. If you are using albuterol and ipratropium, use the albuterol first. Wait at least 5 minutes before inhaling the ipratropium. If you are using albuterol, ipratropium, and a steroid inhaler, use the albuterol first, then the ipratropium, then the steroid inhaler.
- Shake the inhaler well before each dose.
- Blow your nose before using the nasal spray.
- Take a missed dose as soon as possible. However, if it is almost time for the next dose, skip the missed dose and return to your regular dosing schedule.

Precautions:
Do not use if:
- you are allergic to ipratropium or another anticholinergic drug, such as atropine, belladonna, hyoscyamine, or scopolamine.
- you are allergic to peanuts or soybeans.

Talk to your doctor if:
- you have difficulty urinating or have an enlarged prostate.

Side Effects:

Contact your health-care provider immediately if you experience:
- skin rash, hives, or itching.
- ulcers or sores in the mouth or on the lips.
- blurred vision or eye pain.
- difficulty urinating.
- irregular heartbeat.

Commonly reported side effects:
- cough or dryness of the mouth or throat
- headache or dizziness
- nervousness or trembling
- stomach upset or nausea
- metallic or unpleasant taste

Time Required for Drug to Take Effect: Starts to work within 1 to 3 minutes of inhaling a dose.

Symptoms of Overdose:

- blurred vision
- headache
- nervousness
- dry mouth or drying of respiratory secretions
- cough
- nausea

Special Notes:

- Check with your physician and pharmacist before you use any over-the-counter medications while taking this drug.

- Be sure that you keep track of how many inhalations are left, and get your medication refilled about 1 week before you expect to run out.
- Sometimes a spacer device is used with your inhaler. This device helps the medication get beyond the mouth or throat and into the lungs.
- Chewing gum or sucking on ice chips or hard candy may help relieve dry mouth.

ipratropium and albuterol combination

Brand Names: Combivent, DuoNeb

Generic Available: no

Type of Drug: bronchodilator

Used for: Opening of the airways in lung diseases in which spasms cause breathing problems, such as asthma, emphysema, bronchitis, and chronic obstructive pulmonary disease (COPD).

How This Medication Works: Ipratropium and albuterol both work at sites in the airways to relax the muscles and improve oxygen flow.

Dosage Form and Strength:
- inhaler (18 mcg ipratropium/103 mcg albuterol sulfate per actuation)
- solution for nebulizer (3 mg albuterol sulfate/ 0.5 mg ipratropium bromide per 3 mL vial)

Storage:
- room temperature; do not freeze
- protect from light

Administration:
- Shake the inhaler well before use.
- If you are using the inhaler for the first time or if you have not used the inhaler for several days, prime it by spraying it once into the air before administering your dose.
- Read and follow all instructions provided with inhaler; proper use is very important.
- Take a missed dose as soon as possible. However, if it is almost time for the next dose, skip the missed dose and return to your regular dosing schedule.
- If you are using more than one type of inhaler, ask your health-care provider in which order you should use them.

Precautions:
Do not use if:
- you are allergic to soybeans or peanuts and products made from them.
- you are allergic to ipratropium, albuterol, or atropine.

Talk to your doctor if:
- you have diabetes, heart disease, liver disease, high blood pressure (hypertension), a history of seizures, prostate or bladder disease, or open-angle glaucoma.
- you are allergic to any type of nuts or seeds.

- you are taking a monoamine oxidase (MAO) inhibitor (or have taken one in the past 14 days), a beta-blocker, atomoxetine, or digoxin.

Side Effects:

Contact your health-care provider immediately if you experience:
- signs of a life-threatening reaction, which include fever; wheezing; chest tightness; and itching or swelling of face, lips, tongue, or throat.
- pain or pounding in the chest or irregular heartbeat.
- problems with urination.
- fainting or light-headedness.
- continuous tremors or shaking.
- a worsening of your breathing problems.

Commonly reported side effects:
- nervousness or excitability
- headache
- nausea and/or vomiting
- dry mouth or cough
- blurred vision
- insomnia

Time Required for Drug to Take Effect: Starts
relieving symptoms within 15 to 60 minutes of inhaling a dose.

Symptoms of Overdose:
- dry mouth
- blurred vision
- tremor
- nervousness
- headache
- high blood pressure (hypertension)

- chest pain
- seizures

Special Notes:
- Throw away the inhaler after the recommended maximum number of sprays has been used.
- Limit caffeine (such as from tea, coffee, and cola); caffeine use during treatment with this drug may cause nervousness, shakiness, and fast heartbeat.
- Do not keep this medication inside a motor vehicle or anywhere else it could be exposed to extreme heat or cold.

irbesartan

Brand Name: Avapro

Generic Available: no

Type of Drug: antihypertensive (angiotensin II receptor blocker)

Used for: Treatment of high blood pressure (hypertension) and protection of the kidneys in people with diabetes.

How This Medication Works: Lowers blood pressure by blocking the effects of angiotensin, a strong chemical that causes blood vessels to constrict.

Dosage Form and Strength: tablets (75 mg, 150 mg, 300 mg)

Storage:
- room temperature

- protect from light and moisture—do not store in bathroom or kitchen

Administration:
- Usually taken once daily.
- Take at a similar time each day.
- May be taken without regard to meals, but take with food if stomach upset occurs.
- Take a missed dose as soon as possible. However, if it is almost time for the next dose, skip the missed dose and return to your dosing schedule.

Precautions:
Do not use if:
- **you are pregnant or may become pregnant.**
- you are allergic to irbesartan or related drugs, such as candesartan, losartan, or olmasartan.
- you have bilateral renal artery stenosis (blockage of the kidney's blood vessels), severe kidney disease, or hyperaldosteronism.

Talk to your doctor if:
- you are allergic to ACE inhibitors (such as benazepril, enalapril, fosinopril, lisinopril, or ramipril).
- you have liver or kidney disease.
- you have low blood pressure.
- you become dehydrated.
- you are taking allopurinol, lithium, potassium supplements, or spironolactone.

Side Effects:
Contact your health-care provider immediately if you experience:
- chest pain or palpitations.

- signs of a life-threatening reaction, which include fever; wheezing; chest tightness; and itching or swelling of face, lips, tongue, or throat.
- severe dizziness or fainting.
- severe headache.
- a rash.
- swelling of the hands, ankles, or feet.

Commonly reported side effects:
- dizziness or light-headedness
- headache
- diarrhea
- heartburn
- stomach upset

Time Required for Drug to Take Effect: Starts lowering blood pressure within 1 to 2 hours after you take the first dose, but it may take 4 to 6 weeks of treatment to reach maximum effectiveness.

Symptoms of Overdose:
- low blood pressure
- dizziness
- slow pulse

Special Notes:
- Do not use potassium-containing salt substitutes while taking this drug.
- Follow a diet plan and exercise program recommended by your health-care provider.
- To avoid dizziness while taking this medication, rise slowly over several minutes from a sitting or lying position.

- This medication may make you dizzy or drowsy. Avoid driving and other tasks that require alertness until you see how this medicine affects you.

irbesartan and hydrochloro-thiazide combination

Brand Name: Avalide

Generic Available: no

Type of Drug: antihypertensive (angiotensin II receptor blocker and diuretic)

Used for: Treatment of high blood pressure.

How This Medication Works: Irbesartan lowers blood pressure by blocking the effects of angiotensin, a strong chemical that causes blood vessels to constrict. Hydrochlorothiazide (HCTZ) lowers blood pressure (exactly how is unclear) and rids the body of extra salt and water through the kidneys.

Dosage Form and Strength: tablets (150 mg irbesartan/12.5 mg HCTZ, 300 mg/12.5 mg)

Storage:
- room temperature
- protect from light and moisture—do not store in bathroom or kitchen

Administration:
- Usually taken once daily.
- Take early in the day to avoid sleep problems.

- Take at a similar time each day.
- May be taken without regard to meals, but take with food if stomach upset occurs.
- Take a missed dose as soon as possible. However, if it is almost time for the next dose, skip the missed dose and return to your dosing schedule.

Precautions:

Do not use if:

- **you are pregnant or may become pregnant.**
- you are allergic to irbesartan or related drugs, such as candesartan, eprosartan, losartan, or olmasartan.
- you have had an allergic reaction to hydrochlorothiazide or a sulfa drug.
- you are not able to urinate.
- you have bilateral renal artery stenosis (blockage of the kidney's blood vessels), severe kidney disease, or hyperaldosteronism.

Talk to your doctor if:

- you are allergic to ACE inhibitors (such as benazepril, enalapril, lisinopril, or ramipril).
- you have liver or kidney disease or gout.
- you have low blood pressure.
- you become dehydrated.
- you are taking allopurinol, lithium, potassium supplements, or spironolactone.

Side Effects:

Contact your health-care provider immediately if you experience:

- signs of a life-threatening reaction, which include fever; wheezing; chest tightness; and itching or swelling of face, lips, tongue, or throat.

- severe dizziness or fainting.
- chest pain or palpitations.
- severe headache.
- a change in how much or how often you urinate.
- severe dry mouth, increased thirst, constant nausea, or vomiting.
- numbness or tingling or muscle cramps.
- loss of appetite or unusual weakness.

Commonly reported side effects:
- fatigue, dizziness, or light-headedness
- headache
- diarrhea or constipation
- heartburn or stomach upset

Time Required for Drug to Take Effect: This medication starts lowering blood pressure within 3 to 6 hours of taking the first dose, but it may take 4 to 6 weeks of continued treatment to reach maximum effectiveness.

Symptoms of Overdose:
- low blood pressure
- dizziness
- slow pulse
- lethargy
- confusion
- muscle weakness

Special Notes:
- Do not consume salt substitutes that contain potassium while you are taking this medication (check with your pharmacist if you aren't sure).

- Follow a diet plan and exercise program recommended by your health-care provider.
- To avoid dizziness, rise slowly over several minutes from a sitting or lying position.
- This medicine may make you dizzy or drowsy. Avoid driving or other tasks that require alertness until you see how this medicine affects you.
- Use a sunblock with at least SPF 15 when outside, because this drug may increase your sensitivity to the sun.

isosorbide mononitrate

Brand Names:
Imdur
ISMO
Monoket

Generic Available: yes

Type of Drug: vasodilator

Used for: Treatment of congestive heart failure, angina, and heart disease.

How This Medication Works: Relaxes smooth muscle, reducing blood pressure and demand on the heart.

Dosage Form and Strength:
- tablets (10 mg, 20 mg)
- extended-release tablets (30 mg, 60 mg, 120 mg)

Storage:
- room temperature

- tightly closed in original container
- protect from moisture—do not store in bathroom or kitchen

Administration:

- Usually taken once or twice daily.
- It is important to have an 8- to 10-hour period each day that is drug-free. If this drug is taken continuously, tolerance will develop and it will become ineffective. If dosing twice daily, take doses 7 hours apart (for example, at 9 A.M. and 4 P.M.).
- Take each dose of this medication with a full glass of water.
- Take a missed dose as soon as possible. However, if it is almost time for the next dose, skip the missed dose and return to your regular dosing schedule.

Precautions:

Do not use if:

- you are allergic to isosorbide or nitroglycerin.
- you are taking sildenafil (Viagra), tadalafil (Cialis), or vardenafil (Levitra).

Talk to your doctor if:

- you have glaucoma, severe anemia, or head trauma.
- you are taking any other medications for blood pressure.

Side Effects:

Contact your health-care provider immediately if you experience:

- severe dizziness or fainting.

- chest pain.
- blurred vision.
- severe headache.

Commonly reported side effects:
- headache
- nausea or stomach upset
- weakness or dizziness
- diarrhea
- flushing

Time Required for Drug to Take Effect:

Begins to have an effect on blood pressure about 1 hour after a dose is taken.

Symptoms of Overdose:

- very low blood pressure, marked by severe dizziness and light-headedness
- rapid heartbeat or palpitations
- visual disturbances
- shortness of breath

Special Notes:

- Changing positions slowly when sitting and/or standing up may help decrease dizziness caused by this medication.
- If you notice dizziness, avoid activities requiring mental alertness, such as driving a motor vehicle or operating dangerous machinery.
- Do not drink alcohol while you are taking this medication.
- Do not use for acute angina attacks (attacks that are in progress).

labetalol

Brand Names: Normodyne, Trandate

Generic Available: yes

Type of Drug: antihypertensive (alpha- and beta-adrenergic blocking agent [alpha- and beta-blocker])

Used for: Treatment of high blood pressure (hypertension)

How This Medication Works: Inhibits certain hormones that increase heart rate and blood pressure.

Dosage Form and Strength: tablets (100 mg, 200 mg, 300 mg)

Storage:
- room temperature
- protect from moisture—do not store in bathroom or kitchen

Administration:
- **Do not abruptly stop taking this medication because serious side effects may occur.**
- Usually taken twice daily.
- Take labetalol at the same time every day.
- Take a missed dose as soon as possible. However, if it is almost time for the next dose, skip the missed dose and return to your regular dosing schedule.

Precautions:

Do not use if:
- you have ever had an allergic reaction to labetalol or another beta-blocker, such as atenolol or propranolol.
- you have ever had a very slow heartbeat or heart block.

Talk to your doctor if:
- you are taking other blood pressure medications.
- you have lung disease, asthma, or diabetes.

Side Effects:

Contact your health-care provider immediately if you experience:
- skin rash or itching or difficulty breathing.
- problems with sexual ability or desire.
- extreme fatigue or weakness.
- confusion, hallucinations, or nightmares.
- palpitations or irregular heartbeat.
- swelling of the feet, ankles, or lower legs.
- chest discomfort or pressure.
- unusual bleeding or bruising.
- severe dizziness or fainting.
- yellowing of the eyes or skin.

Commonly reported side effects:
- tingling or numbness of the skin, especially the scalp
- low blood pressure, marked by light-headedness or dizziness
- drowsiness
- nervousness, anxiety, or trouble sleeping
- nausea, stomach upset, diarrhea, or constipation

Time Required for Drug to Take Effect: Starts to work within 20 minutes to 2 hours after a dose, but it takes at least 2 to 4 weeks of treatment to reach maximum effectiveness.

Symptoms of Overdose:

- slow, fast, or irregular heartbeat
- severe dizziness or fainting
- difficulty breathing
- seizures
- blue-tinting of nail beds or palms

Special Notes:

- Do not discontinue this medication without first talking with your doctor.
- Labetalol is not a cure, and you may have to take this medication for a long time.
- Changing positions slowly when sitting or standing up may help decrease dizziness caused by this medication.
- Older patients may be more sensitive to cold temperatures while on this medication.
- Check with your physician or pharmacist before using any over-the-counter medications while taking this drug.
- Labetalol may slow the heart rate. Ask your doctor what your safe range is, but call your doctor if your heart rate falls below 50 beats per minute.
- Be careful to avoid becoming dehydrated or overheated while taking this medication.
- If you have diabetes, you will need to monitor your blood sugar levels closely, because this

medication hides the signs (other than sweating) of low blood sugar.

lansoprazole

Brand Names: Prevacid, Prevacid SoluTab

Generic Available: no

Type of Drug: proton pump inhibitor

Used for: Prevention or treatment of heartburn, stomach ulcers, and ulcers of the esophagus (food tube).

How This Medication Works: Prevents symptoms of heartburn and damage to the gastrointestinal tract by reducing stomach acid.

Dosage Form and Strength:
- capsules (15 mg, 30 mg)
- granules for oral suspension (15 mg/packet)
- orally disintegrating tablets, with phenylalanine (15 mg, 30 mg)

Storage:
- room temperature
- protect from moisture—do not store in bathroom or kitchen

Administration:
- Usually taken once or twice daily.
- Take this medicine 30 minutes before a meal.
- Swallow the capsules whole; do not chew, break, or crush. The capsule contents may be sprinkled into soft food (such as applesauce, pudding,

cottage cheese, yogurt, or strained pears) or liquid (such as orange, apple, cranberry, grape, or tomato juice), but the mixture must be consumed immediately.

- Place orally disintegrating tablet on tongue and let dissolve; water is not needed. Do not swallow whole or chew, break, or crush.
- To take oral suspension, empty packet of granules into container with 2 tablespoons of water (do not mix with other liquids or food), stir well, and drink immediately.
- Take a missed dose as soon as possible. However, if it is almost time for the next dose, skip the missed dose and return to your regular dosing schedule.

Precautions:
Do not use if:
- you are allergic to lansoprazole or similar medicines, such as esomeprazole, omeprazole, pantoprazole, or rabeprazole.

Talk to your doctor if:
- you have severe liver disease.
- you are also taking amoxicillin, iron (ferrous sulfate), ketoconazole, sucralfate, or theophylline.

Side Effects:
Contact your health-care provider immediately if you experience:
- signs of a life-threatening reaction, which include fever; wheezing; chest tightness; and itching or swelling of face, lips, tongue, or throat.
- unusual bruising or bleeding.

- extreme dizziness or fainting.
- persistent diarrhea or constipation.
- a rash.

Commonly reported side effects:
- abdominal pain or nausea
- diarrhea, constipation, or flatulence
- dry mouth or change in taste
- headache

Time Required for Drug to Take Effect: Starts
working within 1 to 2 hours of the first dose but may
take 1 to 4 weeks of treatment to reach maximum
effectiveness.

Symptoms of Overdose: No information cur-
rently available; contact poison control center.

Special Notes:
- Do not take sucralfate within 30 minutes of taking
  this medicine.
- Consult your health-care provider or pharmacist
  before starting any other medicine, including
  over-the-counter drugs, while on this medication.
- Avoid smoking and consuming alcohol while you
  are taking this medication; they can aggravate
  your condition.
- Talk to your health-care provider or pharmacist
  about drugs that may make your condition worse,
  such as aspirin and other anti-inflammatories
  (such as ibuprofen and naproxen).

latanoprost

Brand Name: Xalatan

Generic Available: no

Type of Drug: antiglaucoma (ophthalmologic prostaglandin analogue)

Used for: Treatment of glaucoma.

How This Medication Works: Lowers pressure in the eye.

Dosage Form and Strength: solution (0.005%)

Storage:
- protect from light
- refrigerate unopened bottle until ready to use
- store opened bottle at room temperature with cap on; throw away any unused portion after 6 weeks

Administration:
- For use in the eye only.
- Usually used once daily in the evening.
- Wash your hands before and after use of this medication.
- Remove contact lenses before administering medicine.
- Do not touch the tip of the container to the eye or to anything else.
- After administering medicine, keep eyes closed, and apply pressure to inside corner of treated eye (next to nose) for 2 to 3 minutes; this keeps the drug from draining out through the tear duct.

- Wait at least 15 minutes after using medicine to insert contact lenses.
- The eye can hold only one drop at a time; wait at least 5 minutes between each drop if you have more than 1 drop or another medicine to apply.
- Administer a missed dose as soon as possible. However, if it is the next day when you remember, skip the missed dose and return to your regular dosing schedule. Do not administer more than the prescribed number of drops.

Precautions:

Do not use if:
- you are allergic to latanoprost or benzalkonium chloride.

Talk to your doctor if:
- you have or develop an eye infection, require eye surgery, or experience eye trauma.

Side Effects:

Contact your health-care provider immediately if you experience:
- a sudden change in vision, eye pain, or severe eye irritation.
- signs of a life-threatening reaction, which include fever; wheezing; chest tightness; and itching or swelling of face, lips, tongue, or throat.
- chest pain or pressure.
- flashes or sparks of light.

Commonly reported side effects:
- headache
- mild eye irritation or short-term discomfort after administering drug

- sensitivity to bright lights
- change in eye color (brown pigment may increase)
- darkening of eyelashes and skin around eye

Time Required for Drug to Take Effect: Starts lowering eye pressure within 24 hours of taking a dose.

Symptoms of Overdose: No information available; contact your local poison control center for information.

Special Notes:
- Have your eye pressure checked regularly.
- Use caution when driving or doing other tasks that require clear vision if latanoprost causes your vision to blur.
- A medication delivery device (Xal-Ease) is available for use with Xalatan.

leuprolide

Brand Names:

Eligard

Lupron

Lupron Depot

Viadur

Generic Available: no

Type of Drug: gonadotropin-releasing hormone agonist

Used for: Relief of symptoms of prostate cancer and endometriosis.

How This Medication Works: Decreases the levels of testosterone in men and estrogen in women.

Dosage Form and Strength: injection (3.75 mg, 7.5 mg, 11.25 mg, 15 mg, 22.5 mg, 30 mg)

Storage:

Eligard:
- refrigerate

Lupron:
- unopened vials should be refrigerated; a vial in use can be kept at room temperature for several months

Lupron Depot and Viadur:
- room temperature

Administration:
- Dose and injection schedule vary; discuss options with your health-care provider.
- The drug is given as a shot under the skin or into a muscle; discuss proper administration with your health-care provider and have them view your injection technique to ensure you are administering the medication properly.

Precautions:

Do not use if:
- you have had an allergic reaction to leuprolide or gonadorelin.
- you are or may be pregnant or are breast-feeding.
- you have a spinal cord compression.

Talk to your doctor if:
- you are taking any other medication.
- you have osteoporosis, heart failure, or a history of blood clots in the arms or legs.

Side Effects:

Contact your health-care provider immediately if you experience:
- chest pain or pressure.
- arm or leg pain or swelling.
- shortness of breath.
- increased bone pain after 2 to 4 weeks of treatment.
- extreme fatigue or weakness.
- inability to urinate or blood in the urine.

Commonly reported side effects:
- decreased appetite
- depression or change in mood
- bone pain
- breast swelling or tenderness
- nausea, vomiting, or constipation
- decrease in sexual desire or ability
- dizziness
- minor swelling of the feet or lower legs
- hair loss
- hot flashes or flushing
- injection-site irritation

Time Required for Drug to Take Effect:

Becomes effective 2 to 4 weeks after treatment begins but may take up to 12 weeks to reach maximum effectiveness.

Symptoms of Overdose: Same as side effects.

Special Notes:

- Worsening of symptoms (bone pain, urination problems, weakness, and tingling of the arms and legs) may occur in the first 1 to 2 weeks of therapy but should improve in 2 to 4 weeks.

- Decreased bone strength may occur with long-term therapy; consult your health-care provider about calcium supplements or other treatments.

levodopa and carbidopa combination
levodopa
carbidopa

Brand Names:

Levodopa/carbidopa combination:
Parcopa
Sinemet
Sinemet CR

Levodopa:
Dopar, Larodopa
Carbidopa:
Lodosyn

Generic Available: yes

Type of Drug: antiparkinsonian

Used for: Treatment of Parkinson's disease and restless legs syndrome.

How This Medication Works: Replaces the naturally occurring brain chemical dopamine, which is responsible for the coordination of movement.

Dosage Form and Strength:
Levodopa/carbidopa combination:
- tablets (10 mg carbidopa/100 mg levodopa, 25 mg/100 mg, 25 mg/250 mg)

- controlled-release tablets (25 mg carbidopa/ 100 mg levodopa, 50 mg/200 mg)

Levodopa:
- tablets (100 mg, 250 mg, 500 mg)
- capsules (250 mg, 500 mg)

Carbidopa:
- tablets (25 mg)

Storage:
- room temperature
- protect from light and moisture—do not store in bathroom or kitchen

Administration:
Levodopa/carbidopa combination:
- Regular tablet initially taken 2 to 4 times daily depending on response, but may be increased to 8 or more tablets daily.
- Controlled-release tablet initially taken 2 to 3 times daily depending on response, but may be increased to 8 tablets a day in divided doses.
- Controlled-release tablets may be broken, but they should not be crushed or chewed.
- Take a missed dose as soon as possible. However, if it is almost time for the next dose, skip the missed dose and return to your regular dosing schedule.

Levodopa:
- Dosing depends on the needs of the individual patient.

Carbidopa:
- Dosing depends on the needs of the individual patient, but total daily dose is usually not greater than 200 mg.

Precautions:

Do not use if:

- you have had an allergic response to levodopa, carbidopa, or tartrazine dye. (Certain tablets contain tartrazine. Check with your pharmacist.)
- you have used a monoamine oxidase (MAO) inhibitor within the past 14 days.
- you have melanoma (a type of skin cancer).

Talk to your doctor if:

- you have seizures, a history of peptic ulcers, heart disease, asthma, glaucoma, or mental disorders.
- you are taking an antipsychotic (such as haloperidol or thioridazine), metoclopramide, phenytoin, or large doses of vitamin B_6.
- you drink alcohol on a regular or occasional basis.

Side Effects:

Contact your health-care provider immediately if you experience:

- palpitations.
- severe dizziness or fainting.
- unusually high or low blood pressure.
- chest pain.
- abnormal movements or spasms.
- severe constipation with pain.
- severe confusion or hallucinations.
- severe or persistent nausea and vomiting.

Commonly reported side effects:

- dizziness when sitting up or standing up
- decline in mood
- stomach upset or vomiting
- insomnia

Time Required for Drug to Take Effect: Starts
to work within days of first dose but may take weeks to
reach maximum effectiveness.

Symptoms of Overdose:
* very high or very low blood pressure
* abnormal heart rhythm
* psychotic symptoms (hallucinations, delusions)
* unusual movements
* severe nausea or vomiting

Special Notes:
* Nausea or vomiting may occur when starting
  this medicine or when the dose is increased.
  Your doctor may recommend that you take the
  medicine with food or lower the dose until your
  body gets used to the medicine.
* Talk with your doctor before making changes in
  your dosing regimen.
* Levodopa may cause a harmless darkening in the
  color of urine or sweat.
* Your response to levodopa may diminish over
  time, and your dose may need to be increased.
* Patients sometimes develop abnormal body
  movements after taking this medication.
* Keep a record of the times when the medication
  is most effective and least effective. Good record
  keeping will help your doctor adjust your doses
  to provide the maximum benefit for you.
* Taking this medication with large amounts of
  protein may result in decreased absorption of the
  drug into your system.

levofloxacin

Brand Name: Levaquin

Generic Available: no

Type of Drug: antibiotic (quinolone)

Used for: Treatment of bacterial infections.

How This Medication Works: Injures the bacteria by interfering with DNA gyrase, an enzyme important for bacterial cell growth and reproduction.

Dosage Form and Strength: tablets (250 mg, 500 mg, 750 mg)

Storage:
- room temperature
- protect from moisture—do not store in bathroom or kitchen

Administration:
- Usually taken once daily.
- Take until completely gone, even if symptoms have improved.
- May be taken without regard to meals, but take with food if stomach upset occurs. Do not, however, take dairy products, antacids, multivitamins, minerals, nutritional supplements, didanosine, or sucralfate within 2 hours of taking this medicine.
- Drink plenty of caffeine-free liquid while taking this medication unless directed otherwise by your health-care provider.

- Take a missed dose as soon as possible. However, if it is almost time for the next dose, skip the missed dose and return to your regular dosing schedule.

Precautions:

Do not use if:

- you are allergic to levofloxacin or similar medications, such as ciprofloxacin, gatifloxacin, or moxifloxacin.

Talk to your doctor if:

- you are also using a blood thinner, theophylline, oral diabetes medication, a steroid, or erythromycin.
- you have a history of heart disease, heart rhythm problems, kidney disease, stroke, or a seizure disorder (such as epilepsy).

Side Effects:

Contact your health-care provider immediately if you experience:

- signs of a life-threatening reaction, which include fever; wheezing; chest tightness; and itching or swelling of face, lips, tongue, or throat.
- a rash.
- severe nausea, vomiting, or diarrhea.
- numbness, tingling, or pain in the shoulders, elbows, or back of the ankles.
- chest pain or rapid heartbeat.
- nervousness or confusion.
- vaginal itching or discharge.
- a worsening of or lack of improvement in your condition.

Commonly reported side effects:
- stomach upset, nausea, or vomiting
- diarrhea or constipation
- dizziness
- headache

Time Required for Drug to Take Effect:

Begins killing bacteria within hours of first dose, but full course of treatment must be completed, even if symptoms disappear before then.

Symptoms of Overdose:
- kidney failure
- seizures

Special Notes:
- Do not consume alcohol or caffeine while taking this drug.
- Use a sunblock with at least SPF 15 when outside, because this drug may increase your sensitivity to the sun.
- Eating yogurt with active cultures may help eliminate mild diarrhea, but contact your healthcare provider if diarrhea becomes severe or continues.

levothyroxine

Brand Names:

Levothroid	Synthroid
Levoxyl	Unithroid

Generic Available: yes

Type of Drug: hormone (thyroid)

Used for: Treatment of low levels of thyroid hormone (hypothyroidism).

How This Medication Works: Raises low thyroid hormone levels into the normal range.

Dosage Form and Strength: tablets (25 mcg, 50 mcg, 75 mcg, 88 mcg, 100 mcg, 112 mcg, 125 mcg, 137 mcg, 150 mcg, 175 mcg, 200 mcg, 300 mcg)

Storage:
- room temperature
- protect from light and moisture—do not store in bathroom or kitchen

Administration:
- Dosages vary for each person, but usually taken once daily.
- The dosage will be adjusted until the desired level of thyroid hormone is reached. (Doses usually start low and are increased slowly to avoid side effects.)
- Take at a similar time each day unless directed otherwise.
- Take a missed dose as soon as possible. However, if it is almost time for the next dose, skip the missed dose and return to your dosing schedule.
- It is best to take this medication on an empty stomach with a full glass of water.

Precautions:

Do not use if:

- you have had an allergic reaction to levothyroxine, thyroid hormone, thyroglobulin, liothyronine, or liotrix.
- you have high levels of thyroid hormone (hyperthyroidism).

Talk to your doctor if:

- you have heart disease (angina, chest pain, coronary artery disease, heart attack), diabetes, adrenocortical disease, pituitary disease, or malabsorption disease (celiac disease).
- you are taking any other medication, especially a blood thinner, diabetes or cholesterol medication, digoxin, cough or cold medicine, or a seizure medication.

Side Effects:

Contact your health-care provider immediately if you experience:

- hives or a rash.
- changes in appetite or weight loss.
- chest pain or palpitations.
- difficulty breathing.
- hand tremor.
- severe headache.
- flushing.
- irritability, nervousness, or insomnia.
- leg cramps.

Commonly reported side effects:

- weakness
- increased sensitivity to cold
- constipation

- headache
- sleepiness or listlessness
- depression
- nausea and/or vomiting

Time Required for Drug to Take Effect:
Usually takes 1 to 2 months of treatment for thyroid levels to reach normal range.

Symptoms of Overdose:
- weight loss
- nervousness, insomnia
- fast heartbeat
- psychosis

Special Notes:
- Levothyroxine is not a cure, and you may have to take this medication for a long time.
- Do not discontinue taking this drug or change brands (or from a branded to generic product) without first talking with your doctor.
- Your health-care provider will regularly check your thyroid levels to ensure your dose is correct.
- If you also take an antacid, calcium, or iron, separate your dose of it from your dose of levothyroxine by 2 to 4 hours.
- Sound-alike/look-alike warning: Levoxyl can be confused with Lanoxin.

lisinopril

Brand Names: Prinivil, Zestril

Generic Available: yes

Type of Drug: antihypertensive (angiotensin-converting enzyme [ACE] inhibitor)

Used for: Treatment of high blood pressure (hypertension), congestive heart failure, and kidney disease caused by diabetes (diabetic nephropathy), and preservation of heart function after a heart attack.

How This Medication Works: Lowers blood pressure by decreasing production of angiotensin, a strong chemical that causes blood vessels to constrict.

Dosage Form and Strength: tablets (2.5 mg, 5 mg, 10 mg, 20 mg, 30 mg, 40 mg)

Storage:
- room temperature
- protect from moisture—do not store in bathroom or kitchen

Administration:
- Usually taken once daily.
- May be taken without regard to food.
- Take a missed dose as soon as possible. However, if it is almost time for the next dose, skip the missed dose and return to your regular dosing schedule.

Precautions:
Do not use if:
- **you are pregnant or could become pregnant.**
- you are allergic to lisinopril or another ACE inhibitor, such as captopril or enalapril.
- you have kidney disease (bilateral renal artery stenosis).

Talk to your doctor if:
- you are taking a diuretic, a potassium supplement, allopurinol, digoxin, or lithium.
- you have severe aortic stenosis.
- you have severe liver or kidney disease.
- you have low blood pressure (hypotension).
- you become dehydrated.

Side Effects:
Contact your health-care provider immediately if you experience:
- swelling of the mouth, lips, or tongue.
- severe dizziness or fainting.
- a generalized rash.
- chest pain.
- irregular heartbeat.

Commonly reported side effects:
- cough
- headache
- dizziness
- fatigue
- abnormal taste
- nausea and/or vomiting

Time Required for Drug to Take Effect: Starts
to lower blood pressure within several hours of the first dose but sometimes several weeks of therapy are needed for the drug to reach maximum effectiveness.

Symptoms of Overdose:
- very low blood pressure
- extreme muscle weakness
- nausea, vomiting, or diarrhea

Special Notes:
- Avoid salt substitutes containing potassium while you are taking this medication.
- You will need laboratory bloodwork to monitor kidney function and electrolytes (sodium, potassium) in the blood while you are being treated with lisinopril.
- To avoid dizziness while taking this drug, rise slowly from a sitting or reclining position.
- Lisinopril may cause a dry cough. Talk to your doctor if this side effect becomes particularly bothersome.

lithium

Brand Names:
Eskalith
Eskalith-CR
Lithobid

Generic Available: yes

Type of Drug: central nervous system drug

Used for: Treatment of manic depression (bipolar disorder).

How This Medication Works: Affects the transport of sodium and the activity of the brain chemicals norepinephrine and serotonin.

Dosage Form and Strength:
- tablets (300 mg)
- extended-release tablets (300 mg, 450 mg)

- capsules (150 mg, 300 mg, 600 mg)
- oral syrup (approximately 300 mg/5 mL)

Storage:
- room temperature
- protect from moisture—do not store in bathroom or kitchen

Administration:
- Swallow tablets, extended-release tablets, and capsules whole; do not break, crush, or chew.
- Dilute the oral syrup in juice before drinking.
- Take this medication with meals or milk if stomach upset occurs.
- Take a missed dose as soon as possible. However, if it is almost time for the next dose, skip the missed dose and return to your regular dosing schedule.

Precautions:
Do not use if:
- you have had an allergic reaction to lithium.

Talk to your doctor if:
- you are taking any other medications, especially a blood pressure medication, carbamazepine, an antipsychotic or antidepressant, a nonsteroidal anti-inflammatory drug (such as ibuprofen, etodolac, or naproxen), or theophylline.
- you have taken a monoamine oxidase (MAO) inhibitor within the past 14 days.
- you have kidney disease, seizures, diabetes, severe heart disease, schizophrenia, or a history of leukemia.
- you experience diarrhea, a fever, or dehydration.

Side Effects:

Contact your health-care provider immediately if you
experience:
- severe nausea, vomiting, or diarrhea.
- change in thinking or confusion.
- change in balance or severe dizziness.
- drowsiness.
- muscle weakness.
- severe trembling.

Commonly reported side effects:
- drowsiness or light-headedness
- nausea and/or vomiting
- mild trembling of the hands
- headache
- frequent urination

Time Required for Drug to Take Effect: May
require a week or more of treatment before the effects
are evident.

Symptoms of Overdose:
- vision changes
- clumsiness or confusion
- seizures
- dizziness
- severe trembling
- increase in amount of urine

Special Notes:
- **It is important to follow any instructions for
  blood tests while you are on this medication.**
- This medication may cause drowsiness. Use
  caution when driving a motor vehicle or
  operating dangerous machinery.

- Drink at least eight 8-ounce glasses of fluids (water or juice) daily.
- Do not change the amount of salt or caffeine in your diet without consulting your health-care provider.

loratadine

Brand Names:

Alavert

Claritin

Claritin Redi-Tabs

Tavist ND

Generic Available: yes

Type of Drug: nonsedating antihistamine

Used for: Treatment of allergies, hay fever, and hives.

How This Medication Works: Blocks histamine—a substance in the body that causes sneezing, itching, and runny nose.

Dosage Form and Strength:

- tablets and orally disintegrating tablets (10 mg)
- syrup (1 mg/mL)

Storage:

- room temperature
- protect from moisture—do not store in bathroom or kitchen
- once the foil pouch holding the orally disintegrating tablets has been opened, use the contents within 6 months

Administration:

- Take your dose of the regular tablets with a full glass of water.
- Do not exceed the prescribed dose.
- Take this medication with food or milk if stomach upset occurs.
- Place the orally disintegrating tablet on your tongue to dissolve; no water is necessary. Do not break, crush, or chew it.
- Take a dose 1 to 3 hours before expected contact with whatever causes your allergy.
- Take a missed dose as soon as possible. However, if it is almost time for the next dose, skip the missed dose and return to your regular dosing schedule.

Precautions:

Do not use if:

- you are allergic to loratadine or other antihistamine, such as diphenhydramine.
- you have severe liver or kidney disease.

Talk to your doctor if:

- you have asthma, difficulty breathing, liver disease, heart disease, high blood pressure, or an abnormal or irregular heartbeat.
- you are taking any medication that causes drowsiness.

Side Effects:

Contact your health-care provider immediately if you experience:

- skin rash, hives, or itching.
- swelling of the mouth, lips, or face.

- difficulty breathing.
- difficulty urinating.
- extreme constipation.

Commonly reported side effects:
- nervousness
- cough
- fatigue
- headache
- dry mouth
- constipation

Time Required for Drug to Take Effect: Starts
to work within 1 to 2 hours of taking a dose.

Symptoms of Overdose:
- irregular heartbeat
- seizures or convulsions
- drowsiness or dizziness
- dry mouth or throat
- trouble breathing

Special Notes:
- Check with your physician and pharmacist before you use any over-the-counter medications while you are taking this drug.
- Do not drink alcohol or take other medications that cause drowsiness or mental slowing while you are taking this drug.
- This medication may cause drowsiness. Do not operate a motor vehicle or other machinery while you are taking this medication.
- If you experience dry mouth, chew sugarless gum, suck on ice chips or hard candy, or try a saliva substitute.

lorazepam

Brand Name: Ativan

Generic Available: yes

Type of Drug: antianxiety (benzodiazepine)

Used for: Treatment of anxiety.

How This Medication Works: Calms the brain by enhancing the activity of the brain chemical gamma-aminobutyric acid (GABA) in the central nervous system.

Dosage Form and Strength:
- tablets (0.5 mg, 1 mg, 2 mg)
- oral solution (2 mg/mL)

Storage:
- room temperature
- tightly closed
- protect from light and moisture—do not store in bathroom or kitchen

Administration:
- Usually taken 2 to 3 times daily as needed.
- Take this medication with food or milk if stomach upset occurs.
- Take a missed dose as soon as possible. However, if it is almost time for the next dose, skip the missed dose and return to your regular dosing schedule.

Precautions:
Do not use if:
- you have ever had an allergic reaction to lorazepam or another drug in the benzodiazepine family, such as diazepam or temazepam.

Talk to your doctor if:
- you are taking any other substance or medication that can depress the central nervous system, such as alcohol, phenobarbital, or a narcotic (such as codeine or meperidine).
- you have glaucoma, asthma or other lung problem, kidney disease, or liver disease.
- you have been told that you snore or that you have sleep apnea.

Side Effects:
Contact your health-care provider immediately if you experience:
- confusion or hallucinations.
- a change in balance or falls.
- extreme weakness or fatigue.
- wheezing, a rash, or swelling of the face or throat.
- difficulty concentrating.

Commonly reported side effects:
- drowsiness or light-headedness
- dry mouth
- nausea or stomach upset

Time Required for Drug to Take Effect: Effects on anxiety may be seen within 30 to 90 minutes of taking a dose.

Symptoms of Overdose:
- continuing confusion or slurred speech
- severe weakness or drowsiness
- shortness of breath
- increased heart rate
- tremors
- coma

Special Notes:
- Do not drink alcohol while taking this medication.
- This medication may be habit-forming; do not abruptly stop taking it without your doctor's consent.
- If you notice dizziness, avoid activities requiring mental alertness, such as driving a motor vehicle or operating dangerous machinery.
- Sound-alike/look-alike warning: Lorazepam may be confused with diazepam, clonazepam, alprazolam, or temazepam.

losartan

Brand Name: Cozaar

Generic Available: no

Type of Drug: angiotensin II receptor blocker

Used for: Treatment of high blood pressure (hypertension) and congestive heart failure.

How This Medication Works: Inhibits the formation of angiotensin, a substance that causes powerful constriction of blood vessels.

Dosage Form and Strength: tablets (25 mg, 50 mg, 100 mg)

Storage:
- room temperature
- protect from moisture—do not store in bathroom or kitchen

Administration:
- Usually taken once or twice daily.
- Take at a similar time each day.
- May be taken without regard to food.
- Take a missed dose as soon as possible. However, if it is almost time for the next dose, skip the missed dose and return to your regular dosing schedule.

Precautions:

Do not use if:
- **you are pregnant or could become pregnant.**
- you are allergic to losartan or a related drug, such as irbesartan, candesartan, or olmasartan.
- you have renal artery stenosis, severe kidney disease, or hyperaldosteronism.

Talk to your doctor if:
- you have kidney disease or liver disease.
- you have low blood pressure.
- you become dehydrated.
- you are taking a seizure medication, lisinopril, allopurinol, a potassium supplement, or spironolactone.
- you have an allergy to angiotensin-converting enzyme (ACE) inhibitors, such as lisinopril or enalapril.

Side Effects:

Contact your health-care provider immediately if you experience:
- severe dizziness or fainting.
- chest pain or palpitations.
- severe headache.
- unexplained or prolonged fatigue or tiredness.
- swelling of the mouth, lips, or tongue.

Commonly reported side effects:
- dizziness or blurred vision
- constipation
- dry mouth
- muscle pains and headache

Time Required for Drug to Take Effect: Starts
to lower blood pressure within several hours after the first dose, but it usually reaches maximum effectiveness after about 1 week of treatment.

Symptoms of Overdose
- very low blood pressure
- very rapid heartbeat

Special Notes:
- Losartan is not a cure, and you may have to take this medication for a long time.
- Do not use a potassium-containing salt substitute while you are taking this medication.
- To avoid dizziness while you are taking this medication, rise slowly over several minutes from a sitting or reclining position.

losartan and hydrochloro-thiazide combination

Brand Name: Hyzaar

Generic Available: no

Type of Drug: antihypertensive combination (angiotensin II receptor blocker and diuretic)

Used for: Treatment of high blood pressure (hypertension).

How This Medication Works: Losartan lowers blood pressure by blocking the effects of angiotensin, a strong chemical that causes blood vessels to constrict. Hydrochlorothiazide (HCTZ) lowers blood pressure (exactly how is unclear) and rids the body of extra salt and water through the kidneys.

Dosage Form and Strength: tablets (50 mg losartan/12.5 mg HCTZ, 100 mg/25 mg)

Storage:
- room temperature
- protect from light and moisture—do not store in bathroom or kitchen

Administration:
- Usually taken once daily.
- Take early in the day to avoid sleep problems.
- Take at a similar time each day.
- May be taken without regard to meals, but take with food if stomach upset occurs.

- Take a missed dose as soon as possible. However, if it is almost time for the next dose, skip the missed dose and return to your regular dosing schedule.

Precautions:

Do not use if:

- **you are pregnant or could become pregnant.**
- you are allergic to losartan or related drugs, such as irbesartan, candesartan, olmasartan, or eprosartan.
- you have had an allergic reaction to hydrochlorothiazide or a sulfa drug.
- you are not able to urinate.
- you have bilateral renal artery stenosis (blockage of the kidney's blood vessels), severe kidney disease, or hyperaldosteronism.

Talk to your doctor if:

- you have an allergy to ACE inhibitors, such as lisinopril, enalapril, benazepril, fosinopril, or ramipril.
- you have liver or kidney disease.
- you have low blood pressure.
- you become dehydrated.
- you are taking allopurinol, lithium, potassium supplements, or spironolactone.
- you have gout.

Side Effects:

Contact your health-care provider immediately if you experience:

- a rash.

- signs of a life-threatening reaction, which include fever; wheezing; chest tightness; and itching or swelling of face, lips, tongue, or throat.
- severe dizziness or fainting.
- chest pain or palpitations.
- a severe headache.
- a change in amount of urine or frequency of urination.
- severe dry mouth, increased thirst, constant nausea, or vomiting.
- numbness, tingling, or muscle cramps.
- loss of appetite or unusual weakness.

Commonly reported side effects:
- fatigue, dizziness, or light-headedness
- headache
- diarrhea or constipation
- heartburn or stomach upset

Time Required for Drug to Take Effect: Starts lowering blood pressure within 3 to 6 hours after you take the first dose but may take 4 to 6 weeks of treatment to reach maximum effectiveness.

Symptoms of Overdose:
- low blood pressure
- dizziness
- slow pulse
- lethargy
- confusion
- muscle weakness

Special Notes:

- Do not use a potassium-containing salt substitute while taking this medication.
- Follow a diet plan and exercise program recommended by your health-care provider.
- To avoid dizziness, rise slowly over several minutes from a sitting or lying position.
- This medicine may make you dizzy or drowsy. Avoid driving and other tasks that require alertness until you see how this drug affects you.
- Use a sunblock with at least SPF 15 when outside, because this drug may increase your sensitivity to the sun.
- Look-alike/sound-alike warning: Hyzaar may be confused with Cozaar.

lovastatin

Brand Names: Altoprev, Mevacor

Generic Available: yes

Type of Drug: antihyperlipidemic

Used for: Treatment of high blood cholesterol levels and heart disease.

How This Medication Works: Decreases the amount of LDL (bad) cholesterol made by the body.

Dosage Form and Strength:

- tablets (10 mg, 20 mg, 40 mg)
- extended-release tablets (10 mg, 20 mg, 40 mg, 60 mg)

Storage:
- room temperature
- protect from moisture—do not store in bathroom or kitchen

Administration:
- Usually taken once daily.
- Take with the evening meal.
- Swallow the extended-release tablets whole; do not crush, break, or chew.
- Take a missed dose as soon as possible. However, if it is almost time for the next dose, skip the missed dose and return to your regular dosing schedule.

Precautions:
Do not use if:
- you are allergic to lovastatin or a similar drug, such as simvastatin, fluvastatin, or pravastatin.
- you have severe liver disease.
- you are or may be pregnant or you are breast-feeding.

Talk to your doctor if:
- you have liver or kidney disease.
- you are taking any other medication, especially verapamil, an HIV medication, cyclosporine, erythromycin, warfarin, an oral antifungal, or another cholesterol drug.
- you consume alcohol on a daily basis.

Side Effects:
Contact your health-care provider immediately if you experience:
- unexplained muscle aches.
- breathing difficulty.

- swelling of the face, throat, lips, or tongue.
- flulike symptoms.
- unusual bleeding or bruising.
- yellowing of the skin or of the eyes.

Commonly reported side effects:
- insomnia
- abdominal pain, cramps, or diarrhea
- headache
- dizziness
- taste disturbance

Time Required for Drug to Take Effect: Starts
lowering blood cholesterol levels within 1 to 2 weeks of taking the first dose, but it may take 4 to 6 weeks of treatment to reach maximum effectiveness.

Symptoms of Overdose: No specific symptoms.

Special Notes:
- After beginning lovastatin therapy, your doctor will recheck your cholesterol levels and liver enzymes periodically.
- Use a sunblock with at least SPF 15 when outside because lovastatin may increase your sensitivity to the sun.
- Do not drink alcohol while you are taking this medication.
- Follow a diet plan and exercise program recommended by your health-care provider.
- Lovastatin is not a cure, and it must be taken on a long-term basis for its beneficial effect to be maintained.
- Do not consume grapefruit or grapefruit juice while you are taking this medication.

meclizine

Brand Names:
Antivert
Bonamine
Bonine
Dramamine Less Drowsy Formula

Generic Available: yes

Type of Drug: antiemetic/antivertigo

Used for: Treatment of motion sickness and vertigo associated with inner-ear problems.

How This Medication Works: Decreases the sensitivity of the inner ear to motion and sensitivity of the vomit center to messages arriving from the inner ear.

Dosage Form and Strength:
- tablets (12.5 mg, 25 mg, 50 mg)
- chewable tablets (25 mg)

Storage:
- room temperature
- protect from moisture—do not store in bathroom or kitchen

Administration:
- For motion sickness, take 1 tablet 1 hour before beginning travel and once daily during travel.
- For dizziness, take 1 tablet 2 to 3 times daily.
- Take a missed dose as soon as possible. However, if it is almost time for the next dose, skip the missed dose and return to your regular dosing schedule.

Precautions:

Do not use if:

- you have ever had an allergic reaction to meclizine.
- you have glaucoma, colitis, severe constipation, prostate problems, or myasthenia gravis.

Talk to your doctor if:

- you have severe dry mouth, constipation, urinary retention, or breathing problems.
- you take a drug for Parkinson's disease, irregular heartbeat, upset stomach or cramping, hiatal hernia, allergy, sleep problems, anxiety, depression, hallucinations, or other mental condition.
- you are taking metoclopramide, an antipsychotic (such as chlorpromazine or haloperidol), a tricyclic antidepressant (such as amitriptyline, imipramine, or nortriptyline), a muscle relaxant, or a prescription pain medicine.

Side Effects:

Contact your health-care provider immediately if you experience:

- severe constipation.
- difficult or painful urination.
- severe agitation or confusion.
- hot, dry, flushed skin.
- difficulty breathing.

Commonly reported side effects:

- dizziness, drowsiness, or sedation
- weight gain
- dry mouth

- blurred vision
- mild constipation

Time Required for Drug to Take Effect: Starts to work within 30 to 60 minutes of taking a dose.

Symptoms of Overdose:
- nausea and/or vomiting
- inability to urinate
- dizziness
- severe confusion, agitation, or psychosis
- hyperactivity, combativeness
- hot, dry, flushed skin or fever
- severe muscle weakness or cramping
- stupor, coma

Special Notes:
- In general, older adults are more sensitive to the side effects of this medicine; ask your doctor or pharmacist to recommend the lowest dose that is likely to be effective.
- Do not drink alcohol while taking this medication.
- To prevent dehydration, avoid exposure to hot weather for long periods.
- Consult your health-care provider before taking any over-the-counter medication while you are using this drug.

meloxicam

Brand Name: Mobic

Generic Available: yes

Type of Drug: nonsteroidal anti-inflammatory drug, or NSAID

Used for: Relief of pain and inflammation.

How This Medication Works: Blocks the production and release of chemicals that cause pain and inflammation in the body.

Dosage Form and Strength:
- tablets (7.5 mg, 15 mg)
- suspension (7.5 mg/5 mL)

Storage:
- room temperature
- protect from moisture—do not store in bathroom or kitchen

Administration:
- Usually taken once daily, but may also be prescribed for use on an "as-needed" basis.
- May be taken without regard to meals, but take with food if stomach upset occurs.
- Take a missed dose as soon as possible. However, if it is almost time for the next dose, skip the missed dose and return to your regular dosing schedule.

Precautions:
Do not use if:
- **you have recently had "bypass" surgery, or a coronary artery bypass graft (CABG).**
- you are allergic to meloxicam.
- you are allergic to aspirin or other NSAIDs.

• you have the "aspirin triad" (asthma, allergy to aspirin, and nasal polyps).

Talk to your doctor if:

• you have heart disease or heart failure.
• you have kidney or liver disease.
• you have high blood pressure (hypertension).
• you have a history of stomach problems or ulcers.
• you have asthma.
• you take any aspirin-containing product; any other pain medication; a blood thinner; or a supplement of garlic, ginseng, ginkgo, or vitamin E.

Side Effects:

Contact your health-care provider immediately if you experience:

• signs of a life-threatening reaction, which include fever; wheezing; chest tightness; and itching or swelling of face, lips, tongue, or throat.
• a rash.
• severe stomach pain, nausea, or vomiting.
• severe diarrhea.
• unusual bruising or bleeding.
• weight gain or excessive swelling in your feet or hands.
• tarry stools or vomit resembling coffee grounds.

Commonly reported side effects:

• headache
• stomach pain or heartburn
• nausea or vomiting, diarrhea
• slight swelling of the hands and feet
• dizziness

Time Required for Drug to Take Effect: Starts
working within 2 hours of taking a dose.

Symptoms of Overdose:
- confusion
- drowsiness
- agitation
- hallucinations
- nausea and/or vomiting
- stomach pain
- seizures
- coma

Special Notes:
- **This type of drug may increase your risk for heart attack, stroke, stomach ulcer, and stomach bleeds. Discuss the risks vs. benefits with your physician.**
- Avoid driving and other tasks that require alertness until you see how this drug affects you.
- Do not use aspirin, aspirin-containing drugs, or any other anti-inflammatory while on this drug without consulting your doctor or pharmacist first.
- Tell your dentist, surgeon, and other health-care providers that you use this medication.
- Do not consume alcohol while taking this drug.
- If you are taking this drug and a blood thinner, you may require more frequent monitoring.
- Consult your health-care provider or pharmacist before starting any other medicine, including over-the-counter drugs, while on this medication.

memantine

Brand Name: Namenda

Generic Available: no

Type of Drug: NMDA antagonist

Used for: Treatment of some symptoms of Alzheimer's disease.

How This Medication Works: Decreases the amount of the brain chemical glutamate. Too much glutamate is thought to lead to memory, learning, and attention problems.

Dosage Form and Strength: tablets (5 mg, 10 mg)

Storage:
- room temperature
- protect from moisture—do not store in bathroom or kitchen

Administration:
- Usually taken twice daily.
- May be taken without regard to meals, but take with food if stomach upset occurs.
- Take a missed dose as soon as possible. However, if it is almost time for the next dose, skip the missed dose and return to your regular dosing schedule.

Precautions:
Do not use if:
- you are allergic to memantine.

Talk to your doctor if:
- you have a seizure disorder, liver disease, or kidney disease.
- you are taking acetazolamide, methazolamide, or sodium bicarbonate.

Side Effects:

Contact your health-care provider immediately if you experience:
- signs of a life-threatening reaction, which include fever; wheezing; chest tightness; and itching or swelling of face, lips, tongue, or throat.
- severe dizziness or fainting.
- chest pain or palpitations.
- severe nausea, vomiting, or diarrhea.
- hallucinations or aggressiveness.
- a rash.

Commonly reported side effects:
- dizziness
- headache
- constipation

Time Required for Drug to Take Effect: Takes at least 2 weeks for effects to become apparent.

Symptoms of Overdose:
- restlessness
- drowsiness
- confusion
- hallucinations
- loss of consciousness

Special Notes:
- This drug does not cure Alzheimer's disease, but it may reduce some symptoms.
- The prescribed dose usually starts out low and is gradually increased over several weeks.

metformin

Brand Name: Glucophage

Generic Available: yes

Type of Drug: antidiabetic

Used for: Lowering blood glucose (sugar) levels in type 2 (non–insulin-dependent or adult-onset) diabetes.

How This Medication Works: Reduces the amount of sugar made by your body and helps insulin work better.

Dosage Form and Strength:
- tablets (500 mg, 750 mg, 800 mg, 1,000 mg)
- extended-release tablets (500 mg, 750 mg, 1,000 mg)

Storage:
- room temperature
- protect from moisture—do not store in bathroom or kitchen

Administration:
- Usually taken once or twice daily.
- Take with food to avoid stomach upset.

- Individual dosage will vary, depending on your response to the medication. (Total daily dose should not exceed 2,550 mg.)
- Swallow extended-release tablets whole; do not crush, break, or chew.
- Take a missed dose as soon as possible. However, if it is almost time for the next dose, skip the missed dose and return to your regular dosing schedule.

Precautions:

Do not use if:

- you are allergic to metformin.
- you drink excessive amounts of alcohol.
- you become dehydrated.
- you have severe kidney disease, severe heart failure, or an acidic blood condition.

Talk to your doctor if:

- you have kidney disease, respiratory disease, heart disease, or pancreatitis.
- you have ever had liver disease or diabetic ketoacidosis.
- you have type 1 (insulin-dependent or juvenile-onset) diabetes.
- you have more than 2 alcoholic drinks each day.
- you are taking cimetidine, ranitidine, trimethoprim, nifedipine, furosemide, or procainamide.

Side Effects:

Contact your health-care provider immediately if you experience:

- **persistent diarrhea, vomiting, or stomach upset.**
- **malaise or increasing sleepiness.**

- **unexplained muscle aches or cramps.**
- low blood sugar (symptoms of low blood sugar include palpitations, headache, tremor, sweating, light-headedness, irritability, and blurred vision; untreated, the falling sugar level can lead to seizures and coma).
- painful, swollen tongue.

Commonly reported side effects:
- nausea and/or vomiting, loss of appetite
- diarrhea
- change in taste or metallic taste in mouth

Time Required for Drug to Take Effect:
Begins to work within about 3 hours after taking a dose and reaches its maximum effectiveness within 1 or 2 weeks of treatment.

Symptoms of Overdose:
- very low blood sugar (see Side Effects for symptoms)

Special Notes:
- **Metformin can cause a vitamin B$_{12}$ deficiency and a rare but very serious side effect called lactic acidosis. For these reasons, your doctor will take blood tests to monitor your blood count and kidney function.**
- Do not drink alcohol while taking this medication.
- Do not discontinue this medication without first consulting your doctor.
- You may need to stop this medicine before having surgery or certain medical tests; consult your health-care provider.

- Tell the doctor or dentist you are taking metformin if you are going to have emergency treatment or surgery.
- Talk to your doctor or diabetes educator about how to handle sick days.
- When you begin metformin therapy, check your blood glucose level frequently.
- Metformin can be used alone or in combination with other diabetes medication.
- Nausea, vomiting, and diarrhea should disappear with continued use of the drug.
- Remnants of the extended-release tablets may be noticed in the stool; this is normal.

methylphenidate

Brand Names:

Concerta	Metadate ER	Ritalin
Daytrana	Methylin	Ritalin-LA
Metadate CD	Methylin ER	Ritalin-SR

Generic Available: yes (for some formulations)

Type of Drug: stimulant

Used for: Treatment of attention-deficit hyperactivity disorder and narcolepsy. Sometimes prescribed for treatment of depression.

How This Medication Works: Stimulates the central nervous system to decrease sensation of tiredness.

Dosage Form and Strength:

- tablets (5 mg, 10 mg, 20 mg)

- extended-release tablets (10 mg, 18 mg, 20 mg, 27 mg, 30 mg, 36 mg, 40 mg, 54 mg)
- extended-release capsules (10 mg, 20 mg, 30 mg, 40 mg)
- patch (10 mg/9 hours, 15 mg/9 hours, 20 mg/9 hours, 30 mg/9 hours)

Storage:

- room temperature
- protect from light, heat, and moisture—do not store in bathroom or kitchen

Administration:

- Tablets usually taken 2 to 3 times daily (once daily for extended-release tablets).
- Swallow extended-release tablets or capsules whole; do not break, crush, or chew.
- Patch is applied once daily and removed after 9 hours.
- Take with food if stomach upset occurs.
- Take dose early in the day to avoid insomnia.
- Take a missed dose as soon as possible. However, if it is almost time for the next dose, skip the missed dose and return to your regular dosing schedule.

Precautions:

Do not use if:

- you are allergic to methylphenidate.
- you are extremely anxious or agitated.
- you have taken a monoamine oxidase (MAO) inhibitor, such as phenelzine or tranylcypromine, within the past 14 days.
- you have Tourette's syndrome or tics.

Talk to your doctor if:
- **you have a history of drug dependence or alcoholism.**
- you have high blood pressure or heart disease.
- you have seizures or glaucoma.
- you have an intestinal obstruction or problems with your small intestine.

Side Effects:

Contact your health-care provider immediately if you experience:
- **mood changes, especially nervousness, anxiety, or psychotic thinking.**
- increased heart rate or chest pain/pressure.
- weight loss.
- severe headache.
- extreme dizziness.

Commonly reported side effects:
- decreased appetite
- difficulty sleeping
- headache
- nausea and/or vomiting
- dizziness

Time Required for Drug to Take Effect: Effects seen within a few hours of taking a dose.

Symptoms of Overdose:
- confusion
- seizures or tremors
- dry mouth
- increased heart rate
- vomiting

Special Notes:
- **This drug may be habit-forming.**
- Do not discontinue this medication without first talking with your doctor.
- If you have difficulty sleeping, take the last dose of the day before 6 P.M.
- You may notice remnants of the Concerta tablets in your stool; this is normal.
- Avoid excessive caffeine intake while taking this medication; it may cause nervousness or shakiness.
- Consult your health-care provider before using any other medication while you are taking this drug.
- You should monitor your blood pressure periodically while you are taking this drug and notify your doctor if your blood pressure has increased; discuss this with your doctor.

metoclopramide

Brand Name: Reglan

Generic Available: yes

Type of Drug: antiemetic/antivertigo

Used for: Treatment of nausea and vomiting (especially due to cancer chemotherapy), stomach problems in diabetes, and heartburn (gastroesophageal reflux disease [GERD]). Also used in patients with stomach tubes.

How This Medication Works: Increases the movement (muscle contractions) inside the stomach and intestines and inhibits the nausea center in the brain.

Dosage Form and Strength:
- tablets (5 mg, 10 mg)
- syrup (5 mg/5 mL)

Storage:
- room temperature
- protect from moisture—do not store in bathroom or kitchen

Administration:
- Take 15 to 30 minutes before meals and at bedtime.
- Take a missed dose as soon as possible. However, if it is almost time for the next dose, skip the missed dose and return to your regular dosing schedule.

Precautions:
Do not use if:
- you are allergic to metoclopramide.
- you have stomach bleeding or intestinal blockage.

Talk to your doctor if:
- you have a disorder of the stomach or intestines, Parkinson's disease, epilepsy or seizures, kidney disease, or liver disease.
- you are taking any other medication, especially any drug that may make you drowsy, such as an antihistamine, cold medicine, sedative, tranquilizer, sleeping medication, pain reliever, seizure medication, or muscle relaxant.

Side Effects:
Contact your health-care provider immediately if you experience:
- skin rash, hives, or itching.

- shuffling walk.
- trembling of hands.
- confusion.
- difficulty speaking or swallowing.
- severe dizziness or fainting.
- stiffness of the arms or legs; strange movements.

Commonly reported side effects:
- drowsiness
- restlessness and irritability
- breast tenderness or swelling
- constipation or diarrhea
- headache
- nausea
- unusually dry mouth

Time Required for Drug to Take Effect: Starts
to work within 15 to 60 minutes of taking a dose of the medication.

Symptoms of Overdose:
- confusion
- drowsiness
- strange movements or difficulty coordinating movements
- irritability and agitation

Special Notes:
- Check with your physician or pharmacist before using any over-the-counter medication while taking this drug.

- This medication may cause drowsiness. Use caution when driving a motor vehicle or operating dangerous machinery.
- Do not drink alcohol while you are taking this medication.
- Metoclopramide may worsen the symptoms of Parkinson's disease.
- If you experience dry mouth, chew gum, suck on ice chips or hard candy, or try a saliva substitute.

metoprolol

Brand Names: Lopressor, Toprol XL

Generic Available:
- tablets: yes
- extended-release tablets: yes (in some strengths)

Type of Drug: antihypertensive (beta-adrenergic blocking agent, or beta-blocker)

Used for: Relief of angina (chest pressure or discomfort) and treatment of high blood pressure (hypertension), heart attack, and heart rhythm problems.

How This Medication Works: Inhibits certain hormones that increase heart rate and blood pressure.

Dosage Form and Strength:
- tablets (25 mg, 50 mg, 100 mg)
- extended-release tablets (25 mg, 50 mg, 100 mg, 200 mg)

Storage:
- room temperature

- protect from moisture—do not store in bathroom or kitchen

Administration:

- **Do not abruptly stop taking this medication because serious side effects may occur.**
- Usually taken once or twice daily.
- Take at the same time every day.
- Take with food.
- Swallow extended-release tablets whole; do not crush or chew.
- Take a missed dose as soon as possible. However, if it is almost time for the next dose, skip the missed dose and return to your regular dosing schedule.

Precautions:

Do not use if:

- you have ever had an allergic reaction to metoprolol or another beta-blocker, such as atenolol or propranolol.
- you have a very slow heartbeat without a pacemaker.

Talk to your doctor if:

- you are taking any other medication, especially medication for diabetes, asthma, high blood pressure (hypertension), heart disease, or depression.
- you have asthma, lung disease, a slow heart rate, heart disease, a problem with your blood vessels or circulation, diabetes, kidney or liver disease, thyroid disease, or a history of depression.

Side Effects:

Contact your health-care provider immediately if you experience:

- skin rash, itching, or swelling of the face or throat.
- severe dizziness or fainting.
- difficulty breathing.
- significant weight gain.
- confusion, hallucinations, or nightmares.
- palpitations or irregular heartbeat.
- swelling of the feet, ankles, or lower legs.
- chest pressure or discomfort.
- unusual bleeding or bruising.

Commonly reported side effects:

- nervousness, anxiety, and trouble sleeping
- light-headedness, dizziness, and drowsiness
- nausea, stomach upset, diarrhea, or constipation
- change in sexual ability or desire

Time Required for Drug to Take Effect: Starts
to work within 1 to 4 hours of taking a dose, but it takes at least 2 to 4 weeks of treatment to reach maximum effectiveness.

Symptoms of Overdose:

- slow, fast, or irregular heartbeat
- severe dizziness or fainting
- difficulty breathing
- seizures
- blue tint to nail beds or palms

Special Notes:

- Do not stop taking metoprolol without first consulting your doctor.

- Metoprolol is not a cure, and you may have to take this medication for a long time.
- Check with your physician or pharmacist before using any over-the-counter medication while taking this drug.
- Older patients may be more sensitive to cold temperatures while taking metoprolol.
- If you notice dizziness, avoid activities requiring mental alertness, such as driving a motor vehicle or operating dangerous machinery.
- Changing positions slowly when sitting and/or standing up may help decrease dizziness caused by this medication.
- Metoprolol may slow the heart rate. Ask your doctor what your safe range is, but call your doctor if your heart rate falls below 50 beats per minute.
- Be careful to avoid becoming dehydrated or overheated.
- You may see the shell of the extended-release tablet in your stool; this is normal.

metronidazole

Brand Names: Flagyl, Flagyl ER

Generic Available: yes

Type of Drug: anti-infective

Used for: Treatment of Crohn's disease and of infections of the blood, skin, vagina, bone, and respiratory tract caused by susceptible bacteria or protozoa.

How This Medication Works: Appears to enter invading organisms and stop DNA synthesis, fatally injuring the organisms.

Dosage Form and Strength:
- tablets (250 mg, 500 mg)
- extended-release tablets (750 mg)
- capsules (375 mg)

Storage:
- room temperature
- protect from moisture—do not store in bathroom or kitchen

Administration:
- Regular tablets and capsules usually taken 3 to 4 times daily; extended-release tablets usually taken once daily.
- Take at even intervals.
- Take the regular tablets and capsules with food to avoid stomach upset.
- Take the extended-release tablets on an empty stomach, at least 1 hour before or 2 hours after a meal.
- Finish all the medication prescribed for you.
- Do not drink alcohol while taking this medication; doing so may cause cramps and vomiting.
- Take a missed dose as soon as possible. However, if it is almost time for the next dose, skip the missed dose and return to your regular dosing schedule.

Precautions:

Do not use if:
- you are allergic to metronidazole.
- you are less than 12 weeks pregnant.

Talk to your doctor if:
- you have liver or kidney disease, seizures, or heart failure.
- you are taking phenobarbital, warfarin, disulfiram, phenytoin, or lithium.

Side Effects:

Contact your health-care provider immediately if you experience:
- numbness or tingling in the hands or feet.
- seizures.
- a rash.
- wheezing.
- swelling of the face or throat.

Commonly reported side effects:
- metallic taste
- darkening of the urine (to a deep red-brown color)
- dizziness
- stomach upset, nausea, or vomiting
- headache
- diarrhea

Time Required for Drug to Take Effect:

Begins to kill infecting organisms within hours after you take the first dose. However, you must finish all of the prescribed medication, even if your symptoms have disappeared.

Symptoms of Overdose:

- nausea and/or vomiting

- staggering
- seizures

Special Notes:
- Do not drink alcohol while taking this medication or for at least 24 hours after you take the very last dose; otherwise, severe nausea and vomiting may occur.
- Do not use this medication for any infections other than the infection for which it was prescribed.
- This medication may cause your urine to darken; this is a harmless side effect.
- Use this medication only as directed and only for the condition for which it was prescribed.

mirtazapine

Brand Names: Remeron, Remeron SolTab

Generic Available: yes

Type of Drug: antidepressant

Used for: Treatment of depression.

How This Medication Works: Increases the amounts of the naturally occurring chemicals norepinephrine and serotonin in the brain.

Dosage Form and Strength:
- tablets (15 mg, 30 mg, 45 mg)
- orally disintegrating tablets (15 mg, 30 mg, 45 mg)

Storage:
- room temperature

- protect from moisture—do not store in bathroom or kitchen
- protect orally disintegrating tablets from light

Administration:

- Usually taken once daily.
- Usually taken at bedtime because it may cause drowsiness.
- May be taken without regard to meals, but take with food if stomach upset occurs.
- Place orally disintegrating tablet on tongue and let dissolve; water is not needed. Do not swallow whole or chew, break, or crush.
- Take a missed dose as soon as possible. However, if it is almost time for the next dose, skip the missed dose and return to your dosing schedule.

Precautions:

Do not use if:

- you are allergic to mirtazapine.
- you have taken a monoamine oxidase (MAO) inhibitor, such as isocarboxazid, phenelzine, or tranylcypromine, within the past 14 days.

Talk to your doctor if:

- you have a history of mania/hypomania.
- you have a history of seizure disorders.
- you had an allergy to or other adverse effect from other antidepressants.
- you have severe kidney, heart, or liver disease.
- you are using any medicine that makes you drowsy, such as a sleeping pill, cold and allergy medicine, narcotic pain reliever, or sedative.

Side Effects:

Contact your health-care provider immediately if you experience:
- **severe depression or thoughts of suicide or harming yourself.**
- signs of a life-threatening reaction, which include fever; wheezing; chest tightness; and itching or swelling of face, lips, tongue, or throat.
- a rash.
- extreme nervousness, excitability, or confusion.
- extreme dizziness or fainting.

Commonly reported side effects:
- drowsiness or fatigue
- dizziness
- nausea and/or vomiting
- constipation
- blurred vision
- dry mouth
- weight gain

Time Required for Drug to Take Effect: May take 2 to 8 weeks of treatment to reach maximum effectiveness.

Symptoms of Overdose:
- drowsiness
- memory problems
- fast heartbeat

Special Notes:
- The desire to kill yourself is a serious symptom of depression. If you are planning suicide, dial 911 right away.

- Do not take Saint John's wort while you are taking this drug, because it may decrease this drug's effectiveness.
- Once treatment of depression is begun, sleep and appetite may improve quickly. However, other depressive symptoms may take up to 4 to 8 weeks to improve.
- Do not drive or perform other tasks that require alertness until you see how this medication affects you.
- Do not consume alcohol while you are taking this medication.

mometasone

Brand Names: Nasonex, Asmanex

Generic Available: no

Type of Drug: corticosteroid

Used for: Nasal spray (Nasonex) used for treatment of nasal irritation, allergies, or nasal polyps; oral inhaler (Asmanex) used for maintenance treatment of asthma.

How This Medication Works: Reduces irritation and swelling by minimizing or preventing the body's response to what is causing the allergy.

Dosage Form and Strength:
- nasal suspension (50 mcg/spray)
- oral inhaler (220 mcg/inh)

Storage:
- room temperature, with the cap on
- protect from light

Administration:
- Administer a missed dose as soon as possible. However, if it is almost time for the next dose, skip the missed dose and return to your regular dosing schedule.

Nasal spray:
- For use in the nose only.
- Shake well before use.
- Blow nose to clear nostrils before use.
- Before using nasal spray the first time, prime it by pumping or squeezing bottle until some of the medicine sprays out; it is then ready to use.
- Prime spray again after each pump cleaning or if medicine has not been used for 5 or more days.
- After using nasal spray, wipe tip of bottle with clean tissue and put cap back on.

Oral inhaler:
- Carefully read and follow all instructions provided with the inhaler.
- Rinse out mouth after each use.

Precautions:
Do not use if:
- you are allergic to mometasone or benzalkonium chloride.
- you recently injured your nose, had surgery on your nose, or had sores in your nose.

Talk to your doctor if:
- you have asthma, an active infection, tuberculosis, or herpes simplex in your eye.
- you have a history of glaucoma or cataracts.
- you are switching from oral steroids to inhaled steroids.
- you are having surgery or you have an infection.

Side Effects:

Contact your health-care provider immediately if you experience:
- signs of a life-threatening reaction, which include wheezing; chest tightness; and itching or swelling of face, lips, tongue, or throat.
- signs of infection, such as fever, chills, severe sore throat, ear or sinus pain, or cough.
- extreme fatigue, weakness, or irritability.
- sores or white patches in the mouth, throat, or nose.
- a worsening of your allergy symptoms.

Commonly reported side effects:
- headache
- nasal congestion
- nasal irritation or burning

Time Required for Drug to Take Effect: Starts

working within 24 hours after you take the first dose, but it may take up to 2 weeks of treatment to reach maximum effectiveness.

Symptoms of Overdose:
- stomach pain
- muscle weakness
- chest pain
- seizures

Special Notes:
- Do not keep this medicine inside a motor vehicle or anywhere else it could be exposed to extreme heat or cold.
- Consult your health-care provider or pharmacist before starting any other medicine, including over-the-counter drugs, natural products, or vitamins, while you are on this medication.

montelukast

Brand Name: Singulair

Generic Available: no

Type of Drug: leukotriene-receptor antagonist

Used for: Prevention of allergy symptoms or treatment of asthma.

How This Medication Works: Decreases the body's production of a group of chemicals called leukotrienes that worsen asthma and allergic reactions.

Dosage Form and Strength:
- tablets (10 mg)
- chewable tablets (4 mg, 5 mg)
- granules (4 mg/packet)

Storage:
- store in original container at room temperature
- protect from light and moisture—do not store in bathroom or kitchen

Administration:

- Usually taken once daily in the evening.
- May be taken without regard to meals, but take with food if stomach upset occurs.
- Do not swallow chewable tablet whole; chew or crush well.
- Granules may be poured directly in the mouth or mixed with soft foods, such as applesauce or ice cream, but not liquid. Use within 15 minutes of opening packet. Discard any unused granules.
- Take a missed dose as soon as possible. However, if it is almost time for the next dose, skip the missed dose and return to your dosing schedule.

Precautions:

Do not use if:
- you are allergic to montelukast.
- you have phenylketonuria and the chewable tablets have been prescribed for you.

Talk to your doctor if:
- you have severe liver disease.

Side Effects:

Contact your health-care provider immediately if you experience:
- signs of a life-threatening reaction, which include fever; wheezing; chest tightness; and itching or swelling of face, lips, tongue, or throat.
- a rash.
- a persistent cough.
- numbness or tingling of the hands or feet.
- dark urine.
- yellowing of the skin or eyes.
- appetite loss or weight loss.

Commonly reported side effects:
- flulike symptoms, such as headache, weakness, fever, shakes, or muscle aches
- nervousness
- headache
- stomach upset, nausea, or vomiting
- stuffy nose
- dizziness

Time Required for Drug to Take Effect: Starts working within 24 hours of first dose.

Symptoms of Overdose:
- thirst
- drowsiness
- stomach pain

Special Notes:
- This medication should not be used to treat a sudden asthma attack; consult your health-care provider for instructions on treating an asthma attack in progress.
- Take this medication on a regular basis to help avoid asthma and allergy attacks.
- Do not consume grapefruit or grapefruit juice while you are taking this medication.

morphine

Brand Names:

Avinza	Oramorph SR
Kadian	RMS
MS Contin	Roxanol
MSIR	Roxanol/100

Generic Available: yes (for some formulations)

Type of Drug: narcotic analgesic

Used for: Relief of moderate to severe pain and shortness of breath due to heart or lung disease.

How This Medication Works: Acts in the brain to decrease the recognition of pain signals.

Dosage Form and Strength:
- tablets (15 mg, 30 mg)
- sustained-release tablets/capsules (15 mg, 30 mg, 60 mg, 90 mg, 100 mg, 120 mg, 200 mg)
- capsules (15 mg, 30 mg)
- liquid (10 mg/5 mL, 20 mg/5 mL, 20 mg/5 mL, 100 mg/5 mL)
- rectal suppositories (5 mg, 10 mg, 20 mg, 30 mg)

Storage:
- room temperature
- protect from moisture—do not store in bathroom or kitchen

Administration:
- **Do not consume alcoholic beverages while taking Avinza or Kadian, as this may result in a fatal overdose. Use of alcohol with any morphine product may cause increased sedation, confusion, and difficulty breathing.**
- Regular tablets, capsules, solution, and suppositories are usually taken every 4 hours.
- Sustained-release products are usually taken every 12 hours.

- Dosage is individualized for each patient, depending on the pain and previous exposure to morphine.
- Never take a larger dose or more doses per day than your doctor has prescribed.
- Take with milk or food if stomach upset occurs.
- Swallow sustained-release tablets or capsules whole; do not crush, break, or chew.
- The entire contents of the sustained-release capsules may be sprinkled onto applesauce and swallowed at once; do not crush, chew, or dissolve the individual pellets contained in the capsule.

Precautions:

Do not use if:

- you are allergic to morphine or another narcotic, such as hydrocodone, codeine, hydromorphone, or oxycodone.
- you have increased pressure in the brain or an intestinal blockage.

Talk to your doctor if:

- you have alcoholism or other substance-abuse problem; brain disease or a head injury; colitis; seizures; emotional problems or a mental illness; emphysema, asthma, or other lung disease; kidney, liver, or thyroid disease; prostate problems or problems with urination; or gallbladder disease or gallstones.
- you are taking naltrexone, zidovudine, or any other medication, especially any that can cause drowsiness, such as an antihistamine, barbiturate (such as phenobarbital), benzodiazepine (such

as diazepam, alprazolam, or lorazepam), muscle relaxant, or antidepressant.
- you drink alcoholic beverages.

Side Effects:

Contact your health-care provider immediately if you experience:
- a skin rash or hives.
- severe confusion or hallucinations.
- severe dizziness or fainting.
- irregular or difficult breathing.
- painful or difficult urination.
- severe nausea, vomiting, or constipation.
- fast, slow, or pounding heartbeat.
- poor pain control.
- trembling or uncontrolled muscle movements.
- extreme weakness.

Commonly reported side effects:
- constipation
- drowsiness
- dry mouth
- loss of appetite
- nervousness or restlessness
- dizziness or drowsiness

Time Required for Drug to Take Effect: Starts
to work within 30 to 60 minutes after taking a dose.

Symptoms of Overdose:
- cold, clammy skin
- severe confusion or hallucinations
- seizures
- severe dizziness or drowsiness
- continued nausea, vomiting, or diarrhea

- severe nervousness or restlessness
- difficulty breathing
- slowed heartbeat

Special Notes:

- This medication may cause drowsiness. Do not drive a motor vehicle or operate machinery while you are taking this medication.
- Morphine and other narcotics (such as oxycodone and codeine) cause constipation. This side effect may be diminished by drinking 6 to 8 full glasses of water each day. If you are using this medication for chronic pain, adding a stool softener–laxative combination may be necessary.
- Check with your physician or pharmacist before using any over-the-counter medication while you are taking this drug.
- When morphine is used over a long period of time, your body may become tolerant and require larger doses.
- Do not stop taking this medication abruptly because you may encounter the effects of withdrawal.
- Nausea and vomiting may occur, especially after the first few doses. This effect may go away if you lie down for a while.
- If you experience dry mouth, chew gum, suck on ice chips or hard candy, or try a saliva substitute.
- Do not drink alcohol while you are taking this medication.
- Sustained-release tablets should not be used for acute pain relief but to maintain a steady level of

medication in the bloodstream for the treatment of chronic pain.

naproxen

Brand Names:
Aleve
Anaprox
Anaprox DS
EC-Naprosyn

Naprelan
Naprosyn
Pamprin Maximum
   Strength All Day Relief

Generic Available: yes

Type of Drug: nonsteroidal anti-inflammatory drug, or NSAID

Used for: Relief of pain and inflammation.

How This Medication Works: Blocks the production and release of chemicals that cause pain and inflammation in the body.

Dosage Form and Strength:
- tablets (220 mg, 275 mg, 550 mg)
- caplets (220 mg, 275 mg, 550 mg)
- delayed-release tablets (375 mg, 500 mg)
- suspension (125 mg/5 mL)

Storage:
- room temperature
- protect pill forms from light and moisture—do not store in bathroom or kitchen

Administration:

- Usually taken every 8 to 12 hours, but may also be prescribed for use on an "as-needed" basis.
- May be taken without regard to meals, but take with food if stomach upset occurs.
- Swallow delayed-release tablets whole; do not chew, break, or crush.
- Shake suspension well before use.
- Take a missed dose as soon as possible. However, if it is almost time for the next dose, skip the missed dose and return to your dosing schedule.

Precautions:

Do not use if:

- **you have recently had "bypass" surgery, or a coronary artery bypass graft (CABG).**
- you are allergic to naproxen.
- you are allergic to aspirin or other NSAID, such as celecoxib, diclofenac, ibuprofen, indomethacin, meloxicam, or oxaprozin.
- you have the "aspirin triad" (asthma, allergy to aspirin, and nasal polyps).

Talk to your doctor if:

- you have heart disease, heart failure, or high blood pressure (hypertension).
- you have kidney or liver disease.
- you have a history of stomach problems or ulcers.
- you have asthma.
- you take an aspirin-containing product; another pain medicine; a blood thinner; or a supplement containing garlic, ginseng, ginkgo, or vitamin E.

Side Effects:

Contact your health-care provider immediately if you experience:
- signs of a life-threatening reaction, which include fever; wheezing; chest tightness; and itching or swelling of face, lips, tongue, or throat.
- a rash.
- severe stomach pain, nausea, or vomiting.
- severe diarrhea.
- unusual bruising or bleeding.
- weight gain or excessive swelling in your feet or hands.
- tarry stools or vomit that looks like coffee grounds.

Commonly reported side effects:
- headache
- stomach pain or heartburn
- nausea and/or vomiting
- diarrhea
- slight swelling of the hands and feet
- dizziness

Time Required for Drug to Take Effect: Starts working within 1 hour of taking a dose.

Symptoms of Overdose:
- confusion, hallucinations
- drowsiness
- agitation
- nausea and/or vomiting, stomach pain
- seizures
- coma

Special Notes:

- **This type of drug may increase your risk for heart attack, stroke, stomach ulcer, and stomach bleeds. Discuss the risks vs. benefits with your physician.**
- Avoid driving and other tasks that require alertness until you see how this drug affects you.
- Do not use aspirin, aspirin-containing medication, or any other anti-inflammatory medication while on this drug without consulting your doctor or pharmacist.
- Tell your dentist, surgeon, and other health-care providers that you use this medicine.
- If you are taking a blood thinner in addition to this drug, you may require more frequent monitoring.
- Consult your health-care provider or pharmacist before starting any other medicine, including over-the-counter drugs, while on this medication.
- Do not consume alcohol while taking this drug.
- When used for self-medication (over-the-counter use), naproxen should not be used for more than 10 consecutive days or in doses greater than 220 mg twice daily.

niacin

Brand Names:

Niacor   Nicobid
Niaspan   Slo-Niacin

Generic Available: yes (for some formulations)

Type of Drug: vitamin and antihyperlipidemic

Used for: Vitamin supplementation or improvement of blood lipid (fats and cholesterol) profile.

How This Medication Works: Lowers triglyceride levels and total and LDL (bad) cholesterol levels and increases HDL (good) cholesterol levels in the blood.

Dosage Form and Strength:
- tablets (50 mg, 100 mg, 250 mg, 500 mg, 750 mg)
- extended-release capsules (125 mg, 250 mg, 400 mg, 500 mg)
- long-acting tablets (250 mg, 500 mg, 750 mg, 1,000 mg)

Storage:
- room temperature
- protect from moisture—do not store in bathroom or kitchen

Administration:
- If you have been prescribed one dose daily, take it at bedtime.
- Take this medicine with food.
- If you stop using this medicine for several days, talk to your doctor before you start using it again.
- Swallow long-acting or extended-release products whole; do not chew, break, or crush.
- Avoid drinking hot liquids near the time you take a dose of this drug.

Precautions:
Do not use if:
- you are allergic to niacin or niacinamide.
- you have severe liver disease, an active peptic ulcer, or very low blood pressure.

Talk to your doctor if:
- you have diabetes; heart, kidney, liver, thyroid, or gallbladder disease; or gout.
- you take the blood thinner warfarin or blood pressure medication.
- you drink alcohol on a regular basis.

Side Effects:

Contact your health-care provider immediately if you experience:
- signs of a life-threatening reaction, which include fever; wheezing; chest tightness; and itching or swelling of face, lips, tongue, or throat.
- unusual bruising or bleeding.
- yellowing of the skin or eyes.
- a rash.
- severe dizziness or fainting.

Commonly reported side effects:
- headache
- flushing, itching
- stomach upset, nausea, and vomiting

Time Required for Drug to Take Effect: Takes weeks or months of use to affect cholesterol levels.

Symptoms of Overdose:
- flushing, itching
- stomach upset

Special Notes:
- You may experience flushing, a sensation of heat, or headache from this medication; these reactions may be minimized by starting with a low dose of niacin and increasing it gradually or by taking

aspirin 30 minutes prior to taking niacin; discuss
this with your health-care provider.
- Flushing usually diminishes with regular use.
- Consuming alcohol while you are taking this drug
  may increase flushing.
- If you have diabetes, you will need to monitor
  blood glucose closely while on this medication.

nicotine (topical)

Brand Names:
Commit   Nicorette
Nicoderm CQ   Nicotrol

Generic Available: yes

Type of Drug: antismoking aid

Used for: Helping people to quit smoking.

How This Medication Works: Provides nicotine
to prevent smoking withdrawal symptoms.

Dosage Form and Strength:
- gum (2 mg, 4 mg)
- inhaler (10 mg)
- lozenge (2 mg, 4 mg)
- nasal spray (10 mg/mL)
- patch (7 mg, 14 mg, 21 mg)

Storage:
- room temperature
- in original packaging

Administration:

- Closely read and follow directions for proper dosing and use because they vary among nicotine products.

Patch:

- Apply to a clean, dry, nonoily, and hairless area of the upper arms, chest, or stomach once daily.
- Do not put the patch on the same spot each time; rotate patch placement.
- Do not apply on cuts or abrasions.

Gum:

- Chew gum until tingling is felt in the mouth; then store gum between your gums and cheek until the tingling goes away. Repeat this cycle for approximately 30 minutes; do not chew it the way you chew regular gum.

Lozenge:

- Suck on the lozenge and let it slowly dissolve in your mouth; do not bite, chew, or swallow whole.

Inhaler and nasal spray:

- Carefully follow the instructions included in the package.

Precautions:

Do not use if:

- you have had an allergic reaction to nicotine or any type of adhesive dressing or bandage.
- you have phenylketonuria and the lozenge form of this drug has been prescribed for you.
- you are still smoking.
- you have severe angina.
- you have had a recent heart attack.
- you are or may be pregnant.

Talk to your doctor if:
- you experience irregular heart rates or have mild angina; diabetes; high blood pressure (hypertension); hyperthyroidism; stomach ulcer; temporomandibular joint (TMJ), or jaw joint, problems; or a skin disease.
- you have ever had a heart attack.
- you have not stopped smoking after 4 weeks of using this medication.
- you are taking any other medication, especially theophylline, propranolol, insulin, bupropion, or cimetidine.

Side Effects:

Contact your health-care provider immediately if you experience:
- nausea, vomiting, or diarrhea that continues.
- irregular or fast heartbeat that persists.
- stomach pain.
- swelling or irritation of the skin.
- extreme nervousness or irritability.

Commonly reported side effects:
- nausea, vomiting, or heartburn
- fast heartbeat
- mild headache
- increased appetite
- skin irritation (from patch)
- jaw ache (from chewing the gum form)
- insomnia

Time Required for Drug to Take Effect: The
nicotine begins to enter the bloodstream immediately upon dosing.

Symptoms of Overdose:
- confusion, seizures
- diarrhea, nausea, or stomach pain
- dilated pupils or eyes moving from side to side
- fast or irregular heartbeat
- hearing loss or ringing in the ears
- slowed or difficult breathing
- tingling of the arms and legs
- watery eyes and mouth

Special Notes:
- You must stop smoking when using this drug; nicotine overdoses can be fatal.
- Before applying the patch form, wash your hands with water only; soap will increase the absorption of nicotine through the skin of your fingers.
- To not take the patches by mouth; if accidentally taken orally, call your doctor or poison control center.
- Do not eat or drink within 15 minutes (before or after) of using the gum form.
- Nicotine gum may cause problems with dental work.
- Sound-alike/look-alike warning: Nicoderm may be confused with Nitroderm.
- Be sure to keep any form of this medication, but especially the gum or lozenge, out of the reach of children.

nifedipine

Brand Names:
Adalat
Adalat CC
Afeditab
Nifediac CC

Nifedical XL
Procardia
Procardia XL

Generic Available: yes

Type of Drug: cardiovascular (calcium channel blocker)

Used for: Treatment of angina and high blood pressure (hypertension).

How This Medication Works: Inhibits smooth-muscle contraction and causes dilation of the blood vessels.

Dosage Form and Strength:
- sustained-release tablets (30 mg, 60 mg, 90 mg)
- capsules (10 mg, 20 mg)

Storage:
- room temperature
- protect from moisture—do not store in bathroom or kitchen

Administration:
- Swallow sustained-release tablets whole; do not crush or chew.
- Take at the same time every day.
- Take with food if stomach upset occurs.

- Take a missed dose as soon as possible. However, if it is almost time for the next dose, skip the missed dose and return to your dosing schedule.

Precautions:

Do not use if:

- you have ever had an allergic reaction to nifedipine or another calcium channel blocker, such as amlodipine, diltiazem, or verapamil.

Talk to your doctor if:

- you have heart, kidney, or liver disease or problems with your circulation or blood vessels.
- you are taking any other medication, especially carbamazepine, cyclosporine, warfarin, theophylline, an oral antifungal, or a blood pressure medication.

Side Effects:

Contact your health-care provider immediately if you experience:

- fast or irregular heartbeat.
- skin rash, itching, or difficulty breathing.
- severe headache.
- painful or swollen joints or swollen legs.
- chest pressure or discomfort.
- severe dizziness or fainting.

Commonly reported side effects:

- light-headedness, dizziness, or drowsiness
- headache
- change in sexual ability or desire
- flushing
- nausea or constipation
- irritated gums

Time Required for Drug to Take Effect: Starts
to work within 20 to 60 minutes of taking a dose.
However, it takes at least 2 to 4 weeks of treatment to
reach maximum effectiveness.

Symptoms of Overdose:
- nausea and/or vomiting
- weakness, drowsiness, or slurred speech
- dizziness or confusion
- palpitations and low blood pressure
- loss of consciousness

Special Notes:
- The short-acting forms of nifedipine should not be
  used to treat high blood pressure (hypertension).
- Changing positions slowly when sitting and/or
  standing up may help decrease dizziness caused
  by this medication.
- If this medication makes you dizzy, do not
  perform activities requiring mental alertness,
  such as driving a car or operating potentially
  dangerous machinery.
- Check with your physician or pharmacist before
  using any over-the-counter medication while you
  are taking this drug.
- Avoid becoming dehydrated or overheated while
  you are taking this drug.
- Do not consume grapefruit or grapefruit juice
  while you are taking this drug.
- Sometimes the shell of the tablet may show up in
  the stool; this is normal and does not mean that
  the active ingredient in the tablet has not been
  absorbed.

nitrofurantoin

Brand Names:
Furadantin
Macrobid
Macrodantin

Generic Available: yes

Type of Drug: anti-infective

Used for: Treatment of urinary tract infections.

How This Medication Works: Interferes with carbohydrate metabolism in the invading bacteria and disrupts bacterial growth.

Dosage Form and Strength:
- capsules (25 mg, 50 mg, 100 mg)
- suspension (25 mg/5 mL)

Storage:
- room temperature
- protect from moisture—do not store in bathroom or kitchen

Administration:
- Take at even intervals.
- Take with food or milk.
- Take until completely gone, even if symptoms disappear.
- Shake suspension well before measuring dose.
- If you also use an antacid, separate doses of nitrofurantoin and the antacid by 2 hours.
- Take a missed dose as soon as possible. However, if it is almost time for the next dose, skip the

missed dose and return to your regular dosing schedule.

Precautions:

Do not use if:
- you are allergic to nitrofurantoin.

Talk to your doctor if:
- you are taking probenecid, a magnesium supplement, or an antacid.
- you have liver or kidney disease.

Side Effects:

Contact your health-care provider immediately if you experience:
- fever, chills, and cough.
- chest pain or pressure.
- difficulty breathing.
- a rash.
- numbness or tingling of the hands or feet.
- persistent nausea, vomiting, or diarrhea.
- unexplained bruising.
- confusion.

Commonly reported side effects:
- brown discoloration of the urine
- nausea and/or vomiting
- abdominal pain
- headache
- dizziness and drowsiness

Time Required for Drug to Take Effect:

Begins to kill infecting bacteria within hours after the first dose. However, you must finish all of the medication that has been prescribed, even if your symptoms disappear before then.

Symptoms of Overdose:
- vomiting

Special Notes:
- Do not use this drug for infections other than the one for which it was prescribed.
- Drink 6 to 8 glasses of water daily while you are taking this medication, unless directed otherwise by your health-care provider.
- Eating yogurt with active cultures may help eliminate mild diarrhea, but contact your health-care provider if diarrhea becomes severe or continues.

nitroglycerin

Brand Names:
Minitran
Nitrek
Nitro-Bid
Nitro-Bid Ointment
Nitro-Dur

Nitrolingual Spray
NitroQuick
Nitrostat
Transderm-Nitro

Generic Available:
- sublingual tablets: yes
- sublingual spray: no
- ointment: yes
- skin patch: yes
- sustained-release capsules: yes
- sustained-release tablets: no

Type of Drug: vasodilator

Used for: Treatment of chest pain, congestive heart failure, angina, and coronary heart disease.

How This Medication Works: Relaxes smooth muscle, reducing blood pressure and demand on heart.

Dosage Form and Strength:
- sublingual tablets (0.3 mg, 0.4 mg, 0.6 mg)
- sublingual spray (0.4 mg per spray)
- ointment (2%)
- skin patch (0.1 mg/hr, 0.2 mg/hr, 0.3 mg/hr, 0.4 mg/hr, 0.6 mg/hr, 0.8 mg/hr)
- sustained-release capsules (2.5 mg, 6.5 mg, 9 mg)
- sustained-release tablets (2.6 mg, 6.5 mg, 9 mg)

Storage:
- room temperature
- tightly closed in original container
- protect from moisture—do not store in bathroom or kitchen

Administration:
- Oral or sustained-release products are usually taken twice daily.
- Sublingual tablets (or the spray) are taken when necessary to relieve chest pain.
- If you experience chest pain, spray once under the tongue or place 1 sublingual tablet under the tongue and let it dissolve; do not swallow. If pain persists after 5 minutes, take another dose. Repeat again in 5 minutes, if needed. If pain is not relieved after 3 doses, seek immediate medical care (call 911).

- It is important to have an 8- to 10-hour period each day that is nitrate-free. If nitrates (such as nitroglycerin and isosorbide) are taken continuously, tolerance will develop and the medication becomes ineffective. Skin patches should be removed for at least 8 hours daily. Capsules should be taken 8 hours apart, but only 2 times a day (for example, 8 A.M. and 4 P.M.).
- Take on an empty stomach, 1 hour before or 2 hours after a meal.
- Dissolve sublingual tablets under the tongue; do not swallow, crush, or chew.
- Use sublingual products only when seated.
- Patches should be applied to the chest, upper back, or upper arms. Apply to an area that has no cuts, is free of hair, and is not irritated. Try to avoid areas that will be subject to the movement of your arms.
- Sublingual spray or tablets may be used 5 or 10 minutes before an activity that might cause chest pain.
- If you take this medication daily, take a missed dose as soon as possible. However, if it is almost time for the next dose, skip the missed dose and return to your regular dosing schedule.

Precautions:
Do not use if:
- you are allergic to nitroglycerin or other medicine in the nitrate family, such as isosorbide mononitrate or isosorbide dinitrate.
- you are taking sildenafil (Viagra), tadalafil (Cialis), or vardenafil (Levitra).

Talk to your doctor if:
- you have glaucoma, severe anemia, or a head trauma.
- you are taking a calcium channel blocker, such as nifedipine, amlodipine, diltiazem, or verapamil.
- you have allergies to adhesives and the doctor has prescribed the topical patch.

Side Effects:
Contact your health-care provider immediately if you experience:
- severe dizziness or fainting.
- chest pain or pressure.
- severe headache.
- change in type or duration of chest pain.

Commonly reported side effects:
- headache
- dizziness, flushing, or weakness
- nausea, diarrhea, or stomach upset

Time Required for Drug to Take Effect:
Sublingual tablets and spray begin to work in 2 to 5 minutes. Sustained-release capsules begin to work in about 4 hours and continue to work for up to 8 hours.

Symptoms of Overdose:
- very low blood pressure (fainting)
- rapid heartbeat or very slow heartbeat
- throbbing headache
- shortness of breath

Special Notes:
- Talk to your doctor about when to call 911 for angina pain.

- Changing positions slowly when sitting and/or standing up may help decrease dizziness caused by this medication.
- If this medication makes you dizzy, avoid activities requiring mental alertness, such as driving a motor vehicle or operating potentially dangerous machinery.
- Do not drink alcohol while taking this drug.
- Do not change brands of this drug without consulting your pharmacist or physician.
- Use sublingual products for acute angina attacks.
- Do not use oral capsules or transdermal patches for acute angina attacks.
- There will still be some nitroglycerin left in the patch after you remove it. Discard it carefully, being mindful of the safety of children and pets.
- Do not inhale nitroglycerin spray.
- A sublingual tablet that does not burn or sting will still be effective.
- Sound-alike/look-alike warning: Nitro-Dur may be confused with Nicoderm, and Nitrostat may be confused with Nystatin.

nortriptyline

Brand Name: Pamelor

Generic Available: yes

Type of Drug: tricyclic antidepressant

Used for: Treatment of depression, chronic pain, and panic disorder.

How This Medication Works: Increases the action of the brain chemicals norepinephrine and serotonin.

Dosage Form and Strength:
- capsules (10 mg, 25 mg, 50 mg, 75 mg)
- liquid/solution (10 mg/5 mL)

Storage:
- room temperature
- protect from light and moisture—do not store in bathroom or kitchen

Administration:
- Usually taken once daily at bedtime; may also be prescribed to be taken 2 to 3 times daily.
- May be taken with food if stomach upset occurs.
- Use an accurate measuring device (available in pharmacies) to measure liquid medication.
- Take a missed dose as soon as possible. However, if it is almost time for the next dose, skip the missed dose and return to your regular dosing schedule.

Precautions:
Do not use if:
- you are allergic to nortriptyline or another tricyclic antidepressant, such as amitriptyline.
- you have taken a monoamine oxidase (MAO) inhibitor, such as phenelzine or isocarboxazid, in the past 14 days.

Talk to your doctor if:
- you have glaucoma (angle-closure type), heart disease, urinary or prostate problems, severe

constipation, breathing problems, seizures, diabetes, or a thyroid problem.
- you are taking cimetidine, clonidine, methyldopa, reserpine, guanethidine, or a sedative, muscle relaxant, antihistamine, decongestant (including cold medication), or stimulant.
- you drink alcohol.

Side Effects:

Contact your health-care provider immediately if you experience:
- **suicidal thoughts or a desire to harm yourself.**
- severe dizziness or fainting.
- rapid heartbeat.
- chest pain or pressure.
- confusion or hallucinations.
- severe constipation or inability to urinate.
- a rash.
- severe sedation.
- fever.
- restlessness or agitation.

Commonly reported side effects:
- drowsiness or dizziness
- dry mouth
- mild constipation
- weight gain
- unpleasant taste
- stomach upset

Time Required for Drug to Take Effect: May

take 4 to 8 weeks of treatment to reach maximum antidepressant effectiveness; improvement in certain symptoms may occur within 1 to 2 weeks of starting treatment.

Symptoms of Overdose:

- confusion or hallucinations
- seizures
- extreme sedation or agitation
- very slow or rapid heartbeat
- difficulty breathing
- inability to urinate
- severe constipation

Special Notes:

- The desire to harm yourself is a serious symptom of depression. If you are planning to harm yourself in any way, call 911 immediately.
- Know which "target symptoms" (restlessness, depressed mood, worry, fear, or changes in sleep or appetite) you are being treated for and be prepared to tell your doctor if your target symptoms are improving, worsening, or unchanged.
- Do not discontinue this medication or change your dose without consulting your doctor first.
- Check with your physician or pharmacist before using any over-the-counter medications while you are taking this drug.
- If you have diabetes, you may need to check your blood glucose more frequently.
- Use a sunblock with at least SPF 15 when outside because nortriptyline may increase your sensitivity to the sun.

olanzapine

Brand Name: Zyprexa

Generic Available: no

Type of Drug: antipsychotic

Used for: Treatment of schizophrenia, bipolar disorder, mania, and acute agitation. **Patients with dementia-related behavioral disorders who are treated with this class of drugs are at an increased risk of death compared to those taking a placebo (sugar pill).**

How This Medication Works: Blocks certain brain chemicals such as dopamine and serotonin, to clear thinking and improve social interactions, mood, and other symptoms of psychosis.

Dosage Form and Strength:
- tablets (2.5 mg, 5 mg, 7.5 mg, 10 mg, 15 mg, 20 mg)
- orally disintegrating tablets (5 mg, 10 mg, 15 mg, 20 mg)

Storage:
- room temperature
- protect from light and moisture—do not store in bathroom or kitchen

Administration:
- Usually taken once daily.
- May be taken without regard to meals, but take with food if stomach upset occurs.

- Place orally disintegrating tablet on tongue and let dissolve; no water is needed. Do not swallow whole, chew, break, or crush.
- Take a missed dose as soon as possible. However, if it is almost time for the next dose, skip the missed dose and return to your regular dosing schedule.

Precautions:

Do not use if:

- you are allergic to olanzapine.
- you have been prescribed the orally disintegrating tablet and have phenylketonuria.

Talk to your doctor if:

- you have or had a stroke, Parkinson's disease, seizures, brain damage, heart rhythm problems, bone marrow suppression, or breast cancer.
- you have dementia (this drug may increase your risk of stroke and death).
- you have diabetes or kidney, liver, heart, or lung disease.
- you have narrow-angle glaucoma.
- you have problems with urinary retention, BPH (enlarged prostate), GI motility, or GI blockage.

Side Effects:

Contact your health-care provider immediately if you experience:

- signs of a life-threatening reaction, which include wheezing; chest tightness; and itching or swelling of face, lips, tongue, or throat.
- severe dizziness or fainting.
- a significant change in balance.

- shakiness, stiffness, difficulty moving, or strange movements.
- nervousness or excitability.
- extreme weakness or tiredness.
- increased frequency of urination.
- constant hunger or thirst.
- significant weight gain.
- a rash.

Commonly reported side effects:
- drowsiness or light-headedness
- dizziness
- blurred vision
- constipation
- dry mouth
- headache
- change in mood
- weight gain
- insomnia

Time Required for Drug to Take Effect: May cause some sleepiness and calming with the first doses, but can take up to 6 weeks of treatment to reach maximum effectiveness.

Symptoms of Overdose:
- drowsiness
- strange or jerking movements
- low blood pressure, fast heartbeat
- slurred speech
- teeth grinding
- coma

Special Notes:

- Drink plenty of caffeine-free fluids, unless directed otherwise by your health-care provider.
- Avoid driving or other tasks that require alertness until you see how this medicine affects you.
- Avoid alcohol and other medicines or natural products that slow your actions and reactions.
- Use a sunblock with at least SPF 15 when outside, because this medication increases your sensitivity to the sun.
- To avoid dizziness, rise slowly over several minutes from a sitting or lying position.
- If you have diabetes, monitor glucose closely and notify your health-care provider of changes, because this medication may alter glucose levels.

omeprazole

Brand Names: Prilosec, Prilosec OTC

Generic Available: yes

Type of Drug: proton pump inhibitor

Used for: Treatment of heartburn, stomach ulcers, or ulcers of the esophagus (food tube).

How This Medication Works: Inhibits the mechanism that transports acid into the stomach, lowering the amount of acid.

Dosage Form and Strength:

- sustained-release capsules (20 mg)
- tablets (20 mg)

Storage:

- room temperature
- protect from moisture—do not store in bathroom or kitchen

Administration:

- Usually taken once daily.
- Take immediately before a meal, preferably in the morning.
- Swallow the capsule whole (do not crush, break, or chew), or open it and sprinkle the contents onto soft food or liquid (such as applesauce or apple juice).
- Swallow the tablet whole; do not break, crush, or chew.
- Take a missed dose as soon as possible. However, if it is almost time for the next dose, skip the missed dose and return to your regular dosing schedule.

Precautions:

Do not use if:

- you are allergic to omeprazole, esomeprazole, lansoprazole, pantoprazole, or rabeprazole.

Talk to your doctor if:

- you have liver disease.
- you are taking any other medication, especially diazepam, phenytoin, or a blood thinner, such as warfarin.

Side Effects:

Contact your health-care provider immediately if you experience:

- skin rash, hives, or itching.

- ulcers or sores in the mouth.
- difficult or frequent urination.
- fever or sore throat.
- unusual bleeding or bruising.

Commonly reported side effects:
- stomach discomfort
- constipation or diarrhea
- gas or heartburn
- headache
- muscle pain
- nausea and/or vomiting
- drowsiness or dizziness

Time Required for Drug to Take Effect:
Begins to work within several days after treatment is started.

Symptoms of Overdose:
- confusion, drowsiness
- seizures
- fast heartbeat or flushing

Special Notes:
- Consult your doctor or pharmacist before using other over-the-counter drugs with this medication.
- Do not self-treat with omeprazole for more than 14 days; if symptoms persist, see your doctor.
- Avoid medications that may make your ulcer worse, including nonsteroidal anti-inflammatory drugs (such as aspirin, ibuprofen, and naproxen).
- Avoid smoking or drinking alcohol, which can aggravate your condition.

oxybutynin

Brand Names:
Ditropan
Ditropan XL
Oxytrol

Generic Available:
- Ditropan: yes
- Oxytrol: no

Type of Drug: urinary antispasmodic

Used for: Treatment of overactive bladder and neurogenic bladder.

How This Medication Works: Decreases spasms in the bladder.

Dosage Form and Strength:
- tablets (5 mg)
- syrup (5 mg/5 mL)
- extended-release tablets (5 mg, 10 mg, 15 mg)
- transdermal patch (3.9 mg/day)

Storage:
- room temperature
- protect from light and moisture—do not store in bathroom or kitchen

Administration:
- Regular tablets and syrup usually taken 2 to 4 times daily; extended-release tablets usually taken once daily; and patch usually replaced twice weekly.

- Take tablets with food or milk to reduce stomach upset.
- Take a missed dose as soon as possible. However, if it is almost time for the next dose, skip the missed dose and return to your regular dosing schedule.

Precautions:
Do not use if:
- you have had an allergic reaction to oxybutynin.
- you have uncontrolled narrow-angle glaucoma, urinary retention, an enlarged colon, intestinal blockage, ulcerative colitis, or myasthenia gravis.

Talk to your doctor if:
- you have heart disease, kidney or liver disease, a gastrointestinal obstructive disorder, hiatal hernia or reflux disease, paralytic ileus, or prostate enlargement.
- you are taking any other medication, especially an anticholinergic agent, antidepressant, antipsychotic, antihistamine, antiparkinsonian, or antispasmodic.

Side Effects:
Contact your health-care provider immediately if you experience:
- an inability to urinate.
- agitation, nervousness, or restlessness.
- breathing difficulty.
- fever or flushing.
- severe dizziness or fainting.
- hallucinations or confusion.
- increased heart rate.

Commonly reported side effects:
- constipation
- drowsiness or dizziness
- dry mouth, nose, and throat
- weakness
- nausea and/or vomiting
- headache
- decreased sweating
- vision changes (blurred vision or light sensitivity)
- skin irritation (from the patch)

Time Required for Drug to Take Effect: Starts to work within 24 hours after taking the first dose (possibly longer for patch).

Symptoms of Overdose:
- agitation
- breathing difficulty
- confusion, disorientation, or hallucinations
- severe drowsiness or weakness
- fever or flushing
- irregular heartbeat (fast or slow)
- pupil enlargement
- seizures or tremors
- vomiting

Special Notes:
- If you wear dentures, they may not fit as well or may begin to irritate your gums due to the dry mouth often caused by oxybutynin.
- If you experience dry mouth, chew gum, suck on ice chips or hard candy, or try a saliva substitute.
- Do not drink alcohol while you are taking this medication.

- This medication may cause drowsiness. Use caution when driving a motor vehicle or operating potentially dangerous machinery.
- Oxybutynin decreases your body's ability to sweat. Be careful to avoid getting overheated by outdoor activities in the heat, saunas, or hot baths and showers.
- Talk to your doctor about re-evaluating your use of this medication on a regular basis.
- You may notice the shell of the extended-release tablet in your stool; this is normal and does not mean that the active ingredient in the tablet has not been absorbed.

oxycodone
oxycodone and aceta-
minophen combination

Brand Names:

Endocet	Percocet
OxyContin	Roxicet
Oxydose	Roxicodone
OxyFAST	Tylox
OxyIR	

Generic Available: yes

Type of Drug: narcotic analgesic

Used for: Relief of moderate to severe pain.

How This Medication Works: Oxycodone acts in the brain to decrease the recognition of pain impulses. Acetaminophen works in the nervous system and blocks pain signals.

Dosage Form and Strength:

Oxycodone:
- immediate-release tablets (5 mg, 15 mg, 30 mg)
- immediate-release capsules (5 mg)
- controlled-release tablets (10 mg, 20 mg, 40 mg, 80 mg, 160 mg)
- liquid (5 mg/5 mL, 20 mg/mL)

Oxycodone and acetaminophen combination:
- tablets (2.5 mg oxycodone/325 mg acetaminophen, 5 mg/325 mg, 7.5 mg/325 mg, 7.5 mg/500 mg, 10 mg/325 mg, 10 mg/650 mg)
- capsules/caplets (5 mg/500 mg)
- liquid (5 mg/325 mg per 5 mL)

Storage:
- room temperature
- protect from moisture—do not store in bathroom or kitchen

Administration:
- The regular, or immediate-release, tablets, capsules, and liquid are usually taken every 4 hours or as prescribed by a physician. The controlled-release tablets are usually taken every 12 hours.
- The amount of oxycodone per dose is individualized for each patient and depends on the pain being treated and previous exposure to oxycodone.
- Each agent can be harmful if used in excess. Never take a larger dose or more doses per day

than your doctor has prescribed. Never take more than 4,000 mg of acetaminophen per day.
- Take with milk or food if stomach upset occurs.
- Swallow the controlled-release tablets whole; do not break, crush, or chew.
- Do not abruptly stop taking this medication if you have been taking it on a regular basis; contact your doctor first.

Precautions:

Do not use if:
- you are allergic to oxycodone or any other narcotic, such as morphine, hydrocodone, hydromorphone, or codeine.
- you are allergic to acetaminophen.

Talk to your doctor if:
- you have alcoholism or other substance-abuse problem; brain disease or a head injury; colitis; seizures; emotional problems or mental illness; emphysema, asthma, or other lung disease; kidney, liver, or thyroid disease; prostate problems or problems with urination; or gallbladder disease or gallstones.
- you are taking naltrexone, zidovudine, or any other medication, especially any that can cause drowsiness, such as antihistamines, barbiturates (phenobarbital), benzodiazepines (such as diazepam, alprazolam, and lorazepam), muscle relaxants, or antidepressants.

Side Effects:

Contact your health-care provider immediately if you experience:
- poor pain control.

- a skin rash or hives.
- irregular breathing or difficulty breathing.
- fainting or extreme weakness.
- severe confusion or hallucinations.
- painful, difficult, or frequent urination.
- severe dizziness or drowsiness.
- severe nausea, vomiting, or constipation.
- trembling or uncontrolled muscle movements.
- yellowing of the eyes or skin.

Commonly reported side effects:
- constipation
- drowsiness or dizziness
- dry mouth
- nausea and/or vomiting
- loss of appetite
- nervousness, restlessness, or difficulty sleeping

Time Required for Drug to Take Effect: Starts
to work within 10 to 30 minutes after taking a dose. The sustained-release tablets begin to work within 1 hour after taking a dose.

Symptoms of Overdose:
- cold, clammy skin
- seizures
- severe dizziness, drowsiness, or confusion
- continued nausea, vomiting, or diarrhea
- severe nervousness or restlessness
- difficulty breathing
- slowed heartbeat

(Symptoms associated with acetaminophen overdose may not occur until 2 to 4 days after the overdose is taken, but treatment should begin as soon as possible to prevent liver damage or death.)

Special Notes:
- **This drug may be habit-forming.**
- When oxycodone is used for a long period, you may become tolerant and require larger doses.
- This medication may cause drowsiness. Do not drive a motor vehicle or operate dangerous machinery while you are taking this medication.
- Oxycodone and other narcotics cause constipation. This side effect may be diminished by drinking 6 to 8 full glasses of water each day. If using this medication for chronic pain, adding a stool softener–laxative combination may be necessary.
- Check with your physician or pharmacist before using any over-the-counter medications while on this drug.
- Nausea and vomiting may occur, especially after the first few doses. This effect may go away if you lie down for a while.
- To ease dry mouth symptoms, chew gum, suck on ice chips or hard candy, or try a saliva substitute.
- Do not drink alcohol while taking this medication.
- Sustained-release tablets should be used not for acute pain but for the treatment of chronic pain.
- If you think you or anyone else may have taken an overdose, get emergency help immediately.

pantoprazole

Brand Name: Protonix

Generic Available: no

Type of Drug: proton pump inhibitor

Used for: Prevention or treatment of heartburn, stomach ulcers, or ulcers of the esophagus (food tube).

How This Medication Works: Prevents symptoms of heartburn and damage to the gastrointestinal tract by reducing stomach acid.

Dosage Form and Strength: tablets (20 mg, 40 mg)

Storage:
- room temperature
- protect from moisture—do not store in bathroom or kitchen

Administration:
- Usually taken once daily.
- Take 30 minutes before a meal.
- Swallow tablets whole; do not chew, break, or crush.
- Take at the same time each day.
- Take a missed dose as soon as possible. However, if it is almost time for the next dose, skip the missed dose and return to your regular dosing schedule.

Precautions:
Do not use if:
- you have an allergy to pantoprazole or similar medicines such as omeprazole (Prilosec), esomeprazole (Nexium), lansoprazole (Prevacid), or rabeprazole (Aciphex).

Talk to your doctor if:
- you are also taking theophylline, sucralfate, iron (ferrous sulfate), warfarin, phenytoin, ketoconazole, atazanavir, indinavir, or any other medications.

Side Effects:

Contact your health-care provider immediately if you experience:
- signs of a life-threatening reaction, which include fever; wheezing; chest tightness; and itching or swelling of face, lips, tongue, or throat.
- unusual bruising or bleeding.
- severe dizziness or fainting.
- persistent diarrhea or constipation.
- a rash.

Commonly reported side effects:
- abdominal pain or nausea
- diarrhea or constipation, flatulence
- headache

Time Required for Drug to Take Effect: Starts
working within 1 to 2 hours after first dose is taken, but may take 1 to 4 weeks of therapy to reach maximum effectiveness.

Symptoms of Overdose: No information cur-
rently available; contact local poison control center.

Special Notes:
- Do not take sucralfate within 30 minutes of taking this medicine.
- Consult your health-care provider or pharmacist before starting any other medicine, including over-the-counter drugs, while on this medication.

- Do not smoke or consume alcohol, which can aggravate your condition.
- Consult your health-care provider or pharmacist before taking any drug that may make your condition worse, such as aspirin and other anti-inflammatories (for example, naproxen and ibuprofen).

paroxetine

Brand Names: Paxil, Paxil CR

Generic Available: yes

Type of Drug: antidepressant (selective serotonin reuptake inhibitor)

Used for: Treatment of depression, panic disorder, obsessive-compulsive disorder, social anxiety disorder, and post-traumatic stress disorder.

How This Medication Works: Prolongs the effects of the brain chemical serotonin.

Dosage Form and Strength:
- tablets (10 mg, 20 mg, 30 mg, 40 mg)
- controlled-release tablets (12.5 mg, 25 mg, 37.5 mg)
- suspension (10 mg/5 mL)

Storage:
- room temperature
- protect from moisture—do not store in bathroom or kitchen

Administration:

- Usually taken once daily in the morning, although you may be advised to take it in the evening instead if you experience drowsiness.
- Swallow the controlled-release tablets whole; do not break, crush, or chew.
- Do not abruptly stop taking this medication; contact your doctor first.
- Take a missed dose as soon as possible. However, if it is almost time for the next dose, skip the missed dose and return to your dosing schedule.

Precautions:

Do not use if:

- you are allergic to paroxetine or another selective serotonin reuptake inhibitor antidepressant, such as fluvoxamine, sertraline, or citalopram.
- you have taken a monoamine oxidase (MAO) inhibitor, such as phenelzine or tranylcypromine, within the past 14 days.
- you are taking mesoridazine or thioridazine.

Talk to your doctor if:

- you have ever had liver problems, kidney problems, or seizures or have bipolar disorder.
- you are taking phenobarbital, phenytoin, cimetidine, digoxin, procyclidine, a blood thinner (such as warfarin), or tryptophan.

Side Effects:

Contact your health-care provider immediately if you experience:

- **suicidal thougths or a desire to harm yourself.**

- seizures.
- muscle rigidity.
- unusual agitation or restlessness.
- dizziness, light-headedness, or fainting.
- severe nausea or vomiting.
- chest pain or palpitations.

Commonly reported side effects:
- dizziness or drowsiness
- vivid dreams or insomnia
- headache
- tremor
- nausea and vomiting
- change in appetite or weight
- constipation or diarrhea
- decreased sexual function and desire
- tingling in the hands and feet

Time Required for Drug to Take Effect: Some
symptoms may begin to improve within the first few
weeks of treatment, but it may take 4 to 8 weeks to
reach maximum effectiveness.

Symptoms of Overdose:
- seizures
- severe drowsiness
- dilated pupils
- very rapid heartbeat
- severe nausea or vomiting

Special Notes:
- The desire to harm yourself is a serious symptom
  of depression. If you are planning to harm
  yourself, call 911 immediately.

- Know which "target symptoms" (restlessness, depressed mood, worry, fear, or changes in sleep or appetite) you are being treated for and be prepared to tell your doctor if your target symptoms are improving, worsening, or unchanged.
- Paroxetine may interact with several other medicines commonly used by older adults. Show your doctor and pharmacist a complete list of all the medicines you take, including nonprescription drugs and supplements.
- Do not drink alcohol while you are taking this medication.
- Never change your dose or stop taking this medication without consulting your health-care provider first.

penicillin

Brand Names: Pen VK, Veetids

Generic Available: yes

Type of Drug: anti-infective/antibiotic

Used for: Treatment of various bacterial infections.

How This Medication Works: Damages cell walls of bacteria, killing them.

Dosage Form and Strength:
- tablets (250 mg, 500 mg)
- oral suspension (125 mg/5 mL, 250 mg/5 mL)

Storage:
- room temperature
- protect from moisture—do not store in bathroom or kitchen
- refrigerate liquid, and discard unused portion after 2 weeks

Administration:
- Can be dosed 2 to 4 times daily; follow your doctor's instructions.
- Take until gone, even if symptoms improve.
- Take this medicine on an empty stomach—1 hour before or 2 hours after a meal.
- Shake the oral liquid well just before each use.
- Take a missed dose as soon as possible. However, if it is almost time for the next dose, skip the missed dose and return to your regular dosing schedule.

Precautions:
Do not use if:
- you are allergic to penicillin.

Talk to your doctor if:
- you are allergic to cephalosporins (another type of antibiotic).
- you have severe kidney disease.
- you have a history of seizures.

Side Effects:
Contact your health-care provider immediately if you experience:
- signs of a life-threatening reaction, which include fever; wheezing; chest tightness; and itching or swelling of face, lips, tongue, or throat.

- severe nausea or vomiting.
- severe or persistent diarrhea.
- a rash.

Commonly reported side effects:
- nausea and/or vomiting
- diarrhea
- vaginal itching or discharge

Time Required for Drug to Take Effect:

Begins to kill bacteria within hours of the first dose, but you must take all the medication prescribed, even if your symptoms disappear and you start to feel better.

Symptoms of Overdose:

- agitation
- hallucinations
- confusion
- seizures

Special Notes:

- Eating yogurt with active cultures may help eliminate mild diarrhea, but contact your health-care provider if diarrhea becomes severe or continues.
- It is very important to complete the full course of medication prescribed, even if you start to feel better. If you stop taking the medicine, the bacterial infection may recur and be harder to treat.

phenazopyridine

Brand Names:

Azo-Gesic   Pyridium
Azo-Standard   Uristat
Prodium

Generic Available: yes

Type of Drug: urinary tract analgesic

Used for: Relief of urinary burning, itching, and urgency associated with a urinary tract infection or urinary medical procedure.

How This Medication Works: Unknown.

Dosage Form and Strength: tablets (95 mg, 97 mg, 100 mg, 200 mg)

Storage:
- room temperature
- protect from light and moisture—do not store in bathroom or kitchen

Administration:
- Usually taken 3 times daily for 2 days.
- Take after meals.
- Take a missed dose as soon as possible. However, if it is almost time for the next dose, skip the missed dose and return to your dosing schedule.

Precautions:
Do not use if:
- you are allergic to phenazopyridine.
- you have kidney or liver disease.

Talk to your doctor if:
- you are taking any other medication.

Side Effects:

Contact your health-care provider immediately if you experience:
- difficulty breathing.
- chest tightness.
- swelling of the face or throat.
- yellowing of the skin or eyes.
- a skin rash or itching.
- severe stomach upset, nausea, or vomiting.

Commonly reported side effects:
- dizziness or headache
- red or orange urine
- stomach upset

Time Required for Drug to Take Effect: Starts
to work within several hours of taking the first dose.

Symptoms of Overdose:
- anemia
- deeply stained urine or vomit
- liver or kidney failure
- yellowing of the skin or eyes

Special Notes:
- Phenazopyridine is not an antibiotic and will not cure a urinary tract infection.
- Phenazopyridine should not be used for more than 2 days.
- Drink 6 to 8 glasses of water daily while taking this medication, unless directed otherwise by your health-care provider.

- This medication may turn your urine orange or red. Wearing a panty liner may help protect clothing. If clothing or bedding does become stained, try soaking them in a 0.25% solution of sodium dithionite or sodium hydrosulfite.

phenytoin

Brand Names: Dilantin, Phenytek

Generic Available: yes

Type of Drug: anticonvulsant

Used for: Prevention of seizures.

How This Medication Works: Alters the movement of the electrolyte sodium so that it interferes with abnormal electrical activity in the brain, thus calming the brain.

Dosage Form and Strength:
- tablets (50 mg)
- capsules (30 mg, 100 mg, 200 mg, 300 mg)
- oral suspension (125 mg/5 mL)

Storage:
- room temperature
- tightly closed
- protect from moisture—do not store in bathroom or kitchen

Administration:
- Usually taken 1 to 3 times daily, depending on the form of the drug prescribed.

- Shake suspension well before measuring dose.
- Swallow capsules whole; do not break, crush, or chew.
- Tablets may be crushed or chewed.
- May be taken with or without food, but always be consistent—either always take your dose with food or always take it without food.
- If you are also using an antacid, separate doses of phenytoin and the antacid by 2 hours.
- Take a missed dose as soon as possible. However, if it is almost time for the next dose, skip the missed dose and return to your dosing schedule.

Precautions:
Do not use if:
- you are allergic to phenytoin or fosphenytoin.

Talk to your doctor if:
- you are taking any drug, especially allopurinol, cimetidine, isoniazid, omeprazole, trimethoprim, valproic acid, phenobarbital, carbamazepine, rifampin, theophylline, sucralfate, haloperidol, quinidine, digoxin, amiodarone, doxycycline, or lithium or a benzodiazepine (such as diazepam or clonazepam), salicylate (such as aspirin), tricyclic antidepressant (such as amitriptyline, imipramine, or desipramine), or antacid.
- you have kidney disease, liver disease, or a fever, or you are malnourished.

Side Effects:
Contact your health-care provider immediately if you experience:
- shortness of breath, chest tightness, itching, or swelling of the face or throat.

- confusion, dizziness, or slurred speech.
- a rash.
- severe nausea or vomiting.
- a change in balance or a loss of balance leading to falls.

Commonly reported side effects:
- nausea and/or vomiting
- constipation
- drowsiness or dizziness
- increased hair growth on the face and body
- bleeding gums or a change in the gums

Time Required for Drug to Take Effect:

Begins to work within hours of taking a dose and decreases the number and/or frequency of seizures as long as treatment is continued.

Symptoms of Overdose:

- blurred or double vision
- severe dizziness, drowsiness, or confusion
- slurred speech
- difficulty breathing
- coma

Special Notes:

- Regular dental visits and good oral hygiene may help prevent or delay bleeding or tender gums caused by this drug.
- Do not discontinue this medication without first consulting with your doctor or pharmacist.
- Check with your physician or pharmacist before using any over-the-counter medication while you are taking this drug.

- You will occasionally have blood drawn to monitor the amount of phenytoin in your blood.
- Talk to your health-care provider about the need for calcium and vitamin D supplementation while you are taking this medication.

pioglitazone

Brand Name: Actos

Generic Available: no

Type of Drug: antidiabetic (thiazolidinedione)

Used for: Lowering of blood glucose levels in type 2 (non–insulin-dependent) diabetes.

How This Medication Works: Increases insulin's activity in the body.

Dosage Form and Strength: tablets (15 mg, 30 mg, 45 mg)

Storage:
- room temperature
- protect from moisture and heat—do not store in bathroom or kitchen

Administration:
- Usually taken once daily.
- May be used alone or in combination with other diabetes medicines.
- Take at a similar time each day.

- May be taken without regard to meals, but take with food if stomach upset occurs.
- Take a missed dose as soon as possible. However, if it is almost time for the next dose, skip the missed dose and return to your regular dosing schedule.

Precautions:

Do not use if:

- you are allergic to pioglitazone, rosiglitazone, or troglitazone.
- you have active liver disease.
- you have type 1 diabetes or ketoacidosis.

Talk to your doctor if:

- you have heart failure or swelling of the arms or legs (edema).
- you have anemia or a history of liver problems.
- you have macular edema or diabetic retinopathy.
- you are premenopausal or have not been ovulating.
- you have a history of osteoporosis or falls or you have an increased risk for fractures.

Side Effects:

Contact your health-care provider immediately if you experience:

- signs of a life-threatening reaction, which include fever; wheezing; chest tightness; and itching or swelling of face, lips, tongue, or throat.
- significant weight gain.
- significant swelling of the arms or legs.
- difficulty breathing.
- very low or very high blood glucose.
- severe stomach pain, nausea, or vomiting.

- yellowing of the skin or eyes.
- extreme fatigue or weakness.
- a rash.

Commonly reported side effects:
- headache
- swelling
- fatigue
- weight gain

Time Required for Drug to Take Effect: Takes
at least 4 weeks of treatment to begin lowering blood glucose levels.

Symptoms of Overdose:
- low blood glucose (signs include shaking, anger, fast heartbeat, confusion, dizziness, and sweating)

Special Notes:
- Using this medication may increase your risk for bone fractures.
- This drug may restart ovulation in perimenopausal and menopausal women, increasing the risk of pregnancy.
- Follow a diet plan and exercise program recommended by your health-care provider.
- Always keep a fast-acting sugar source (such as hard candy, glucose tablets or gel, fruit juice, or nondiet soda) handy.
- Teach your family, friends, and coworkers how to help you if you have low blood glucose.
- Do not drive if you recently had low blood glucose—your risk of an accident is higher.
- Do not consume alcohol while taking this drug.

- Check your blood glucose as directed by your health-care provider.
- Have yearly eye and foot examinations performed by health-care professionals.

polyethylene glycol (PEG 3350) PEG 3350 and electrolyte solution (PEG-ES)

Brand Names:

Without electrolytes:
Miralax

With electrolytes:
Colyte
GoLYTELY
NuLYTELY

Generic Available: yes

Type of Drug: laxative

Used for: Polyethylene glycol (PEG 3350) without added electrolytes is used for the treatment of constipation. PEG 3350 with added electrolytes is used to clean out the gastrointestinal (GI) tract prior to certain medical procedures.

How This Medication Works: Polyethylene glycol pulls water into the colon (also referred to as the large bowel or lower intestine), which in turn softens stools and increases the number of bowel movements. When it is combined with electrolytes, polyethylene glycol causes liquid stools or mild diarrhea, which serves to clean out the colon and allow clearer views of the colon during medical procedures.

Dosage Form and Strength: Powder for reconstitution, which is available in one-time use and multiple-use packaging.

Storage:
- room temperature
- refrigerate reconstituted liquid; discard unused portion after 2 days

Administration:
For constipation:
- Usually taken once daily, but take only as directed by your health-care provider.
- The powder may be mixed in water, juice, soda, coffee, or tea.
- Do not take more medicine or take it more often than your doctor tells you to.
- This medicine is not usually prescribed for long-term use.
- Do not take any other oral medication (medication by mouth) within the hour preceding your use of this medication.

For bowel preparation prior to procedures:
- Follow the directions for use given to you by your health-care provider.
- Ask your health-care provider to specify which liquids you are allowed to use to reconstitute (dissolve) the powder.
- Do not add flavorings unless they are provided with the medication.

- After mixing the liquid with the powder, shake the container well to be sure that all of the powder has been dissolved.
- Drink the liquid quickly if possible.
- Do not eat within the 2 to 4 hours just prior to taking this medication.
- Do not take any other oral medication (medication by mouth) within the hour preceding your use of this medication.
- You may chill the solution to improve its taste, but keep in mind that the solution is only good for 48 hours once it has been mixed.

Precautions:
Do not use if:
- you are allergic to polyethylene glycol.
- you have a blockage in your gastrointestinal (GI) tract.

Talk to your doctor if:
- you have ulcerative colitis or persistent nausea, vomiting, or bloating.

Side Effects:
Contact your health-care provider immediately if you experience:
- signs of a life-threatening reaction, which include fever; wheezing; chest tightness; and itching or swelling of face, lips, tongue, or throat.
- severe dizziness or fainting.
- severe stomach pain.
- black or bloody stools.
- a rash.

Commonly reported side effects:
- nausea and/or vomiting
- stomach pain, cramping, or feeling of fullness
- flatulence

Time Required for Drug to Take Effect: May take from 1 to 10 hours for the colon to be cleaned out when the medication is being used to prepare the colon for a medical procedure. It can take several days of treatment for the medication to relieve constipation.

Symptoms of Overdose:
- diarrhea (when used to treat constipation)
- dehydration

Special Notes:
- Follow the instructions supplied with the drug or by your health-care provider exactly; directions will differ according to the specific brand and the purpose for which this medication is taken.
- When using this drug to prepare your colon for a medical procedure, continue drinking liquid until watery stools are clear.

potassium chloride

Brand Names:

K+8	K-Lor	Klotrix
K+10	Klor-Con	K-Tab
Kay Ciel	Klor-Con 8	Micro-K
K+Care	Klor-Con 10	Micro-K 10
K-Dur 10	Klor-Con/25	
K-Dur 20	Klor-Con M	

Generic Available: yes

Type of Drug: electrolyte supplement (potassium supplement)

Used for: Replacement of potassium in the body.

How This Medication Works: Potassium is an important electrolyte found throughout the body; keeping a specific level of potassium in the body is necessary for brain and body function.

Dosage Form and Strength:
- extended-release tablets (8 mEq, 10 mEq, 20 mEq)
- extended-release capsules (8 mEq, 10 mEq)
- oral solution (20 mEq/15 mL, 40 mEq/15 mL)
- powder for oral solution (20 mEq/packet)

Storage:
- room temperature
- protect from moisture and heat—do not store in bathroom or kitchen

Administration:
- Your doctor will determine your dose based on your body's needs.
- Take this medicine with food.
- Drink plenty of caffeine-free liquids unless directed otherwise by your health-care provider.
- Swallow extended-release tablets or capsules whole—do not chew, break, or crush.
- Mix the liquid or powder for oral solution with at least ½ cup of water.
- Take a missed dose as soon as possible. However, if it is almost time for the next dose, skip the

missed dose and return to your regular dosing schedule.

Precautions:

Do not use if:

- you are allergic to potassium chloride.
- you have Addison's disease.
- you already have high potassium levels.

Talk to your doctor if:

- you have severe kidney disease.
- you have an intestinal blockage or a slow-moving gastrointestinal tract.
- you are taking an angiotensin-converting enzyme (ACE) inhibitor, such as lisinopril, enalapril, or ramipril, or angiotensin receptor blocker (ARB), such as losartan, irbesartan, or candesartan.
- you take digoxin.
- you are taking a potassium-sparing diuretic, such as spironolactone or triamterene, or another potassium supplement.
- you become dehydrated.

Side Effects:

Contact your health-care provider immediately if you experience:

- signs of a life-threatening reaction, which include fever; wheezing; chest tightness; and itching or swelling of face, lips, tongue, or throat.
- fast heartbeat.
- severe dizziness or fainting.
- weakness, numbness, or tingling.
- severe nausea, vomiting, or diarrhea.

- severe stomach or throat pain.
- a rash.

Commonly reported side effects:
- stomach discomfort
- nausea and/or vomiting
- diarrhea or flatulence

Time Required for Drug to Take Effect: Starts
to increase potassium level within hours of first dose.

Symptoms of Overdose:
- muscle weakness
- paralysis
- palpitations
- heart arrhythmia

Special Notes:
- If you are taking a water pill (diuretic) and it is stopped, you may not need this drug; consult your health-care provider.
- Do not use potassium-containing salt substitutes or other potassium supplements while taking this medication.
- The outer shell of the extended-release products may show up in the stool; this is normal. The active ingredients have already been absorbed by the body.

pravastatin

Brand Name: Pravachol

Generic Available: yes

Type of Drug: antihyperlipidemic agent (HMG-CoA reductase inhibitor)

Used for: Treatment of high blood cholesterol levels and prevention of heart attack and stroke.

How This Medication Works: Reduces LDL (bad) cholesterol and triglyceride production in the body.

Dosage Form and Strength: tablets (10 mg, 20 mg, 40 mg, 80 mg)

Storage:
- room temperature
- protect from light and moisture—do not store in bathroom or kitchen

Administration:
- Usually taken once daily.
- Take at a similar time each day.
- May be taken without regard to meals, but take with food if stomach upset occurs.
- Take a missed dose as soon as possible. However, if it is almost time for the next dose, skip the missed dose and return to your dosing schedule.
- Take this medicine even if you feel well. Most people with this condition do not feel sick.

Precautions:
Do not use if:
- you are allergic to pravastatin or any other part of this medicine.
- you have severe liver disease.
- you are or may be pregnant.

Talk to your doctor if:
- you have active liver disease or increased liver enzymes.
- you take any other cholesterol medication, niacin, cyclosporine, erythromycin, amiodarone, or an oral antifungal.

Side Effects:

Contact your health-care provider immediately if you experience:
- signs of a life-threatening reaction, which include fever; wheezing; chest tightness; and itching or swelling of face, lips, tongue, or throat.
- severe muscle pain or weakness.
- yellowing of the skin or eyes.
- flulike symptoms.
- unusual bruising or bleeding.
- a rash.

Commonly reported side effects:
- headache
- mild aches and pains
- nausea and/or vomiting
- constipation or diarrhea

Time Required for Drug to Take Effect: Starts
lowering cholesterol within 72 hours of first dose, but may take 2 to 4 weeks of treatment to reach maximum effectiveness.

Symptoms of Overdose: No specific symptoms.

Special Notes:
- Follow a diet plan and exercise program recommended by your health-care provider.

- Do not take colestipol or cholestyramine within 4 hours of taking this medicine.
- Limit alcohol intake while on this medication.
- Use a sunblock with at least SPF 15 when outside, because this drug may increase your sensitivity to the sun.
- You will need periodic blood work to check liver function and cholesterol levels while you are taking this drug.

prednisone

Brand Names:
Deltasone
Meticorten
Sterapred

Generic Available: yes

Type of Drug: corticosteroid

Used for: Treatment of rheumatoid arthritis, lung diseases, lupus, ulcerative colitis, eye disorders, skin problems, poison ivy, some cancers, and other conditions in which inflammation is present.

How This Medication Works: Prednisone is a cortisonelike substance naturally produced in the body. For most conditions, its mechanism of action is unknown, but often the benefits are a result of decreased inflammation.

Dosage Form and Strength:
- tablets (1 mg, 2.5 mg, 5 mg, 10 mg, 20 mg, 25 mg, 50 mg)
- solution (1 mg/mL, 5 mg/mL)
- syrup (5 mg/5 mL)

Storage:
- room temperature
- protect from light and moisture—do not store in bathroom or kitchen

Administration:
- If you are taking prednisone once daily, take it in the morning.
- Take with food or milk to avoid stomach upset.
- If you are taking the medication more than once daily and you miss a dose, take the dose as soon as you remember it; if you do not remember until it is time for the next dose, double the dose and return to your regular schedule.
- If you are taking this drug once daily and you miss a dose, take the dose as soon as you remember, unless it is the next day; if it is the next day when you remember the missed dose, do not double the dose; take your regular dose and return to your regular dosing schedule.
- If you are taking the medication every other day and you miss a dose, take the dose as soon as you remember it that day; if it is the day after the dose was to be taken, take the dose and start over on the every-other-day schedule, skipping the next day and taking a dose the following day.
- If you miss more than one dose, call your doctor.

- If you have been taking prednisone for more than 5 days, do not abruptly stop taking it; consult your health-care provider first.
- If you take the solution, it must be measured with a dropper or special medication-measuring spoon or cup; a kitchen spoon is not accurate enough.

Precautions:

Do not use if:

- you have had a serious allergic reaction to prednisone, dexamethasone, prednisolone, beta-methasone, cortisone, dexamethasone, hydro-cortisone, triamcinolone, or any other steroid.

Talk to your doctor if:

- you have bone disease, diabetes, emotional problems, glaucoma, a fungal infection, heart disease, high blood pressure (hypertension), high cholesterol, kidney disease, liver disease, myasthenia gravis, stomach problems (ulcers or gastritis), thyroid disease, tuberculosis, or ulcerative colitis.

- you are taking any medication, especially aspirin or a nonsteroidal anti-inflammatory drug (such as ibuprofen or indomethacin), an anticoagulant (such as warfarin), cholestyramine, colestipol, or a diabetes medication, diuretic, seizure medication, or tuberculosis medication.

- you have chicken pox or another infection.

Side Effects:

Contact your health-care provider immediately if you experience:

- confusion or agitation.
- unusual or frequent bleeding or bruising.

- bloody or black, tarry stools.
- blurred vision, eye pain, or headaches.
- fever, sore throat, chills, or other signs of infection.
- slow wound healing.
- mood changes.
- muscle weakness or wasting.
- rapid weight gain (3 to 5 pounds in a week).
- seizures.
- shortness of breath.
- stomach enlargement or pain.
- increased thirst or increased urination.

Commonly reported side effects:
- nervousness and insomnia
- dizziness
- increased appetite or change in body fat
- indigestion, nausea, or vomiting
- increased sweating
- acne or reddening of the skin on the face
- restlessness and sleep disorders
- unusual hair growth

Time Required for Drug to Take Effect: Varies depending on the condition being treated.

Symptoms of Overdose:
- agitation
- mania or psychotic behavior

Special Notes:
- Talk to your health-care provider about the need for calcium and vitamin D supplementation while you are taking this drug.

- You may need dosage adjustments during stressful times. Tell your doctor if you experience a serious infection or injury or if you need surgery.
- If you must take prednisone for a long period of time, be sure to have routine eye examinations; long-term use of prednisone may cause glaucoma and cataracts.
- Taking prednisone for long periods may increase blood sugar levels and may even cause diabetes.
- While you are taking prednisone, you should not receive live vaccinations or immunizations.

prochlorperazine

Brand Names: Compazine, Compro

Generic Available: yes

Type of Drug: antiemetic

Used for: Prevention or relief of severe nausea and vomiting. Sometimes used to treat anxiety or psychosis.

How This Medication Works: Blocks the effects of the brain chemical dopamine, which is responsible for stimulating the vomiting center in the brain.

Dosage Form and Strength:
- tablets (5 mg, 10 mg)
- sustained-release capsules (10 mg, 15 mg)
- syrup (5 mg/5 mL)
- suppositories (2.5 mg, 5 mg, 25 mg)

Storage:
- room temperature
- protect from moisture—do not store in bathroom or kitchen

Administration:
- Tablets usually taken 2 to 4 times daily.
- Capsules usually taken once or twice daily.
- Syrup usually taken 2 to 4 times daily.
- Suppositories usually inserted once or twice daily.
- This medication may be prescribed on an "as-needed" basis.
- Swallow the sustained-release capsules whole; do not open, break, crush, or chew.
- To insert the suppository, you can moisten the tip with water; do not use anything else, because it may reduce the effectiveness of the medicine.

Precautions:
Do not use if:
- you have ever had an allergic reaction to prochlorperazine.

Talk to your doctor if:
- you are taking medicine for Parkinson's disease, seizures, depression, sleep problems, or anxiety.
- you have heart disease, liver disease, glaucoma (angle-closure type), or bone marrow disease.
- you have prostate problems, urinary problems, or decreased gastrointestinal (GI) motility.

Side Effects:
Contact your health-care provider immediately if you experience:
- seizures.

- stiff, rigid muscles or shakiness.
- fever.
- difficulty breathing.
- sweating.
- loss of bladder control or inability to urinate.
- severe constipation.
- eye pain or change in vision.
- significant change in balance or loss of balance leading to falls.
- severe agitation or restlessness.
- a severe rash.

Commonly reported side effects:
- dizziness or drowsiness
- light-headedness
- change in sexual ability or desire
- dry mouth
- mild constipation

Time Required for Drug to Take Effect: Relief of symptoms can occur within 30 to 90 minutes after taking a dose but may take longer.

Symptoms of Overdose:
- severe drowsiness or fainting
- severe agitation or restlessness
- strange movements

Special Notes:
- If vomiting is severe and not relieved by this medicine, you may become dehydrated, which is a serious problem; call your doctor for advice.
- If you use the syrup form of this medicine, take care to avoid contact with skin since it may cause

irritation. If you get the medicine on your skin, rinse the area well with water.

- Use a sunblock with at least SPF 15 when outside because prochlorperazine may increase your sensitivity to the sun.
- Do not drink alcohol while taking this medication.
- Sound-alike/look-alike warning: Prochlorperazine may be confused with chlorpromazine.

promethazine and codeine combination

Brand Names: Phenergan with Codeine, Pherazine with Codeine

Generic Available: yes

Type of Drug: antihistamine and cough suppressant

Used for: Relief of symptoms of the common cold or allergies with runny nose and cough.

How This Medication Works: Promethazine prevents the effects of histamine—a substance produced in the body that causes sneezing, itching, and runny nose. Codeine inhibits the cough center in the brain while decreasing the ability of the body to cough.

Dosage Form and Strength: liquid (6.25 mg promethazine/10 mg codeine per 5 mL)

Storage:
- room temperature

- protect from moisture—do not store in bathroom or kitchen

Administration:
- Take each dose with plenty of water.
- May be taken with or without food.

Precautions:
Do not use if:
- you are allergic to promethazine or a similar medication, such as diphenhydramine, chlorpheniramine, or pheniramine.
- you are allergic to codeine or another narcotic, such as morphine or hydrocodone.

Talk to your doctor if:
- you have emphysema, chronic bronchitis, asthma, or other breathing problems; seizures; gallbladder disease or gallstones; or glaucoma.
- you have Parkinson's disease, bone marrow disease, prostate problems, urinary retention, or brain damage.
- you have kidney, liver, or thyroid disease.
- you are taking any other medication.

Side Effects:
Contact your health-care provider immediately if you experience:
- a skin rash, hives, itching, or difficulty breathing.
- cold, clammy skin or flushing of the face.
- confusion or hallucinations.
- difficult or painful urination.
- severe drowsiness or dizziness.
- severe nervousness.

- pinpoint pupils in the eyes.
- irregular heartbeat.
- seizures.

Commonly reported side effects:
- constipation
- decreased sweating
- slight dizziness or light-headedness
- dryness of the mouth, nose, or throat
- nausea and/or vomiting
- nightmares
- thickening of mucus

Time Required for Drug to Take Effect: Starts to work within 20 minutes of taking a dose.

Symptoms of Overdose:
- difficulty breathing
- severe drowsiness, dizziness, or tiredness
- excitability or irritability
- dilated pupils

Special Notes:
- Consult your doctor or pharmacist before using any over-the-counter drugs with this drug.
- Do not drink alcohol or take medications that cause drowsiness or mental slowing while you are taking this drug.
- Avoid activities requiring mental alertness, such as driving a motor vehicle or operating dangerous machinery, while taking this drug.
- If you experience dry mouth, chew gum, suck on ice chips or hard candy, or try a saliva substitute.

- Tell the doctor or dentist you are taking this drug before having surgery or emergency treatment.
- Sound-alike/look-alike warning: Phenergan may be confused with Phenaphen or Phrenilin.

propoxyphene napsylate and acetaminophen combination

Brand Names:

Darvocet-N 50

Darvocet-N 100

Pronap-100

Propacet 100

Generic Available: yes

Type of Drug: narcotic analgesic

Used for: Relief of pain.

How This Medication Works: Propoxyphene acts in the brain to decrease the recognition of pain impulses. Acetaminophen works in the nervous system and blocks pain signals.

Dosage Form and Strength: tablets (50 mg propoxyphene napsylate/325 mg acetaminophen, 100 mg/500 mg, 100 mg/650 mg)

Storage:

- room temperature
- protect from moisture—do not store in bathroom or kitchen

Administration:

- Take with milk or food if the medication causes stomach upset.
- Take this medication as prescribed and do not exceed the maximum number of doses per day. Each drug in this combination can be harmful if used in excess. Never take more tablets per dose than your doctor has prescribed.
- This medication may be prescribed on an "as-needed" basis.
- Do not take more than six 100 mg/650 mg-strength tablets daily.

Precautions:

Do not use if:

- you are allergic to propoxyphene or related narcotics.
- you are allergic to acetaminophen.

Talk to your doctor if:

- you have alcoholism or other substance-abuse problems; brain disease or a head injury; colitis; seizures; emotional problems or mental illness; or emphysema, asthma, or other lung disease.
- you have kidney, liver, or thyroid disease; prostate problems or problems with urination; or gallbladder disease or gallstones.
- you are taking naltrexone, zidovudine, or any other medication, especially any that can cause drowsiness, such as an antihistamine, phenobarbital, a benzodiazepine (such as diazepam or lorazepam), a muscle relaxant, an antidepressant, warfarin, or carbamazepine.

- you are taking other medications for pain, including acetaminophen.

Side Effects:

Contact your health-care provider immediately if you experience:

- severe depression or suicidal thoughts.
- a skin rash or hives.
- irregular breathing or difficulty breathing.
- fast, slow, or pounding heartbeat.
- painful or difficult urination.
- poor pain control.
- severe confusion or hallucinations.
- depression.
- severe nausea or vomiting.
- unusual bruising or bleeding.
- trembling or uncontrolled muscle movements.
- yellowing of the eyes or skin.

Commonly reported side effects:

- constipation
- drowsiness
- dry mouth
- loss of appetite, nausea, or vomiting
- nervousness or restlessness
- difficulty sleeping

Time Required for Drug to Take Effect: Starts
to work within 10 to 30 minutes of taking a dose and reaches maximum effectiveness about 2 hours after dosing.

Symptoms of Overdose:

- cold, clammy skin
- seizures

- severe dizziness, drowsiness, or confusion
- continued nausea, vomiting, or diarrhea
- severe nervousness or restlessness
- difficulty breathing
- slowed heartbeat

(Symptoms associated with acetaminophen overdose may not occur until 2 to 4 days after the overdose is taken, but it is important to begin treatment as soon as possible after the overdose to prevent liver damage or death.)

Special Notes:

- This medication may cause drowsiness. Do not drive a motor vehicle or operate dangerous machinery while you are taking this medication.
- Propoxyphene causes constipation. This side effect may be diminished by drinking 6 to 8 full glasses of water each day. If you are using this medication for chronic pain, you may also need to take a stool softener–laxative combination.
- Monitor yourself closely for sedation or confusion, and contact your health-care provider if you don't "feel like yourself."
- Check with your physician or pharmacist before using any over-the-counter medication while you are taking this drug.
- When propoxyphene is used over a long period of time, your body may become tolerant and require larger doses.
- Consult your doctor before stopping this drug.
- Do not take more than 4,000 mg of acetaminophen daily on an ongoing basis.
- Do not drink alcohol while taking this medication.

- Nausea and vomiting may occur, especially after the first few doses. They may go away if you lie down for a while.
- If you think you or anyone else may have taken an overdose, get emergency help immediately.

pseudoephedrine and guaifenesin combination

Brand Names:

Congestac Caplets
Deconsal II
Entex PSE
Guaifenex PSE
Guaituss

Maxifed
Mucinex-D
Pseudovent
Respaire

Generic Available: yes

Type of Drug: decongestant and expectorant

Used for: Relief of stuffy nose, congestion, and cough associated with the common cold.

How This Medication Works: Pseudoephedrine causes the blood vessels to become smaller, which can relieve a stuffy nose or congestion. Guaifenesin loosens mucus, or phlegm, in the lungs.

Dosage Form and Strength:

- tablets (60 mg pseudoephedrine/400 mg guaifenesin, 120 mg/400 mg)
- extended-release tablets (60 mg/600 mg, 60 mg/1,000 mg, 120 mg/500 mg, 120 mg/600 mg)

- extended-release capsules (30 mg/200 mg, 60 mg/200 mg, 60 mg/300 mg, 120 mg/250 mg, 120 mg/500 mg)
- liquid (30 mg/100 mg per 5 mL, 30 mg/200 mg per 5 mL)

Storage:

- room temperature
- protect from moisture—do not store in bathroom or kitchen

Administration:

- Drink a glass of water with each dose of this medication.
- Swallow extended-release capsules and tablets whole; do not crush or chew.
- Take a missed dose as soon as possible. However, if it is almost time for the next dose, skip the missed dose and return to your regular dosing schedule.

Precautions:

Do not use if:

- you have an allergy to pseudoephedrine or guaifenesin or other similar medication, such as phenylpropanolamine, phenylephrine, or epinephrine.
- you have taken a monoamine oxidase (MAO) inhibitor (such as isocarboxazid or phenelzine) in the past 14 days.

Talk to your doctor if:

- you have heart disease, high blood pressure (hypertension), diabetes, glaucoma, kidney disease, liver disease, or thyroid disease.

- you are taking any other medication, especially medication for heart disease, high blood pressure, glaucoma, diabetes, thyroid disease, or weight loss.

Side Effects:

Contact your health-care provider immediately if you experience:

- a skin rash, hives, or itching.
- confusion, hallucinations, or excessive anxiety.
- a cough that continues for more than 1 week.
- seizures.
- chest pain or pressure or irregular heartbeat.
- headache.
- severe nausea or vomiting.
- problems with urination.
- difficulty breathing.

Commonly reported side effects:

- dizziness, light-headedness, or drowsiness
- nightmares or trouble sleeping
- nervousness

Time Required for Drug to Take Effect: Starts to work within 15 to 30 minutes after taking a dose.

Symptoms of Overdose:

- nausea and vomiting
- seizures or hallucinations
- irregular heartbeat
- nervousness or irritability

Special Notes:

- Check with your physician or pharmacist before using any over-the-counter medication while taking this drug.

- Phenylephrine has replaced pseudoephedrine in many over-the-counter products.
- Do not take diet aids or medications for weight loss while you are using this medication.
- Drink plenty of water to help loosen mucus in your lungs.
- If your cough has not improved within 7 days or if you have a high fever, skin rash, headache, or sore throat with a cough, contact your doctor.
- Tell your doctor or dentist that you are taking this medication before having any surgery or emergency treatment.

quetiapine

Brand Name: Seroquel

Generic Available: no

Type of Drug: antipsychotic

Used for: Treatment of schizophrenia, bipolar disorder, and mania. **Patients with dementia-related behavioral disorders who are treated with this class of drugs are at an increased risk of death compared to those taking a placebo (sugar pill).**

How This Medication Works: Blocks certain brain chemicals such as dopamine and serotonin to clear thinking and improve social interactions, mood, and other symptoms of psychosis.

Dosage Form and Strength: tablets (25 mg, 50 mg, 100 mg, 200 mg, 300 mg, 400 mg)

Storage:
- room temperature
- protect from light and moisture—do not store in bathroom or kitchen

Administration:
- Usually taken twice daily.
- May be taken without regard to meals, but take with food if stomach upset occurs.
- Drink plenty of caffeine-free liquids unless directed otherwise by your health-care provider.
- Take a missed dose as soon as possible. However, if it is almost time for the next dose, skip the missed dose and return to your regular dosing schedule.

Precautions:
Do not use if:
- you have an allergy to quetiapine.
- you have bone marrow disease, severe liver disease, or a low blood cell count.

Talk to your doctor if:
- you have dementia. This drug may increase risk of death in elderly patients with dementia.
- you have or have had a stroke, Parkinson's disease, seizures, brain damage, heart rhythm problems, or breast cancer.
- you have diabetes or kidney, liver, heart, or lung disease.
- you have narrow-angle glaucoma.
- you have urinary retention, BPH (enlarged prostate), problems with gastrointestinal motility, or gastrointestinal blockage.

- you are taking cimetidine, an oral antifungal (such as fluconazole, itraconazole, or ketoconazole), erythromycin, or valproic acid.

Side Effects:

Contact your health-care provider immediately if you experience:

- signs of a life-threatening reaction, which include fever; wheezing; chest tightness; and itching or swelling of face, lips, tongue, or throat.
- a rash.
- severe dizziness or fainting.
- a significant change in balance.
- shakiness, stiffness, difficulty moving, or strange movements.
- nervousness or excitability.
- extreme fatigue or weakness.
- increased frequency of urination.
- constant hunger or thirst.
- significant weight gain.

Commonly reported side effects:

- drowsiness or light-headedness
- dizziness
- blurred vision
- constipation
- dry mouth
- headache
- change in mood
- difficulty sleeping
- weight gain

Time Required for Drug to Take Effect: May
cause some sedation and calming with the first doses,

but can take up to 6 weeks of treatment to reach maximum effectiveness.

Symptoms of Overdose:

- drowsiness
- strange or jerking movements
- low blood pressure
- fast heartbeat
- slurred speech
- teeth grinding
- coma

Special Notes:

- Drink plenty of caffeine-free liquids while taking this medication, unless directed otherwise by your health-care provider.
- Avoid driving a motor vehicle or engaging in other tasks that require alertness until you see how this medicine affects you.
- Avoid alcohol and other medicines or natural products that slow your actions and reactions while taking this drug.
- Use a sunblock with at least SPF 15, because this drug may increase your sensitivity to the sun.
- To avoid dizziness, rise slowly over several minutes from a sitting or lying position.
- Do not consume grapefruit or grapefruit juice while taking this drug.
- This medication can affect your blood glucose levels; if you have diabetes, monitor your blood glucose closely and notify your health-care provider if it rises.

quinapril

Brand Name: Accupril

Generic Available: yes

Type of Drug: angiotensin-converting enzyme (ACE) inhibitor

Used for: Treatment of high blood pressure (hypertension), heart failure, and kidney problems due to diabetes.

How This Medication Works: Lowers blood pressure by decreasing production of angiotensin II, a strong chemical that causes blood vessels to constrict.

Dosage Form and Strength: tablets (5 mg, 10 mg, 20 mg, 40 mg)

Storage:
- room temperature
- protect from light and moisture—do not store in bathroom or kitchen

Administration:
- Usually taken once daily.
- Take at a similar time each day.
- May be taken without regard to meals, but take with food if stomach upset occurs.
- Take a missed dose as soon as possible. However, if it is almost time for the next dose, skip the missed dose and return to your regular dosing schedule.

Precautions:

Do not use if:

- **you are pregnant or could become pregnant.**
- you have an allergy to quinapril or other ACE inhibitor, such as lisinopril, enalapril, or ramipril.
- you have bilateral renal artery stenosis.

Talk to your doctor if:

- you have severe aortic stenosis.
- you have severe liver or kidney disease.
- you have low blood pressure.
- you become dehydrated.
- you are taking allopurinol, lithium, a potassium supplement, or spironolactone.

Side Effects:

Contact your health-care provider immediately if you experience:

- signs of a life-threatening reaction, which include fever; wheezing; chest tightness; and itching or swelling of face, lips, tongue, or throat.
- severe dizziness or fainting.
- severe headache.
- a rash.

Commonly reported side effects:

- dizziness or light-headedness
- headache
- constipation
- abnormal taste
- mild swelling of the feet, ankles, or legs
- cough

Time Required for Drug to Take Effect: Starts to lower blood pressure within 24 hours of first dose.

Symptoms of Overdose:
- low blood pressure
- slow pulse
- nausea and/or vomiting
- confusion

Special Notes:
- Do not use potassium-containing salt substitutes while taking this drug.
- Follow a diet plan and exercise program recommended by your health-care provider.
- To avoid dizziness, rise slowly over several minutes from a sitting or lying position.
- Notify your health-care provider if you develop a persistent cough that becomes bothersome.
- Do not consume alcohol while taking this drug.
- Drink plenty of fluids in hot weather to prevent dehydration while taking this drug.

rabeprazole

Brand Name: Aciphex

Generic Available: no

Type of Drug: proton pump inhibitor

Used for: Prevention or treatment of heartburn, stomach ulcers, or ulcers of the esophagus (food tube).

How This Medication Works: Prevents symptoms of heartburn and damage to the gastrointestinal tract by reducing stomach acid.

Dosage Form and Strength: tablets (20 mg)

Storage:
- room temperature
- protect from moisture—do not store in bathroom or kitchen

Administration:
- Usually taken once daily.
- Take this medicine 30 minutes before your first meal of the day.
- Swallow tablets whole; do not chew, break, or crush.
- Take a missed dose as soon as possible. However, if it is almost time for the next dose, skip the missed dose and return to your regular dosing schedule.

Precautions:
Do not use if:
- you have an allergy to rabeprazole or a similar medicine, such as omeprazole (Prilosec), esomeprazole (Nexium), pantoprazole (Protonix), or lansoprazole (Prevacid).

Talk to your doctor if:
- you have severe liver disease.
- you are also taking diazepam, phenytoin, sucralfate, iron (ferrous sulfate), ketoconazole, atazanavir, or indinavir.

Side Effects:

Contact your health-care provider immediately if you experience:
- signs of a life-threatening reaction, which include fever; wheezing; chest tightness; and itching or swelling of face, lips, tongue, or throat.
- unusual bruising or bleeding.
- severe dizziness or fainting.
- persistent diarrhea or constipation.
- a rash.

Commonly reported side effects:
- abdominal pain or nausea
- diarrhea or constipation
- flatulence
- headache

Time Required for Drug to Take Effect:

Starts working within 1 to 2 hours after taking the first dose, but may take 1 to 4 weeks of treatment to reach maximum effectiveness.

Symptoms of Overdose: No information currently available.

Special Notes:
- Do not take sucralfate within 30 minutes of taking this medicine.
- Consult your health-care provider or pharmacist before starting any other medicine, including over-the-counter drugs, while taking this drug.
- Do not smoke or consume alcohol; they can aggravate your condition.
- Talk to your health-care provider or pharmacist about medications that may make your condition

worse, such as aspirin-containing products and other anti-inflammatories (naproxen and ibuprofen, for example).

raloxifene

Brand Name: Evista

Generic Available: no

Type of Drug: selective estrogen receptor modulator, or SERM

Used for: Prevention and treatment of osteoporosis (thinning of the bones) in postmenopausal women.

How This Medication Works: Raloxifene is similar to estrogen and mimics some of estrogen's action in the body, including strengthening bones.

Dosage Form and Strength: tablets (60 mg)

Storage:
- room temperature
- protect from moisture—do not store in bathroom or kitchen

Administration:
- This medication is taken once daily.
- Take at a similar time each day.
- May be taken without regard to meals, but take with food if stomach upset occurs.
- Take a missed dose as soon as possible. However, if it is almost time for the next dose, skip the missed dose and return to your dosing schedule.

Precautions:

Do not use if:
- you have an allergy to raloxifene.
- you are or may be pregnant.
- you currently have blood clots (thromboembolic disease).

Talk to your doctor if:
- you have a history of or are at high risk for blood clots in the arms, legs, or lungs.
- you have heart, kidney, or liver disease.
- you have or have had high triglyceride levels.
- you have a history of cervical or uterine cancer.
- you currently take another form of estrogen or hormone replacement.
- you become bedridden or immobile for more than 72 hours.

Side Effects:

Contact your health-care provider immediately if you experience:
- signs of a life-threatening reaction, which include fever; wheezing; chest tightness; and itching or swelling of face, lips, tongue, or throat.
- abnormal thinking, anxiety, or lack of interest in life.
- chest pain or pressure.
- difficulty breathing.
- swelling or pain in the leg or arm.
- severe headache.
- severe nausea, vomiting, or diarrhea.
- significant weight gain.

- a sudden change in vision, eye pain, or eye irritation.
- a lump in the breast or breast tenderness.
- menstrual changes (increased bleeding, spotting, or bleeding between periods).
- vaginal itching or discharge.

Commonly reported side effects:
- hot flashes
- headache
- nausea, vomiting, or diarrhea
- leg or joint pain
- insomnia

Time Required for Drug to Take Effect:
Requires months of therapy to effectively prevent or treat bone loss.

Symptoms of Overdose: No information available.

Special Notes:
- This medicine works best as part of a three-pronged approach to treating osteoporosis that also includes supplements of calcium and vitamin D and weight-bearing exercise (such as walking) or physical therapy.
- This drug fights osteoporosis; it will not reduce hot flashes or flushing due to menopause.
- Do not consume alcohol while taking this drug.
- If you know you will be bedridden or immobile for some time, such as after surgery, talk to your health-care provider about stopping this drug 72 hours prior to your confinement.

ramelteon

Brand Name: Rozerem

Generic Available: no

Type of Drug: sedative/hypnotic (sleeping pill)

Used for: Treatment of insomnia.

How This Medication Works: Calms the brain by activating melatonin receptors.

Dosage Form and Strength: tablets (8 mg)

Storage:
- room temperature
- protect from light and moisture—do not store in bathroom or kitchen

Administration:
- Usually one 8 mg tablet is taken 30 minutes before sleep.
- This drug may be taken with or without food, but avoid taking it with a very high-fat meal.
- Take with food to avoid an upset stomach.
- Do not take more often than every 24 hours, unless instructed by your health-care provider.

Precautions:
Do not use if:
- you are taking fluvoxamine (Luvox).

Talk to your doctor if:
- you have any type of mental illness or depressive condition.
- you have liver disease or lung disease.

- you drink alcohol or take other sedating medications or herbal products.
- you are or may be pregnant.

Side Effects:

Contact your health-care provider immediately if you experience:

- signs of a life-threatening reaction, which include wheezing; chest tightness; itching; or swelling of face, lips, tongue, or throat.
- anxiety, nervousness, feelings of depression, or suicidal thoughts.
- a change in ability to think clearly and logically.

Commonly reported side effects:

- feeling light-headed, sleepy, tired, or weak
- altered taste sensations
- blurred vision
- change in balance
- headache
- change in sexual ability or desire, or changes in menstrual pattern

Time Required for Drug to Take Effect:

Begins to work 30 to 60 minutes after dosing.

Symptoms of Overdose:

- excessive sleepiness

Special Notes:

- Avoid driving or engaging in tasks that require alertness until you know how your body responds to this drug.
- Avoid alcohol and other sedating medications.
- Talk to your health-care provider before taking any new medicine, including over-the-

counter drugs, natural products, or vitamins, in conjunction with this drug.

- An increased risk for hazardous sleep-related activities, such as sleep-driving, eating/cooking while asleep, and making phone calls while asleep have been observed.
- Keep good sleep habits by avoiding naps during the day; getting up and going to bed at the same time every day; only using your bed for sleeping; making sure your bed and bedroom are quiet and comfortable; and avoiding alcohol, heavy meals, and caffeine in the evenings.

ramipril

Brand Name: Altace

Generic Available: no

Type of Drug: angiotensin-converting enzyme (ACE) inhibitor

Used for: Treatment of high blood pressure (hypertension), heart failure, and kidney problems due to diabetes.

How This Medication Works: Lowers blood pressure by decreasing production of angiotensin II, a strong chemical that causes blood vessels to constrict.

Dosage Form and Strength: capsules (1.25 mg, 2.5 mg, 5 mg, 10 mg)

Storage:
- room temperature

- protect from light and moisture—do not store in bathroom or kitchen

Administration:

- Usually taken once or twice daily.
- Take at a similar time each day.
- May be taken without regard to meals, but take with food if stomach upset occurs.
- Capsule contents may be sprinkled on soft food or into liquid.
- Take a missed dose as soon as possible. However, if it is almost time for the next dose, skip the missed dose and return to your dosing schedule.

Precautions:

Do not use if:

- **you are pregnant or could become pregnant.**
- you have an allergy to ramipril or other ACE inhibitor (such as lisinopril or quinapril).
- you have bilateral renal artery stenosis.

Talk to your doctor if:

- you have severe aortic stenosis.
- you have severe liver or kidney disease.
- you have low blood pressure.
- you become dehydrated.
- you are taking allopurinol, lithium, a potassium supplement, or spironolactone.

Side Effects:

Contact your health-care provider immediately if you experience:

- signs of a life-threatening reaction, which include fever; wheezing; chest tightness; and itching or swelling of face, lips, tongue, or throat.

- severe dizziness or fainting.
- severe headache.
- a rash.

Commonly reported side effects:
- dizziness or light-headedness
- headache
- constipation
- abnormal taste
- mild swelling of the feet, ankles, or legs
- cough

Time Required for Drug to Take Effect: Starts lowering blood pressure within 24 hours after taking the first dose.

Symptoms of Overdose:
- low blood pressure
- slow pulse
- nausea and/or vomiting
- confusion

Special Notes:
- Do not use potassium-containing salt substitutes while taking this drug.
- Follow a diet plan and exercise program recommended by your health-care provider.
- To avoid dizziness while you are taking this medication, rise slowly over several minutes from a sitting or lying position.
- Notify your health-care provider if you develop a persistent cough that becomes bothersome while you are being treated with this drug.

- Do not consume alcohol while taking this drug.
- Drink plenty of fluids in hot weather to prevent dehydration while taking this drug.
- Your doctor should periodically perform blood tests to monitor this therapy.

ranitidine

Brand Names: Zantac, Zantac 75

Generic Available: yes

Type of Drug: gastrointestinal (histamine H_2 blocker)

Used for: Treatment of excess acid production in the stomach, ulcers, and heartburn (gastroesophageal reflux disease [GERD]).

How This Medication Works: Blocks the binding of histamine to sites in the stomach that would cause acid secretion.

Dosage Form and Strength:
- tablets (75 mg, 150 mg, 300 mg)
- effervescent tablets (25 mg, 150 mg)
- capsules (150 mg, 300 mg)
- syrup (15 mg/mL)

Storage:
- room temperature
- protect from moisture—do not store in bathroom or kitchen

Administration:

- If you are taking multiple doses daily, take with or immediately after meals unless your doctor has given you different instructions.
- If you are only taking 1 dose daily, it is best to take it before bedtime unless your doctor has given you different instructions.
- Take ranitidine at least 1 hour before or 2 hours after taking an antacid.
- Drop the effervescent tablet in ¾ cup water, let it dissolve, then drink the solution.
- Take a missed dose as soon as possible. However, if it is almost time for the next dose, skip the missed dose and return to your dosing schedule.

Precautions:

Do not use if:

- you are allergic to ranitidine, cimetidine, famotidine, or nizatidine.
- you have phenylketonuria and the effervescent tablet has been prescribed for you.

Talk to your doctor if:

- you have kidney or liver disease.
- you are taking any other medication, especially theophylline, an anticoagulant (such as warfarin), an antidepressant, ketoconazole, itraconazole, an antibiotic, phenytoin, or medication for heart disease or high blood pressure.

Side Effects:

Contact your health-care provider immediately if you experience:

- a skin rash, hives, or itching.

- confusion or hallucinations.
- irregular heartbeat and tightness in the chest.
- severe abdominal pain.
- dark, tarry stool or vomit that resembles coffee grounds.
- unusual bleeding or bruising.

Commonly reported side effects:
- constipation or diarrhea
- dizziness or drowsiness
- headache
- dry mouth
- nausea and/or vomiting

Time Required for Drug to Take Effect: Starts to work within 1 to 3 hours after taking a dose, but ulcer healing may require 4 to 12 weeks of treatment with this medication.

Symptoms of Overdose:
- difficulty breathing
- irregular heartbeat
- tremors or difficulty walking
- vomiting or diarrhea
- light-headedness

Special Notes:
- Check with your physician or pharmacist before using any over-the-counter medication while you are taking this drug.
- Avoid medications that may make your ulcer worse, including nonsteroidal anti-inflammatory drugs (such as aspirin, ibuprofen, and naproxen).

- If you are using over-the-counter ranitidine and your symptoms do not improve or they get worse, contact your health-care provider.
- Smoking and alcohol consumption can aggravate your condition and should be avoided.
- This medication may cause drowsiness. Use caution when driving a car or operating dangerous machinery.
- Avoid other medication that may make you drowsy or dizzy, such as antihistamines, sedatives, tranquilizers, pain relievers, seizure medications, and muscle relaxants.
- To ease dry mouth symptoms, chew gum, suck on ice chips or hard candy, or try a saliva substitute.
- Sound-alike/look-alike warning: Zantac may be confused with Xanax or Zyrtec, and ranitidine may be confused with rimantadine.

risedronate

Brand Name: Actonel

Generic Available: no

Type of Drug: bisphosphonate

Used for: Prevention or treatment of osteoporosis, and treatment of Paget's disease.

How This Medication Works: Reduces the rate of bone loss (resorption), making bones stronger.

Dosage Form and Strength: tablets (5 mg, 30 mg, 35 mg)

Storage:
- room temperature
- protect from moisture—do not store in bathroom or kitchen

Administration:
- Usually taken once daily or once weekly, depending on dose.
- Take this medicine in the morning, with a full glass of water, at least 30 minutes before the first food, drink, or other medicine of the day.
- Do not drink or eat for at least 30 minutes after taking this medicine.
- Do not lie down for at least 30 minutes after taking this medicine, to prevent irritation to the esophagus (food tube).
- Swallow tablets whole; do not chew, break, or crush.
- For daily or weekly dosing: If you miss a dose or forget to take the medication in the morning, skip the missed dose and take a dose the following morning. If you take this drug once a week and miss a dose, take it the next day and return to your regularly scheduled dosing day the following week.

Precautions:
Do not use if:
- you are allergic to risedronate or alendronate.
- you have low calcium levels, severe kidney disease, narrowing of the esophagus, or slow movement through the esophagus.
- you are unable to stand or sit upright for 30 minutes after taking this medicine.

Talk to your doctor if:
- you have kidney disease.
- you have ulcers of the stomach or throat.

Side Effects:
Contact your health-care provider immediately if you experience:
- signs of a life-threatening reaction, which include fever; wheezing; chest tightness; and itching or swelling of face, lips, tongue, or throat.
- severe nausea or vomiting, severe heartburn, stomach pain, or painful swallowing.
- dark, tarry stools or vomit that resembles coffee grounds.
- jaw pain or severe bone pain.

Commonly reported side effects:
- flulike symptoms (such as weakness, fever, aches, and pains)
- headache
- nausea and/or vomiting
- diarrhea or constipation
- bone pain

Time Required for Drug to Take Effect: Takes
3 to 6 weeks of treatment to begin affecting osteoporosis and 3 to 6 months to affect Paget's disease.

Symptoms of Overdose:
- upset stomach
- heartburn
- irritated throat
- stomach pain
- ulcers

Special Notes:
- Consult your health-care provider about also taking calcium and vitamin D supplements and doing weight-bearing exercises, such as walking.
- Wait at least 1 hour after you take risedronate to take calcium, mineral supplements, or antacids that contain aluminum, magnesium, or calcium.

risperidone

Brand Names: Risperdal, Risperdal M-Tabs

Generic Available: no

Type of Drug: antipsychotic

Used for: Treatment of psychotic disorders such as schizophrenia, mania, and bipolar disorder. **Patients with dementia-related behavioral disorders who are treated with this class of drugs are at an increased risk of death compared to placebo.**

How This Medication Works: Mechanism is unknown, but the drug may block the activity of the brain chemicals dopamine and serotonin.

Dosage Form and Strength:
- tablets (0.25 mg, 0.5 mg, 1 mg, 2 mg, 3 mg, 4 mg)
- orally disintegrating tablets (0.5 mg, 1 mg, 2 mg)
- solution (1 mg/mL)

Storage:
- room temperature

- protect from light and moisture—do not store in bathroom or kitchen

Administration:
- Usually taken twice daily.
- The solution can be mixed with water, orange juice, coffee, or low-fat milk (but not cola or tea).
- The orally disintegrating tablet should be taken immediately after you remove it from its packaging. It should be placed on the tongue to dissolve and then swallowed; it should not be split or chewed.
- Take a missed dose as soon as possible. However, if it is almost time for the next dose, skip the missed dose and return to your dosing schedule.

Precautions:
Do not use if:
- you have ever had an allergic reaction to risperidone.
- you have phenylketonuria and Risperdal M-Tabs have been prescribed for you.

Talk to your doctor if:
- you are taking any other medication.
- you have had a stroke or have heart problems, seizures, kidney or liver disease, Alzheimer's or Parkinson's disease, or bone marrow problems.
- you have diabetes, prostate problems, or decreased gastrointestinal (GI) motility.
- you have dementia (this drug may increase your risk of stroke).

Side Effects:

Contact your health-care provider immediately if you experience:
- restlessness or agitation.
- severe dizziness or fainting.
- twitching movements, strange movements, or muscle spasms.
- extreme nervousness or excitability.
- significant weight gain or loss.
- difficulty swallowing.

Commonly reported side effects:
- fatigue
- constipation or diarrhea
- insomnia
- dry mouth
- headache
- drowsiness or dizziness

Time Required for Drug to Take Effect: This medication may need to be taken for several weeks before the desired effect is seen.

Symptoms of Overdose:
- drowsiness
- seizures
- increased heart rate
- uncontrolled movements

Special Notes:
- Do not drink alcohol while taking this medication.
- Changing positions slowly when sitting and/or standing up may help decrease dizziness caused by this medication.

- This medication may increase the risk of death in elderly people who have dementia.
- Do not discontinue this medication without first talking with your doctor.
- Use a sunblock with at least SPF 15 when outside because risperidone may increase your sensitivity to the sun.

rivastigmine

Brand Name: Exelon

Generic Available: no

Type of Drug: acetylcholinesterase inhibitor

Used for: Treatment of mild to moderate Alzheimer's disease.

How This Medication Works: Increases the amount of acetylcholine, a chemical in the brain. Lack of acetylcholine in the brain is thought to contribute to Alzheimer's disease.

Dosage Form and Strength:
- capsules (1.5 mg, 3.0 mg, 4.5 mg, 6.0 mg)
- solution (2 mg/mL)

Storage:
- room temperature; do not freeze the solution
- protect from moisture—do not store in bathroom or kitchen

Administration:
- Usually taken twice daily.

- Treatment is usually begun at a lower dose. After a few weeks, the doctor may increase your dose until the best dose for you is reached.
- If you miss taking this medicine for more than 3 days, contact your doctor; the dose may need to be changed.
- Swallow the capsule whole with meals; do not chew, break, or crush.
- A liquid (solution) form of the medicine is available if you have difficulty with pills. Take it alone, or mix it with water, juice, or soda, then stir well and drink within 4 hours of mixing.
- Take a missed dose as soon as possible with a meal. However, if it is almost time for the next dose, skip the missed dose and return to your regular dosing schedule.

Precautions:

Do not use if:
- you are allergic to rivastigmine.

Talk to your doctor if:
- you have lung or heart disease, because you may be more sensitive to this medicine.
- you have kidney disease or liver disease.
- you have seizures, a slow heartbeat, stomach ulcers, or stomach problems.
- you experience weight loss after starting this medication.
- you take any of the following: atropine, benztropine, dicyclomine, glycopyrrolate, hyoscyamine, scopolamine, tolterodine, oxybutynin, trihexyphenidyl, or trimethobenzamide.

Side Effects:

Contact your health-care provider immediately if you experience:
- signs of a life-threatening reaction, which include fever; wheezing; chest tightness; and itching or swelling of face, lips, tongue, or throat.
- severe headache.
- severe nausea, vomiting, or diarrhea.
- difficulty breathing.
- symptoms of depression, nervousness, abnormal thinking, anxiety, or lack of interest in life.
- severe dizziness or fainting.
- a rash.

Commonly reported side effects:
- nausea and/or vomiting
- headache or dizziness
- loss of appetite
- increased salivation and/or urination
- diarrhea

Time Required for Drug to Take Effect: May take up to 3 months of treatment to reach maximum effectiveness.

Symptoms of Overdose:
- severe nausea and/or vomiting
- severe salivation and/or sweating
- low blood pressure, slow pulse, slow breathing
- seizures

Special Notes:
- This drug does not cure Alzheimer's disease, but it may reduce some symptoms.

- Eating small, frequent meals; getting regular dental care; and sucking hard candy or chewing gum may help minimize nausea and vomiting.
- Nausea and vomiting often decrease once the dose of this medication has been stabilized.
- To avoid dizziness, rise slowly over several minutes from a sitting or lying position.

rosiglitazone

Brand Name: Avandia

Generic Available: no

Type of Drug: antidiabetic (thiazolidinedione)

Used for: Lowering blood glucose levels in type 2 (non–insulin-dependent) diabetes.

How This Medication Works: Increases insulin's activity in the body.

Dosage Form and Strength: tablets (2 mg, 4 mg, 8 mg)

Storage:
- room temperature
- protect from heat and moisture—do not store in bathroom or kitchen

Administration:
- Usually taken once or twice daily.
- May be used alone or in combination with other diabetes medicine.
- Take at a similar time each day.

- May be taken without regard to meals, but take with food if stomach upset occurs.
- Take a missed dose as soon as possible. However, if it is almost time for the next dose, skip the missed dose and return to your regular dosing schedule.

Precautions:

Do not use if:

- you are allergic to rosiglitazone, pioglitazone, or troglitazone.
- you have active liver disease.
- you have type 1 diabetes or ketoacidosis.

Talk to your doctor if:

- you have heart failure or swelling of the arms or legs (edema).
- you have anemia or a history of liver problems.
- you have macular edema or diabetic retinopathy.
- you have osteoporosis or you are at risk for falls or fractures.
- you are premenopausal or have not been ovulating.

Side Effects:

Contact your health-care provider immediately if you experience:

- signs of a life-threatening reaction, which include fever; wheezing; chest tightness; and itching or swelling of face, lips, tongue, or throat.
- significant weight gain.
- significant swelling of the arms or legs.
- difficulty breathing.
- very low or very high blood glucose.
- severe stomach pain, nausea, or vomiting.

- yellowing of the skin or eyes.
- extreme fatigue or weakness.
- a rash.

Commonly reported side effects:
- increased blood cholesterol
- headache
- swelling
- weight gain
- nasal irritation or cough

Time Required for Drug to Take Effect: Takes
at least 4 weeks of treatment to start lowering blood glucose.

Symptoms of Overdose:
- low blood glucose (signs include shaking, anger, fast heartbeat, confusion, dizziness, and sweating)

Special Notes:
- This medication may restart ovulation in perimenopausal and menopausal women, increasing the risk of pregnancy.
- This medication may increase the risk for bone fractures.
- Follow a diet plan and exercise program recommended by your health-care provider.
- Always keep a fast-acting sugar source (such as hard candy, glucose tablets or gel, fruit juice, or nondiet soda) handy.
- Teach your family, friends, and coworkers how to help you if you have low blood sugar.
- Do not drive if you recently had low blood glucose—your risk of an accident is higher.
- Do not consume alcohol while taking this drug.

- Check your blood glucose as directed by your health-care provider.
- Have yearly eye and foot exams performed by health-care professionals.

salmeterol

Brand Name: Serevent Diskus

Generic Available: no

Type of Drug: bronchodilator (beta-agonist)

Used for: Maintenance treatment of asthma and bronchospasms. **This drug may increase risk of asthma-related death and should only be used as an additional therapy by those who cannot gain control of their asthma symptoms by using other medications.**

How This Medication Works: Works in the lungs to relax the muscles and improve oxygen flow.

Dosage Form and Strength: Diskus (50 mcg/ dose)

Storage:
- room temperature
- protect from heat and moisture—do not store in bathroom or kitchen
- discard the device and any unused medicine 6 weeks after removing it from its foil package

Administration:
- For inhalation through the mouth only.

- Usual dose is one puff twice daily (every 12 hours).
- Never use it more often than every 12 hours.
- Have your doctor or pharmacist demonstrate the proper procedure for using your inhaler, and practice your technique in front of them.
- If you have more than one inhaler, it is important to administer your inhalers in the correct order. Consult your health-care provider for specific instructions.
- Take a missed dose as soon as possible. However, if it is almost time for the next dose, skip the missed dose and return to your dosing schedule.
- Never wash the Diskus inhaler device.

Precautions:
Do not use if:
- you are having a sudden attack of difficult breathing.
- you have had an allergic reaction to salmeterol, albuterol, epinephrine, metaproterenol, or terbutaline.
- you have taken a monoamine oxidase (MAO) inhibitor, such as phenelzine or isocarboxazid, within the past 14 days.

Talk to your doctor if:
- you have diabetes, heart disease, high blood pressure (hypertension), problems with your circulation or blood vessels, seizures, thyroid disease, diabetes, glaucoma, or liver disease.
- you are taking any other medication, especially medication for heart disease, high blood pressure (hypertension), migraines, or depression.

Side Effects:

Contact your health-care provider immediately if you experience:
- a skin rash, itching, or hives.
- wheezing or difficulty breathing.
- bluish coloring of your skin.
- swelling of the face, lips, or eyelids.
- dizziness or fainting.
- chest discomfort or pressure.
- extreme nervousness or excitability.
- hallucinations.

Commonly reported side effects:
- nervousness, tremor, trembling, or insomnia
- coughing
- dryness or irritation of the mouth or throat
- unpleasant taste
- headache
- nausea and/or vomiting

Time Required for Drug to Take Effect: Starts
to work within 20 minutes of taking a dose, and continues to work for 12 hours.

Symptoms of Overdose:
- chest discomfort or pressure
- seizures
- irregular heartbeat
- severe nausea or vomiting
- severe breathing difficulty
- tremor

Special Notes:
- Salmeterol should not be used for acute asthma attacks.

- Check with your physician or pharmacist before using any over-the-counter medications while you are taking this drug.
- Keep track of how many inhalations are left and get your medication refilled about 1 week before you expect to run out.
- Limit caffeine intake while you are taking this medication; it may increase nervousness and shakiness.

salmeterol and fluticasone combination

Brand Name: Advair Diskus

Generic Available: no

Type of Drug: corticosteroid and beta-agonist combination

Used for: Prevention of symptoms of asthma or other lung diseases in which spasms may cause breathing problems.

How This Medication Works: Salmeterol works in the lungs to relax the muscles and improve oxygen flow. Fluticasone reduces irritation and swelling in the lungs to help minimize or prevent lung spasms.

Dosage Form and Strength: Diskus (50 mcg salmeterol/100 mcg fluticasone, 50 mcg/250 mcg, 50 mcg/500 mcg)

Storage:
- room temperature; do not freeze
- protect from heat, light, and moisture—do not store in bathroom or kitchen
- discard the device and any unused medicine 1 month after removing it from its foil package

Administration:
- For inhalation through the mouth only.
- Usual dose is one puff twice daily (every 12 hours).
- Never use this medication more often than every 12 hours.
- Have your doctor or pharmacist demonstrate the proper procedure for using your inhaler, and practice your technique in front of them.
- If you have more than one inhaler, it is important to administer your inhalers in the correct order. Consult your health-care provider for specific instructions.
- Take a missed dose as soon as possible. However, if it is almost time for the next dose, skip the missed dose and return to your dosing schedule.
- Never wash the Diskus inhaler device.

Precautions:
Do not use if:
- you are allergic to fluticasone or salmeterol.
- you are having a sudden attack of difficult breathing.
- you have taken a monoamine oxidase (MAO) inhibitor, such as phenelzine or isocarboxazid, within the past 14 days.

<u>*Talk to your doctor if:*</u>
- you are switching from oral steroids to inhaled steroids.
- you have heart disease or a fast or abnormal heartbeat.
- you have an overactive thyroid.
- you have a history of seizures.

Side Effects:

<u>*Contact your health-care provider immediately if you experience:*</u>
- signs of a life-threatening reaction, which include fever; wheezing; chest tightness; and itching or swelling of face, lips, tongue, or throat.
- signs of infection, such as fever, chills, severe sore throat, ear or sinus pain, or cough.
- extreme tiredness, weakness, or irritability.
- trembling or a fast heartbeat.
- confusion or dizziness.
- sores or white patches in your mouth, throat, or nose.
- nervousness and excitability.
- a worsening of your asthma or breathing problems.
- an increased need for your short-acting inhaler.
- a rash.

<u>*Commonly reported side effects:*</u>
- headache
- nausea and/or vomiting
- cough
- sore throat or hoarseness

Time Required for Drug to Take Effect: Takes
1 to 2 weeks of treatment to see improvement in symptoms.

Symptoms of Overdose:
- muscle weakness
- tremor
- high blood pressure
- chest pain
- seizure

If overdose has been occurring for more than several doses, do not stop medication abruptly. Contact health-care provider or poison control center for instructions.

Special Notes:
- Do not use this medication for emergency relief of an asthma or breathing attack.
- This medicine gets into your lungs through the force of your breath, not as a puff of air as with a traditional inhaler. As long as you take a deep breath when you inhale your dose, you are getting medicine into your lungs.
- Do not keep this medicine inside a car or anywhere else it could be exposed to extreme heat or cold.
- Avoid exposure to chicken pox or measles. If exposed, inform your prescriber as soon as possible.
- Limit your caffeine intake during treatment with this drug, because it may cause shakiness, nervousness, and a fast heartbeat.

- Always rinse out your mouth with plain water after using this medicine.

selegiline

Brand Names:
Eldepryl
Emsam
Zelapar

Generic Available: yes

Type of Drug: antiparkinsonian (monoamine oxidase B [MAO-B] inhibitor)

Used for: Treatment of Parkinson's disease (Emsam patch used for treatment of depression).

How This Medication Works: Prolongs the action of the brain chemical dopamine by preventing its breakdown.

Dosage Form and Strength:
- tablets and capsules (1.25 mg, 5 mg)
- patch (6 mg/24 hours, 9 mg/24 hours, 12 mg/24 hours)

Storage:
- room temperature
- protect from moisture—do not store in bathroom or kitchen

Administration:
Tablets and capsules:
- Usually taken once or twice daily.

- Take in the morning and at noon (if prescribed twice daily).
- Take with food.
- Take a missed dose as soon as possible. However, if it is almost time for the next dose, skip the missed dose and return to your regular dosing schedule.

Patch:
- Applied once daily.
- Apply to clean, dry skin on the torso.
- Apply a forgotten patch as soon as possible. However, if it is almost time for the next dose, skip the forgotten patch and return to your regular dosing schedule. Do not apply extra patches to make up for the missed one.

Precautions:

Do not use if:
- you have ever had an allergic reaction to selegiline.
- you are taking meperidine or have taken a monoamine oxidase (MAO) inhibitor, such as phenelzine or isocarboxazid, in the past 14 days.

Talk to your doctor if:
- you are taking metoclopramide, an antidepressant, or an antipsychotic, such as haloperidol or thioridazine.
- you have ever been treated for peptic ulcers.
- your prescribed dose of selegilene is more than 10 mg daily, because you may need to avoid foods that contain tyramine.

Side Effects:

Contact your health-care provider immediately if you experience:

- **suicidal thoughts or a desire to harm yourself.**
- severe flushing.
- chest pain.
- palpitations or fast heartbeat.
- unusually severe headache.
- severe dizziness or fainting.
- severe nausea or vomiting.
- inability to urinate.
- black, tarry stools or severe constipation.
- unusual changes in behavior or thinking, extreme excitability, or if you make unusual movements.

Commonly reported side effects:

- light-headedness or dizziness
- nausea and/or vomiting
- insomnia or nightmares
- dry mouth
- constipation

Time Required for Drug to Take Effect: Mild improvement in symptoms may be noted within several days after starting treatment, but it may take weeks of therapy to reach maximum effectiveness.

Symptoms of Overdose:

- unusually low or high blood pressure
- fast heartbeat or palpitations
- dizziness leading to falls
- unusual changes in behavior or memory
- unusual agitation or irritability
- severe muscle spasms, twitches, or seizures

Special Notes:
- Selegiline may be prescribed to slow Parkinson's disease, but it is not a cure for the disease.
- Do not exceed the recommended dose of selegiline.
- When selegiline is added to a regimen that includes levodopa, it may be necessary to reduce the dose of levodopa.
- Do not drink alcohol while taking this medication.
- Drink 6 to 8 glasses of water daily while taking this drug, unless instructed otherwise by your health-care provider.
- Avoid products with Saint John's wort or tyramine.

sertraline

Brand Name: Zoloft

Generic Available: yes

Type of Drug: antidepressant (selective serotonin reuptake inhibitor)

Used for: Treatment of depression, panic disorder, obsessive-compulsive disorder, post-traumatic stress disorder, premenstrual dysphoric disorder, and social anxiety disorder.

How This Medication Works: Prolongs the effects of the brain chemical serotonin by interfering with its reuptake into nerve cells in the brain.

Dosage Form and Strength:
- tablets (25 mg, 50 mg, 100 mg)
- oral concentrate (20 mg/mL)

Storage:
- room temperature
- protect from moisture—do not store in bathroom or kitchen

Administration:
- Usually taken once daily in the morning or at bedtime (if you experience drowsiness).
- If taking the solution, mix the liquid with ½ cup water, orange juice, lemonade, or ginger ale before swallowing.
- Take a missed dose as soon as possible. However, if it is almost time for the next dose, skip the missed dose and return to your regular dosing schedule.

Precautions:
Do not use if:
- you have ever had an allergic reaction to sertraline or other selective serotonin reuptake inhibitors, such as paroxetine or fluoxetine.
- you have taken a monoamine oxidase (MAO) inhibitor, such as phenelzine or tranylcypromine, within the past 14 days.
- the solution form of sertraline has been prescribed for you and you also take disulfiram.

Talk to your doctor if:
- you have liver problems, kidney problems, seizures, or bipolar disorder.
- you are taking a benzodiazepine (such as alprazolam or diazepam), lithium, desipramine, warfarin, carbamazepine, an amphetamine,

dextromethorphan (found in cough medicines), meperidine, or pimozide.

Side Effects:

Contact your health-care provider immediately if you experience:

- **suicidal thoughts or a desire to harm yourself.**
- a rash, hives, itching, or chest tightness.
- a fever.
- unusual agitation, restlessness, or excitement.
- dizziness or fainting.

Commonly reported side effects:

- headache
- sleeping problems or vivid dreams
- drowsiness or dizziness
- nervousness
- tremor
- fatigue or weakness
- decreased sexual interest and function
- stomach pain, nausea, or diarrhea
- dry mouth
- blurred vision
- urinary problems

Time Required for Drug to Take Effect: May start to improve some symptoms within the first few weeks of treatment, but it may take from 4 to 8 weeks to reach maximum effectiveness.

Symptoms of Overdose:

- severe agitation or excited behavior
- palpitations or chest pain
- drowsiness
- nausea and vomiting

Special Notes:
- The desire to harm yourself is a serious symptom of depression. If you plan to harm yourself, call 911 immediately.
- Know which "target symptoms" (restlessness, depressed mood, worry, fear, or changes in sleep or appetite) you are being treated for and be prepared to tell your doctor if your target symptoms are improving, worsening, or unchanged.
- Do not drink alcohol while taking this medication.
- Never increase your dose or stop taking this medication without consulting your doctor first.

sildenafil

Brand Name: Viagra

Generic Available: no

Type of Drug: phosphodiesterase–5 enzyme inhibitor

Used for: Treatment of impotence, or erectile dysfunction (ED).

How This Medication Works: Improves response to stimulation by relaxing penile smooth muscle and increasing blood flow to the penis.

Dosage Form and Strength: tablets (25 mg, 50 mg, 100 mg)

Storage:
- room temperature

- protect from moisture—do not store in bathroom or kitchen

Administration:

- Take this medicine 30 minutes to 4 hours before sexual intercourse.
- This medication is taken on an "as-needed" basis.
- Do not take sildenafil more often than once every 24 hours, unless approved by your health-care provider.

Precautions:

Do not use if:

- you have an allergy to sildenafil.
- you are taking isosorbide dinitrate, isosorbide mononitrate, or nitroglycerin or using the nitroglycerin patch.

Talk to your doctor if:

- you have heart disease, sickle-cell anemia, multiple myeloma, or leukemia.
- you have cirrhosis, liver disease, or kidney disease.
- you have a deformation of the penis.
- you take an alpha-blocker, such as alfuzosin, doxazosin, tamsulosin, terazosin, or prazosin.
- you are taking any medication or herbal product used to treat changes in sexual ability or desire.

Side Effects:

Contact your health-care provider immediately if you experience:

- signs of a life-threatening reaction, which include fever; wheezing; chest tightness; and itching or swelling of face, lips, tongue, or throat.

- a penile erection that lasts longer than 4 hours.
- chest pain or pressure or fast heartbeat.
- severe dizziness or fainting.
- vision changes or loss of vision.

Commonly reported side effects:

- flushing
- headache
- stomach discomfort or heartburn
- vision changes (color changes, blurred or increased sensitivity to light)
- dizziness

Time Required for Drug to Take Effect: Starts working within 10 minutes to 2 hours after you take a dose.

Symptoms of Overdose: At this time, the overdose information is limited, but the symptoms that have been seen have been similar to the commonly reported side effects, but they are more frequent and severe.

- headache
- flushing
- tremor
- vision changes
- dizziness
- chest pain or heart attack

Special Notes:

- If an erection lasts longer than 4 hours, contact your health-care provider immediately because this effect can cause permanent damage to the penis.

- Sildenafil provides no protection against sexually transmitted diseases, including HIV. Use a latex condom to protect against sexually transmitted diseases.
- This drug will not work in the absence of sexual stimulation.
- Do not consume grapefruit or grapefruit juice while taking this drug.

simvastatin

Brand Name: Zocor

Generic Available: yes

Type of Drug: antihyperlipidemic

Used for: Treatment of high blood cholesterol levels and heart disease.

How This Medication Works: Decreases the amount of cholesterol made by the liver.

Dosage Form and Strength: tablets (5 mg, 10 mg, 20 mg, 40 mg, 80 mg)

Storage:
- room temperature
- protect from moisture—do not store in bathroom or kitchen

Administration:
- Usually taken once daily, in the evening.
- May be taken with or without food.

- Take a missed dose as soon as possible. However, if it is almost time for the next dose, skip the missed dose and return to your regular dosing schedule.

Precautions:
Do not use if:
- you are allergic to simvastatin or a similar drug, such as lovastatin, pravastatin, or atorvastatin.
- you are or may be pregnant.

Talk to your doctor if:
- you have liver disease.
- you are taking any other medication, especially an oral antifungal, a protease inhibitor, cyclosporine, erythromycin, warfarin, niacin, or gemfibrozil.

Side Effects:
Contact your health-care provider immediately if you experience:
- unexplained muscle aches, especially if accompanied by weakness or flulike symptoms.
- breathing difficulty.
- swelling of the face, throat, lips, or tongue.
- yellowing of the skin or eyes.
- confusion or memory loss.

Commonly reported side effects:
- insomnia
- stomach pain or diarrhea
- headache
- constipation
- taste disturbance

Time Required for Drug to Take Effect: Starts lowering blood cholesterol levels within 1 to 2 weeks after beginning treatment but may take 4 to 6 weeks to reach maximum effectiveness.

Symptoms of Overdose: No specific symptoms.

Special Notes:
- After beginning therapy, your doctor will periodically check your blood cholesterol levels and liver function.
- Use a sunblock with at least SPF 15 when outside because simvastatin may increase your sensitivity to the sun.
- Do not drink alcohol while taking this medication.
- Follow a diet plan and exercise program recommended by your health-care provider.
- Do not donate blood while taking this drug.
- Do not consume grapefruit or grapefruit juice while you are taking this medication.

solifenacin

Brand Name: VESIcare

Generic Available: no

Type of Drug: cholinergic antagonist

Used for: Treatment of overactive bladder symptoms.

How This Medication Works: Blocks the action of a chemical that causes spasms of the bladder, which causes symptoms of urgency, increased trips to the bathroom, and incontinence.

Dosage Form and Strength: tablets (5 mg, 10 mg)

Storage:
- room temperature
- protect from heat, light, and moisture—do not store in bathroom or kitchen

Administration:
- Usually taken once daily.
- May be taken without regard to meals, but take with food if stomach upset occurs.
- Swallow tablet whole; do not break, crush, or chew.
- Take a missed dose as soon as possible. However, if it is almost time for the next dose, skip the missed dose and return to your regular dosing schedule.

Precautions:
Do not use if:
- you are allergic to solifenacin.
- you have uncontrolled narrow-angle glaucoma, urinary retention, or myasthenia gravis.

Talk to your doctor if:
- you have a bladder disorder or gastric obstructive disorder.
- you are being treated for narrow-angle glaucoma.
- you have kidney disease or liver disease.

Side Effects:

Contact your health-care provider immediately if you experience:
- signs of a life-threatening reaction, which include wheezing; chest tightness; itching; or swelling of face, lips, tongue, or throat.
- the inability to start urinating.
- a racing heartbeat.
- confusion or become unable to think clearly.

Commonly reported side effects:
- dry mouth
- headache
- dizziness
- constipation
- upset stomach

Time Required for Drug to Take Effect: It

may take 1 to 2 weeks of treatment to reach maximum effectiveness.

Symptoms of Overdose:
- blurred vision
- hallucinations
- racing heartbeat
- chest pain

Special Notes:
- This medication can cause dizziness, so avoid driving or engaging in tasks that require alertness until you know how your body responds to this drug.
- Chewing gum, sucking on hard candy, or brushing your teeth may help with the side effect of dry mouth.

- Drink plenty of noncaffeinated liquids, unless told otherwise by your health-care provider.
- Do not consume grapefruit or grapefruit juice while you are taking this medication.

spironolactone

Brand Name: Aldactone

Generic Available: yes

Type of Drug: diuretic

Used for: Treatment of fluid retention (edema), high blood pressure (hypertension), hyperaldosteronism, heart failure, low potassium levels (hypokalemia), and cirrhosis.

How This Medication Works: Inhibits the formation of a protein necessary for sodium transport in the kidneys, resulting in loss of water through urine.

Dosage Form and Strength: tablets (25 mg, 50 mg, 100 mg)

Storage:
- room temperature
- protect from moisture—do not store in bathroom or kitchen

Administration:
- Usually taken 1 or 2 times daily.
- Take with food to increase absorption.
- Take a missed dose as soon as possible. However, if it is almost time for the next dose, skip the

missed dose and return to your regular dosing schedule.

Precautions:

Do not use if:
- you are allergic to spironolactone.
- you have high potassium levels.

Talk to your doctor if:
- you have kidney disease.
- you are taking triamterene, amiloride, warfarin, digoxin, a potassium supplement, or an angiotensin-converting enzyme (ACE) inhibitor, such as lisinopril or enalapril.

Side Effects:

Contact your health-care provider immediately if you experience:
- seizures or extreme weakness.
- chest pain or irregular heartbeat.
- severe dizziness or fainting.
- severe nausea, vomiting, or diarrhea.
- menstrual changes or spotting.
- a skin rash or swelling of the face or throat.

Commonly reported side effects:
- dry mouth
- nausea and/or vomiting
- headache
- change in sexual ability or desire
- enlargement of the breasts (in men and women)
- hair growth and deepening of the voice

Time Required for Drug to Take Effect: Starts acting very gradually, reaching maximum effectiveness after 3 days of treatment.

Symptoms of Overdose:
- drowsiness or confusion
- nausea and vomiting
- diarrhea
- extreme muscle weakness

Special Notes:
- Avoid salt substitutes containing potassium while you are taking this medication. Spironolactone may cause your body to retain potassium.
- Your doctor will check your blood count, kidney function, and electrolyte (sodium and potassium) levels periodically during therapy.
- Unless otherwise instructed by your doctor, it is important to drink 6 to 8 eight-ounce glasses of water every day while you are taking this medication. This will help prevent dehydration.
- Use a sunblock with at least SPF 15 when outside because spironolactone may increase your sensitivity to the sun.
- To ease dry mouth symptoms, chew gum, suck on ice chips or hard candy, or try a saliva substitute.
- If you gain or lose significant weight while you are taking this medication, contact your doctor.
- Changing positions slowly when sitting and/or standing up may help decrease dizziness caused by this drug.
- If this drug makes you dizzy, avoid activities requiring mental alertness, such as driving a car or operating dangerous machinery.
- Do not drink alcohol while taking this medication.

sulfamethoxazole and trimethoprim combination

Brand Names:

Bactrim   Septra
Bactrim DS   Septra DS

Generic Available: yes

Type of Drug: antibiotic

Used for: Treatment of bacterial infections.

How This Medication Works: Kills bacteria by inhibiting the bacteria's production of important chemicals.

Dosage Form and Strength:

- tablets (80 mg trimethoprim/400 mg sulfamethoxazole, 160 mg/800 mg)
- suspension (40 mg trimethoprim/200 mg sulfamethoxazole per 5 mL)

Storage:

- room temperature
- protect from moisture—do not store in bathroom or kitchen

Administration:

- Usually taken twice daily, but dose and length of treatment will depend on the infection being treated.
- Take at even intervals (such as every 12 hours) and at the same time every day.
- Shake suspension well before measuring dose.

- Take each dose with a full glass of water.
- Take with food or milk.
- Take all the medication prescribed, even if symptoms disappear before it is all gone.
- Take a missed dose as soon as possible. However, if it is almost time for the next dose, skip the missed dose and return to your dosing schedule.

Precautions:
Do not use if:
- you are allergic to sulfamethoxazole, trimethoprim, or sulfa.

Talk to your doctor if:
- you are taking an anticoagulant (such as warfarin), a diuretic (such as furosemide or hydrochlorothiazide), cyclosporine, dapsone, methotrexate, phenytoin, zidovudine, or an oral diabetes medication (such as glyburide or glipizide).
- you have kidney or liver disease.

Side Effects:
Contact your health-care provider immediately if you experience:
- yellowing of the skin or eyes.
- a rash, hives, or shortness of breath.
- unexplained bruising or bleeding.
- difficult or painful urination.
- severe nausea or vomiting.
- confusion or hallucinations.

Commonly reported side effects:
- stomach upset, nausea, or vomiting
- headache
- abdominal pain and diarrhea

Time Required for Drug to Take Effect:
Begins to kill infecting bacteria within hours after you take the first dose. However, you must finish all the medication that was prescribed, even if your symptoms disappear before it is gone.

Symptoms of Overdose:
- nausea or vomiting
- dizziness
- unconsciousness
- difficult or painful urination

Special Notes:
- Do not use for infections other than the one for which it was prescribed.
- Long-term use may lead to bacterial resistance.
- Use a sunblock with at least SPF 15 when outside because this medication may increase your sensitivity to the sun.
- Call your doctor if you get another infection or this infection does not get better.
- Eating yogurt with active cultures may help ease mild diarrhea, but contact your health-care provider if diarrhea continues.

tamoxifen

Brand Name: Nolvadex

Generic Available: yes

Type of Drug: antineoplastic

Used for: Prevention of recurrence of breast cancer and treatment of advanced breast cancer. **Serious events, such as stroke, blood clots, and uterine cancer, may occur at higher rates for people taking this medication.**

How This Medication Works: Prevents estrogen in the body from feeding estrogen-dependent cancer.

Dosage Form and Strength: tablets (10 mg, 20 mg)

Storage:
- room temperature
- protect from light and moisture—do not store in bathroom or kitchen

Administration:
- Usual dose is 10 to 20 mg twice daily (morning and evening).
- Take with or without food.
- Take a missed dose as soon as possible. However, if it is almost time for the next dose, skip the missed dose and return to your regular dosing schedule.

Precautions:
Do not use if:
- you are allergic to tamoxifen.

Talk to your doctor if:
- you have cataracts, low white blood cell count (leukopenia), or low platelet level (thrombocytopenia).
- you are taking any other medication, especially an antacid, cimetidine, famotidine, nizatidine, ranitidine, estrogens, or birth control pills.

- you take warfarin or have a history of stroke or blood clots.

Side Effects:

Contact your health-care provider immediately if you experience:
- confusion.
- pain and swelling in the legs or arms.
- shortness of breath.
- vaginal bleeding or yeast infection.
- severe nausea, vomiting, or diarrhea.
- weakness on one side of your body or slurred speech.

Commonly reported side effects:
- changes in menstruation
- change in sexual desire or ability
- genital itching, rash, or dryness
- headache or mood changes
- hot flashes and bone pain
- nausea and/or vomiting
- weight gain or loss

Time Required for Drug to Take Effect:

Begins to work after 1 to 3 months of treatment but may require several more months to see full effect.

Symptoms of Overdose:

- cataracts
- fever and chills
- low white blood cell count
- swelling of the arms or legs (edema)

Special Notes:

- If you are still menstruating, you should use nonhormonal birth control to prevent pregnancy.

- Notify your doctor immediately if you become or think you may be pregnant.
- Periodic breast and gynecologic examinations are necessary while you are taking this medication.

tamsulosin

Brand Name: Flomax

Generic Available: no

Type of Drug: alpha–1 blocker

Used for: Treatment of the symptoms of an enlarged prostate.

How This Medication Works: Relaxes the muscles of the prostate, improving urinary symptoms.

Dosage Form and Strength: capsules (0.4 mg)

Storage:
- room temperature
- protect from light and moisture—do not store in bathroom or kitchen

Administration:
- Usually taken once daily.
- Take this medicine 30 minutes after the same meal (breakfast, lunch, or dinner) every day.
- Swallow capsules whole; do not chew, break, or crush.
- Drink plenty of noncaffeinated liquids, unless told otherwise by your health-care provider.

- Take a missed dose as soon as possible. However, if it is almost time for the next dose, skip the missed dose and return to your regular dosing schedule.

Precautions:
Do not use if:
- you are allergic to tamsulosin.

Talk to your doctor if:
- you are on blood pressure medication.
- you take another alpha blocker, such as prazosin (Minipress), terazosin (Hytrin), or doxazosin (Cardura).
- you are taking a medication for erectile dysfunction, such as sildenafil (Viagra), tadalafil, (Cialis), or vardenafil (Levitra).
- you have an allergy to sulfa.

Side Effects:
Contact your health-care provider immediately if you experience:
- signs of a life-threatening reaction, which include fever; wheezing; chest tightness; and itching or swelling of face, lips, tongue, or throat.
- severe dizziness or fainting.
- severe headache.
- worsening of urinary symptoms or an inability to pass urine.
- a rash.

Commonly reported side effects:
- dizziness
- headache

- nasal congestion or runny nose
- abnormal ejaculation

Time Required for Drug to Take Effect: Starts working within 8 hours after first dose, but may take up to 1 week of treatment to relieve symptoms.

Symptoms of Overdose:

- headache
- low blood pressure

Special Notes:

- This drug may cause dizziness when you first start therapy or if you restart therapy after several missed doses.
- Avoid driving or other tasks that require alertness until you see how this medicine affects you; it may cause drowsiness, dizziness, or impaired judgment.
- Drink plenty of fluids in hot weather to prevent dehydration.
- Check your blood pressure regularly.
- Avoid taking saw palmetto in combination with this medicine unless both are prescribed by the same health-care professional.
- This medication is usually prescribed for men. If you are a woman and your health-care provider has prescribed this medication, ask to make sure this is the right medication for you.
- Sound-alike/look-alike warning: Flomax may be confused with Fosamax or Volmax.

temazepam

Brand Name: Restoril

Generic Available: yes

Type of Drug: sedative (benzodiazepine)

Used for: Treatment of insomnia.

How This Medication Works: Enhances the activity of the brain chemical gamma-aminobutyric acid (GABA) to calm the brain.

Dosage Form and Strength: capsules (7.5 mg, 15 mg, 30 mg)

Storage:
- room temperature
- protect from moisture—do not store in bathroom or kitchen

Administration:
- Usually taken once daily at bedtime.
- Take approximately 30 minutes before the time you want to fall asleep.
- It may be prescribed on an "as-needed" basis.

Precautions:
Do not use if:
- you have had an allergic reaction to temazepam or a similar drug, such as diazepam, lorazepam, or oxazepam.
- you are or may be pregnant.

Talk to your doctor if:
- you are taking any other substance that can depress the central nervous system, such as alcohol, phenobarbital, or a narcotic (such as codeine).
- you have asthma, other lung problems, kidney disease, liver disease, or depression.
- you have sleep apnea or you have been told that you snore.
- you feel you need to take this drug for more than 7 days.

Side Effects:

Contact your health-care provider immediately if you experience:
- confusion or hallucinations.
- seizures or extreme weakness.
- a rash, difficulty breathing, or swelling of the face or throat.
- a "hangover" feeling or falls.

Commonly reported side effects:
- unsteadiness or drowsiness
- slurred speech or blurred vision

Time Required for Drug to Take Effect: Starts to have an effect within 15 to 45 minutes of taking a dose.

Symptoms of Overdose:
- continuing confusion or slurred speech
- severe weakness or drowsiness
- shortness of breath
- uncoordinated or difficult movement

Special Notes:

- If you have been taking this drug on a regular basis, consult your doctor before stopping.
- This drug may cause a "hangover" effect the next day, with daytime drowsiness or sedation. Avoid tasks that require alertness, such as driving, until you see how this drug affects you.
- Do not drink alcohol while taking this medication.
- The use of temazepam should be limited to 7 to 10 days to prevent worsening severity of insomnia upon discontinuation.
- Consult your pharmacist or health-care provider before using any over-the-counter drugs or herbal products while you are taking this drug.

terazosin

Brand Name: Hytrin

Generic Available: yes

Type of Drug: alpha–1 blocker

Used for: Treatment of high blood pressure or the symptoms of an enlarged prostate (benign prostate hyperplasia, or BPH).

How This Medication Works: Lowers blood pressure by relaxing arteries. It also relaxes the muscles of the prostate, improving urinary symptoms.

Dosage Form and Strength: capsules (1 mg, 2 mg, 5 mg, 10 mg)

Storage:
- room temperature
- protect from light and moisture—do not store in bathroom or kitchen

Administration:
- Usually taken once daily at bedtime.
- May be taken without regard to meals, but take with food if stomach upset occurs.
- Drink plenty of caffeine-free liquids while taking this medication, unless directed otherwise by your health-care provider.
- Take a missed dose as soon as possible. However, if it is almost time for the next dose, skip the missed dose and return to your regular dosing schedule.
- Do not stop using this medicine without consulting your health-care provider first. If you have not taken this medication in several days, you will need to use a lower dose when you do resume taking it; again, consult your health-care provider for more information.

Precautions:
Do not use if:
- you are allergic to terazosin, doxazosin, or prazosin.
- you are taking medication for erectile dysfunction, such as sildenafil (Viagra), tadalafil (Cialis), or vardenafil (Levitra).

Talk to your doctor if:
- you are taking another blood pressure drug.

- you take another alpha-blocker, such as prazosin (Minipress), tamsulosin (Flomax), doxazosin (Cardura), or alfuzosin (Uroxatral).

Side Effects:

Contact your health-care provider immediately if you experience:

- signs of a life-threatening reaction, which include fever; wheezing; chest tightness; and itching or swelling of face, lips, tongue, or throat.
- severe dizziness or fainting.
- severe headache.
- chest pain or discomfort.
- worsening of urinary symptoms or an inability to pass urine.
- a rash.

Commonly reported side effects:

- dizziness or weakness
- headache
- nasal congestion or runny nose
- change in sexual ability or desire

Time Required for Drug to Take Effect: Starts
working within several hours of taking the first dose, but may take up to 1 week of treatment to relieve symptoms.

Symptoms of Overdose:

- headache
- drowsiness
- low blood pressure

Special Notes:
- This drug may cause dizziness when you start therapy or if you restart therapy after missing doses.
- Avoid tasks that require alertness until you see how this medicine affects you; it may cause drowsiness, dizziness, or impaired judgment.
- Drink plenty of fluids in hot weather to prevent dehydration.
- Check your blood pressure regularly; consult your health-care provider for advice and instructions if you do not know how.
- Avoid taking saw palmetto in combination with this medicine unless both are prescribed by the same health-care provider.

theophylline

Brand Names:

Elixophyllin	Theo–24
Quibron	Theo-Dur
Slo-bid	T-Phyl
Slo-Phyllin	Uniphyl

Generic Available: yes

Type of Drug: bronchodilator

Used for: Treatment of asthma, chronic bronchitis, emphysema, and chronic obstructive pulmonary disease (COPD).

How This Medication Works: Causes the passageways in the lungs to dilate and strengthens the diaphragm muscle to help in breathing.

Dosage Form and Strength:
- tablets (100 mg, 125 mg, 200 mg, 250 mg, 300 mg, 400 mg, 450 mg)
- capsules (100 mg, 200 mg, 300 mg, 400 mg)
- solution (80 mg/15 mL)

Storage:
- room temperature
- protect from moisture—do not store in bathroom or kitchen

Administration:
- Swallow tablets and capsules whole; do not crush or chew.
- Certain theophylline products need to be taken on an empty stomach, while others work better or cause less stomach upset when taken with food. Make sure to ask your doctor and pharmacist how to take your theophylline: with or without food or with a full glass of water on an empty stomach.
- This medication is used to prevent breathing problems. It must be taken on a continual basis to ensure adequate concentrations in the blood.
- Take a missed dose as soon as possible. However, if it is almost time for the next dose, skip the missed dose and return to your regular dosing schedule.

Precautions:

Do not use if:

- you have had an allergic reaction to theophylline or another xanthine-related substance, such as caffeine.

Talk to your doctor if:

- you have liver, thyroid, or breast disease; a respiratory infection; diarrhea; an enlarged prostate; heart disease; high blood pressure (hypertension); or ulcers, heartburn, or other stomach problems.
- you smoke.
- you are taking any other medication, especially a steroid, antibiotic, nicotine replacement product, or medication for heart disease, high blood pressure, stomach problems, or seizures.

Side Effects:

Contact your health-care provider immediately if you experience:

- a skin rash, hives, or itching.
- dizziness or light-headedness.
- irregular or fast heartbeat or difficulty breathing.
- trembling or muscle twitching.
- nausea, vomiting, diarrhea, or stomach cramps.
- irritability or trouble sleeping.
- seizures.

Commonly reported side effects:

- nausea and/or vomiting
- nervousness
- tremor

Time Required for Drug to Take Effect: Starts
to work 1½ to 3 hours after taking the first dose, but
you must take theophylline on a continual basis to help
prevent breathing problems.

Symptoms of Overdose:
- dizziness or light-headedness
- difficulty breathing
- irregular or fast heartbeat
- headache
- irritability
- loss of appetite
- trembling or muscle twitching
- nausea, vomiting, diarrhea, or stomach cramps
- seizures

Special Notes:
- Check with your physician or pharmacist before
  using any over-the-counter medications while you
  are taking this drug.
- Theophylline has caffeinelike effects. Therefore,
  avoid consuming large amounts of caffeine while
  you are taking theophylline.
- You will need to have blood tests while you are
  being treated with theophylline to determine how
  much of the medication is in your bloodstream.
- Certain medications, cigarette smoking, and
  eating charcoal-broiled foods can increase your
  liver's ability to metabolize theophylline. Consult
  your doctor or pharmacist before taking any
  new medication. Also, consult your health-care
  provider about your diet and, if you smoke, about
  methods for quitting.

timolol

Brand Names:
Istalol
Timoptic
Timoptic-XE

Generic Available: yes

Type of Drug: topical ophthalmologic agent

Used for: Treatment of glaucoma (increased eye pressure).

How This Medication Works: Appears to lower the pressure in the eye by decreasing fluid production and possibly encouraging fluid outflow from the eye.

Dosage Form and Strength: ophthalmic solution and gel-forming solution (0.25%, 0.5%)

Storage:
- room temperature; do not freeze
- keep cap on when not in use
- protect from light and heat

Administration:
- Usually administered in both eyes once or twice daily, depending on the formulation.
- Wash your hands thoroughly with soap and water before and after administering this drug.
- Remove contact lenses before administering medication; wait at least 15 minutes after the full dose is administered to insert lenses.
- Avoid touching the dropper tip of the bottle to your eye or anything else.

- While tilting your head back, pull down the lower eyelid with your index finger to form a pocket.
- With the other hand, hold the bottle (tip down) as close to the eye as possible without touching it.
- Gently squeeze the dropper so that one drop falls into the pocket made by the lower eyelid.
- After administering the drug, keep your eyes gently closed, and apply pressure to the inside corner of the treated eye for 2 to 3 minutes to keep the medication from draining out through the tear duct.
- Replace and tighten the cap right away and do not wipe or rinse the dropper tip.
- The eye can hold only one drop at a time; wait at least 5 minutes between drops if you have more than one drop or another medicine to apply.
- Take a missed dose as soon as possible. However, if it is almost time for the next dose, skip the missed dose and return to your dosing schedule.

Precautions:

Do not use if:
- you have had an allergic reaction to timolol or another beta-blocker, such as acebutolol, atenolol, betaxolol, carteolol, labetalol, metoprolol, nadolol, propranolol, or sotalol.
- you have severe asthma or other lung disease, heart failure, heart block, cardiac shock, or slow heart rate.

Talk to your doctor if:
- you have experienced heart failure.
- you have breathing problems, kidney disease, a history of heart block, diabetes, an overactive

thyroid (hyperthyroidism), myasthenia gravis, or peripheral vascular disease.
- you are taking any other medication, especially a beta-blocker (such as acebutolol, atenolol, betaxolol, carteolol, labetalol, metoprolol, nadolol, propranolol, or sotalol), asthma or breathing medications (such as inhalers or theophylline), verapamil, or nifedipine.

Side Effects:
Contact your health-care provider immediately if you experience:
- severe irritation, redness, or swelling of the eye or eyelid.
- a skin rash, hives, or itching.
- wheezing or trouble breathing.
- anxiety or confusion.
- chest pain.
- slow heart rate.
- headache.
- severe dizziness.

Commonly reported side effects:
- stinging of the eye upon administration of the drug; this should stop in a few minutes
- dizziness or light-headedness

Time Required for Drug to Take Effect:
Begins to work immediately after a dose is administered, but controls glaucoma only as long as treatment is continued.

Symptoms of Overdose:
- severe dizziness or light-headedness
- slow heart rate

- wheezing or trouble breathing
- low blood pressure

Special Notes:

- Eyedrops are hard to use; have someone help you put them in if possible. Tell your doctor if you cannot put them in yourself and have no one to help you.
- Tell the doctor or dentist you are taking timolol if you are going to have surgery or emergency treatment.
- Timolol may cause light sensitivity; wear sunglasses when outdoors during daylight hours.
- If you are using the gel-forming timolol solution and you also use another eye medicine, apply the other medicine first and wait at least 10 minutes before applying the timolol.

tiotropium

Brand Name: Spiriva

Generic Available: no

Type of Drug: anticholinergic agent

Used for: Treatment of lung diseases, such as chronic obstructive pulmonary disease (COPD) and emphysema.

How This Medication Works: Relaxes the muscles that surround the airways, allowing them to widen and open; however, tiotropium is not to be used as a rescue medication or for immediate relief.

Dosage Form and Strength: inhaler (using
18 mcg capsules)

Storage:
- room temperature
- protect from light and moisture—do not store in bathroom or kitchen
- store capsules in original container and use right after opening

Administration:
- Do not swallow capsule—it is to be inhaled using the HandiHaler device.
- Taken once daily.
- Take at a similar time each day.
- May be taken without regard to meals.
- Take a missed dose as soon as possible. However, if it is almost time for the next dose, skip the missed dose and return to your regular dosing schedule. To gain the most benefit, do not miss doses.

How to use:
- Read and follow all instructions provided with inhaler; proper use is very important.
- Remove capsule from foil blister just before using.
- Place capsule in the capsule chamber at the base of the HandiHaler inhaler.
- Close mouthpiece until you hear a click, leaving dustcap open. Push green button to pierce capsule.
- Exhale fully, but do not exhale into inhaler.
- Tilt head slightly back and inhale slowly and deeply; the capsule may vibrate inside the inhaler.
- Hold breath as long as possible.

- Keeping the same capsule in the device, exhale and inhale again (in case any medication was left behind).

Precautions:
Do not use if:
- you are allergic to tiotropium or any other part of this medicine.
- you are having a breathing attack and need immediate relief.

Talk to your doctor if:
- you have uncontrolled narrow-angle glaucoma, urinary retention, or myasthenia gravis.

Side Effects:
Contact your health-care provider immediately if you experience:
- signs of a life-threatening reaction, which include wheezing; chest tightness; itching; or swelling of face, lips, tongue, or throat.
- difficulty breathing.
- significant nasal irritation.
- eye irritation or sudden change in vision.

Commonly reported side effects:
- constipation
- dry mouth
- sore throat
- muscle aches
- high blood-sugar levels (talk with your doctor to determine what blood-sugar levels are high for you)

Time Required for Drug to Take Effect: May take 3 hours to up to 1 week to reach maximum effec-

tiveness. Tiotropium should not be used as a rescue medication for immediate relief of symptoms.

Symptoms of Overdose:

- red itchy eyes
- dry mouth/throat
- nausea
- cough
- headache
- nervousness
- fast heartbeat

Special Notes:

- This medication should not be used as a rescue medication for immediate relief of symptoms.
- Use a new HandiHaler inhaler device with each new refill of capsules.
- Chewing gum, sucking on hard candy, or brushing your teeth may help with the side effect of dry mouth.
- Do not get tiotropium in your eyes. If you do and experience eye pain, blurred vision, or other vision changes, contact your doctor immediately.

tolterodine

Brand Names: Detrol, Detrol LA

Generic Available:

- Detrol: yes
- Detrol LA: no

Type of Drug: cholinergic antagonist

Used for: Treatment of overactive bladder.

How This Medication Works: Blocks the action of a chemical that causes the bladder to spasm, decreasing symptoms of urgency, frequent urination, and incontinence.

Dosage Form and Strength:
- tablets (1 mg, 2 mg)
- long-acting capsules (2 mg, 4 mg)

Storage:
- room temperature
- protect from heat, light, and moisture—do not store in bathroom or kitchen

Administration:
- Detrol is usually taken twice daily; Detrol LA is usually taken once daily.
- May be taken without regard to meals, but take with food if stomach upset occurs.
- Do not break, chew, or crush the long-acting (LA) form of this medicine.
- Take a missed dose as soon as possible. However, if it is almost time for the next dose, skip the missed dose and return to your regular dosing schedule.

Precautions:
Do not use if:
- you are allergic to tolterodine.

- you have uncontrolled narrow-angle glaucoma, urinary retention, an enlarged colon, intestinal blockage, ulcerative colitis, or myasthenia gravis.

Talk to your doctor if:
- you have a bladder or gastric obstructive disorder.
- you are being treated for narrow-angle glaucoma.
- you have kidney or liver disease.
- you are taking erythromycin, clarithromycin, itraconazole, ketoconazole, or vinblastine.

Side Effects:

Contact your health-care provider immediately if you experience:
- signs of a life-threatening reaction, which include fever; wheezing; chest tightness; and itching or swelling of face, lips, tongue, or throat.
- inability to urinate or pain when urinating.
- a racing heartbeat.
- severe dizziness or fainting.
- a significant change in your ability to think clearly and logically.
- nervousness and excitability.
- severe flushing.
- increasing memory problems or confusion.

Commonly reported side effects:
- dry mouth
- headache
- dizziness or drowsiness
- constipation
- abdominal pain
- blurred vision

Time Required for Drug to Take Effect: Can take from 1 to 4 weeks of treatment to reach maximum effectiveness.

Symptoms of Overdose:
- low blood pressure
- tremor or irritability
- psychotic behavior
- hallucinations
- flushing
- difficulty breathing
- paralysis
- seizures
- coma

Special Notes:
- Avoid driving until you see how this medicine affects you; it may cause dizziness.
- Do not take Saint John's wort while you are taking this medication.
- Chewing gum, sucking on ice chips or hard candy, or using a saliva substitute may help relieve dry mouth.
- The outer shell of the long-acting capsule may show up in the stool; this is normal—the active ingredients in the capsule will have already been absorbed by the body.
- Avoid alcohol or other medicines and natural products that slow your actions and reactions while you are taking this medication.
- Consult your health-care provider or pharmacist before starting any other medicine, including

over-the-counter drugs, natural products, or vitamins, while you are on this medication.
- Consult your doctor about re-evaluating your use of this medication on a regular basis.

tramadol

Brand Names: Ultram, Ultram ER

Generic Available:
- Ultram: yes
- Ultram ER: no

Type of Drug: analgesic

Used for: Relief of pain.

How This Medication Works: Decreases the feeling of pain and the body's response to pain.

Dosage Form and Strength:
- tablets (50 mg)
- extended-release tablets (100 mg, 200 mg, 300 mg)

Storage:
- room temperature
- protect from moisture—do not store in bathroom or kitchen

Administration:
- Take with milk or food if stomach upset occurs.
- Do not exceed the maximum number of doses per day. Never take more tablets per dose than your doctor has prescribed.

- Swallow extended-release tablets whole; do not crush or chew.
- This medication may be prescribed on an "as-needed" basis.

Precautions:

Do not use if:
- you are allergic to tramadol or any opioid drug.

Talk to your doctor if:
- you have alcoholism or other substance-abuse problem; brain disease, head injury, or increased pressure in the brain; colitis; a history of seizures; emotional problems or mental illness; emphysema, asthma, or other lung disease; kidney, liver, or thyroid disease; prostate or urination problems; or gallbladder disease or gallstones.
- you are taking any other medication, especially naltrexone or a medication that can cause drowsiness, such as an antihistamine, phenobarbital, a benzodiazepine, a muscle relaxant, or an antidepressant.

Side Effects:

Contact your health-care provider immediately if you experience:
- a skin rash or hives.
- irregular breathing or difficulty breathing.
- seizures or fainting.
- painful or difficult urination.
- severe nausea, vomiting, or constipation.
- poor pain control.
- hallucinations or confusion.
- trembling or uncontrolled muscle movements.

Commonly reported side effects:
- constipation
- drowsiness or dizziness
- dry mouth
- loss of appetite
- headache
- nervousness or restlessness

Time Required for Drug to Take Effect: Starts to work within 30 to 60 minutes after taking a dose.

Symptoms of Overdose:
- cold, clammy skin
- seizures
- severe dizziness, drowsiness, or confusion
- continued nausea or vomiting
- severe nervousness or restlessness
- difficulty breathing
- slowed heartbeat or stopping of heart

Special Notes:
- This medication may make you drowsy or dizzy. Do not drive a motor vehicle or operate potentially dangerous machinery while you are taking this medication.
- Tramadol will cause constipation. This side effect may be diminished by drinking 6 to 8 full glasses of water each day. Add more fresh fruit to your diet. If using tramadol for chronic pain, ask your doctor about a stool softener–laxative combination.
- Check with your physician or pharmacist before using any over-the-counter medication while you are taking this drug.

- It is not known whether tramadol can be habit-forming (causing mental or physical dependence); discuss this with your health-care provider.
- Do not stop taking this medication abruptly.
- Nausea and vomiting may occur after the first few doses; this effect should diminish with time.
- Do not drink alcohol while you are taking this medication.
- If you think you or anyone else may have taken an overdose of this drug, get emergency help immediately.
- Use this medication as prescribed; do not take a larger dose or use the drug more frequently than prescribed by your doctor.

tramadol and acetaminophen combination

Brand Name: Ultracet

Generic Available: yes

Type of Drug: analgesic combination

Used for: Short-term (5-day maximum) management of acute pain.

How This Medication Works: Tramadol and acetaminophen alter the body's perception of pain, decreasing pain sensations.

Dosage Form and Strength: tablets (37.5 mg tramadol/325 mg acetaminophen)

Storage:
- room temperature
- protect from moisture—do not store in bathroom or kitchen

Administration:
- Your dose will depend on your pain and your medical condition(s). It may be prescribed on an "as-needed" basis.
- Never take more tablets than your health-care provider has prescribed.
- May be taken without regard to meals, but take with food if stomach upset occurs.
- Drink plenty of caffeine-free liquids unless directed otherwise by your health-care provider.

Precautions:
Do not use if:
- you are allergic to tramadol, acetaminophen, or opioid narcotics.
- you have severe liver disease.

Talk to your doctor if:
- you have a history of seizures, alcohol or drug abuse, liver or kidney disease, lung disease, head trauma, or increased pressure on the brain.
- you take other pain medication, sleeping pills, or any drug for depression or a mental problem.

Side Effects:
Contact your health-care provider immediately if you experience:
- signs of a life-threatening reaction, which include fever; wheezing; chest tightness; and itching or swelling of face, lips, tongue, or throat.

- severe dizziness or fainting.
- difficulty breathing.
- confusion.
- poor pain control.
- severe nausea or vomiting.
- severe constipation.
- extreme fatigue or weakness.
- a rash.

Commonly reported side effects:
- dizziness or drowsiness
- blurred vision and dry mouth
- headache
- nausea and/or vomiting
- constipation

Time Required for Drug to Take Effect: Starts working within 30 to 60 minutes after a dose has been taken.

Symptoms of Overdose:
- slowed breathing
- confusion
- drowsiness
- seizures
- coma

Symptoms associated with acetaminophen overdose may not occur until 2 to 4 days after the overdose is taken, but it is extremely important to begin treatment for acetaminophen overdose as soon as possible in order to prevent liver damage and even death.

Special Notes:
- If you are 65 or older, use this medicine with caution; you may experience more side effects.
- Avoid alcohol and other medicines or natural products that slow your actions and reactions, such as sedatives, mood stabilizers, antihistamines, and other pain medicines, while you are taking this drug.
- Avoid driving or other tasks that require alertness until you see how this medicine affects you.
- Constipation, a minor side effect, may be relieved by drinking more water, eating foods that are high in fiber (vegetables, fruits, bran), and exercising.
- Tramadol may be habit-forming. If you are taking this medication on a daily basis, do not abruptly discontinue it without first consulting your health-care provider.

travoprost

Brand Name: Travatan

Generic Available: no

Type of Drug: ophthalmologic prostaglandin analogue

Used for: Decreasing elevated eye pressure in patients with glaucoma or ocular hypertension.

How This Medication Works: Lowers pressure in the eye.

Dosage Form and Strength: solution (0.004%)

Storage:

- room temperature
- with cap on
- discard unused portion after 6 weeks
- protect from light and heat

Administration:

- For use in the eye only.
- Usually used once daily in the evening.
- Wash hands before and after use.
- Remove contact lenses before using medicine.
- Do not touch the container tip to the eye or to anything else.
- After administering the drug, keep your eyes gently closed, and apply pressure to the inside corner of the treated eye for 2 to 3 minutes to keep the drug from draining out through the tear duct.
- Do not wipe or rinse the dropper tip.
- The eye can hold only one drop at a time; wait at least 5 minutes between drops if you have more than one drop or another medicine to apply.
- Wait at least 15 minutes after using this medicine to insert contact lenses.
- Administer a missed dose as soon as possible. However, if it is the next day when you remember, skip the missed dose and return to your regular dosing schedule; do not use more than your usual dose for the day.

Precautions:

Do not use if:
- you are allergic to travoprost or benzalkonium chloride.

Talk to your doctor if:
- you have an eye infection or have had recent eye surgery or eye trauma.

Side Effects:

Contact your health-care provider immediately if you experience:
- signs of a life-threatening reaction, which include fever; wheezing; chest tightness; and itching or swelling of face, lips, tongue, or throat.
- a sudden change in vision, eye pain, or irritation.
- chest pain or pressure.
- sparks or flashes of light.

Commonly reported side effects:
- headache
- eye irritation or short-term discomfort after use
- eye irritation from bright lights
- eye color change with use
- darkening of eyelashes and skin around the eye

Time Required for Drug to Take Effect: Starts lowering eye pressure within 24 hours after first dose.

Symptoms of Overdose: No information currently available; contact local poison control center.

Special Notes:
- Have your eye pressure checked regularly.

- Use caution when driving or doing other tasks that require clear vision if this medication causes your vision to blur.
- Wear sunglasses if bright light irritates your eyes.
- Darkening of the eyelashes or skin around the eye is harmless but may be permanent.

trazodone

Brand Name: Desyrel

Generic Available: yes

Type of Drug: antidepressant

Used for: Treatment of depression, anxiety, and sleep problems associated with depression.

How This Medication Works: Increases the action of serotonin and other brain chemicals.

Dosage Form and Strength: tablets (50 mg, 100 mg, 150 mg, 300 mg)

Storage:
- room temperature
- protect from moisture—do not store in bathroom or kitchen

Administration:
- Initial dose given once daily at bedtime for older adults, but may be increased to 2 to 3 times daily.
- Take with food to reduce stomach upset.
- Take a missed dose as soon as possible. However, if it is almost time for the next dose, skip the

missed dose and return to your regular dosing schedule.

Precautions:

Do not use if:
- you have had an allergic reaction to trazodone.

Talk to your doctor if:
- you have heart disease or have recently had a heart attack.
- you have ever had liver or kidney problems.
- you are taking medication for high blood pressure (hypertension), depression, anxiety, a sleep disorder, seizures, or mental illness of any type.

Side Effects:

Contact your health-care provider immediately if you experience:
- **suicidal thoughts or a desire to harm yourself.**
- confusion, agitation, or extreme excitement.
- dizziness or fainting when standing up.
- chest pain.
- shortness of breath.
- inability to urinate.
- prolonged painful penile erection.

Commonly reported side effects:
- drowsiness or dizziness
- vivid dreams
- dry mouth or unpleasant taste
- headache
- nausea and/or vomiting, constipation
- blurred vision
- muscle aches or pains or fatigue

Time Required for Drug to Take Effect: Some
symptoms may improve within the first few weeks
of treatment, but it may take 4 to 8 weeks to reach
maximum effectivess.

Symptoms of Overdose:
- weakness, severe drowsiness
- severe nausea or vomiting
- dizziness or fainting when standing up
- headache
- urinary accidents

Special Notes:
- The desire to harm yourself is a serious symptom
  of depression. If you are planning to harm
  yourself, call 911 immediately.
- Know which "target symptoms" (restlessness,
  depressed mood, worry, fear, or changes in
  sleep or appetite) you are being treated for
  and be prepared to tell your doctor if your
  target symptoms are improving, worsening, or
  unchanged.
- Do not drink alcohol while using this medicine.
- Never increase your dose or discontinue this
  drug without consulting your doctor first. This
  medication should be withdrawn gradually.

triamterene and hydrochloro-
thiazide combination

Brand Names: Dyazide, Maxzide
Generic Available: yes

Type of Drug: diuretic

Used for: Treatment of fluid retention (edema) and high blood pressure (hypertension).

How This Medication Works: Interferes with sodium reabsorption in the kidneys, thereby increasing water excretion. Triamterene is used in combination with hydrochlorothiazide to prevent the loss of potassium.

Dosage Form and Strength:
- tablets (37.5 mg triamterene/25 mg hydro-chlorothiazide, 75 mg/50 mg)
- capsules (37.5 mg/25 mg, 50 mg/25 mg)

Storage:
- room temperature
- protect from moisture—do not store in bathroom or kitchen

Administration:
- Usually taken once daily, in the morning.
- May be taken without regard to meals, but take with food or milk if stomach upset occurs.
- Take a missed dose as soon as possible. However, if it is almost time for the next dose, skip the missed dose and return to your regular dosing schedule.

Precautions:
Do not use if:
- you are allergic to triamterene.
- you are allergic to hydrochlorothiazide or other thiazide diuretic, such as chlorthalidone or metolazone.

- you are allergic to sulfa drugs, including diabetes medication (tolazamide, glipizide, or glyburide), acetazolamide, loop diuretics (such as furosemide or bumetanide), or sulfa antibacterial medication (such as sulfamethoxazole).

Talk to your doctor if:
- you have liver disease, kidney disease, or gout.
- you are taking allopurinol, warfarin, digoxin, lithium, a diuretic, methyldopa, an oral diabetes drug (such as tolazamide, glipizide, or glyburide), insulin, cholestyramine, a potassium supplement, amantadine, an angiotensin-converting (ACE) enzyme inhibitor (such as captopril, enalapril, lisinopril, or benazepril), or cimetidine.

Side Effects:

Contact your health-care provider immediately if you experience:
- extreme weakness, muscle cramps, or tingling.
- severe nausea or vomiting.
- seizures.
- chest pain or pressure.
- severe dizziness or fainting.
- a skin rash or swelling of the face or throat.

Commonly reported side effects:
- dry mouth
- drowsiness or dizziness
- headache

Time Required for Drug to Take Effect: Starts

to work 2 to 4 hours after the first dose, but may take several days of treatment to reach maximum effect.

Symptoms of Overdose:
- nausea, vomiting, and diarrhea
- confusion
- extreme muscle weakness
- very low blood pressure

Special Notes:
- Avoid potassium-containing salt substitutes while taking this drug. Triamterene may cause your body to retain potassium.
- Your doctor will check your blood count, kidney function, and electrolyte (sodium and potassium) levels periodically during therapy.
- Use a sunblock with at least SPF 15 when outside because this medication may increase your sensitivity to the sun.
- To ease dry mouth symptoms, chew gum, suck on ice chips or hard candy, or try a saliva substitute.
- Weigh yourself periodically while you are taking this drug. If you gain or lose significant weight, call your doctor.
- Changing positions slowly when sitting and/or standing up may help decrease dizziness caused by this medication.
- If you notice dizziness or drowsiness, avoid activities requiring mental alertness, such as driving a motor vehicle or operating dangerous machinery.
- If you have diabetes, you may need to check your blood glucose more frequently while taking this medication.

trospium

Brand Name: Sanctura

Generic Available: no

Type of Drug: cholinergic antagonist

Used for: Treatment of overactive bladder symptoms.

How This Medication Works: Blocks the action of a chemical that causes the bladder to spasm, which causes symptoms of urgency, frequent urination, and incontinence.

Dosage Form and Strength: tablets (20 mg)

Storage:
- room temperature
- protect from heat, light, and moisture—do not store in bathroom or kitchen

Administration:
- Usually taken twice daily, but older individuals can take it once daily (talk with your doctor to see if you fit a once-daily profile).
- This medicine should be taken on an empty stomach, 1 hour before or two hours after a meal.
- Take a missed dose as soon as possible. However, if it is almost time for the next dose, skip the missed dose and return to your regular dosing schedule.

Precautions:

Do not use if:

- you are allergic to trospium.
- you have uncontrolled narrow-angle glaucoma, urinary retention, or myasthenia gravis.

Talk to your doctor if:

- you have a bladder disorder or gastric obstructive disorder.
- you are being treated for narrow-angle glaucoma.
- you have kidney disease or liver disease.
- you take metformin (Fortamet, Glucophage, Glucophage XR, Riomet) or morphine (Avinza, Kadian, MS Contin, MSIR, Oramorph SR, Rescudose, Roxanol, Roxanol 100).

Side Effects:

Contact your health-care provider immediately if you experience:

- signs of a life-threatening reaction, which include wheezing; chest tightness; itching; or swelling of face, lips, tongue, or throat.
- the inability to start urinating.
- a racing heartbeat.
- confusion or become unable to think clearly.

Commonly reported side effects:

- dry mouth
- headache
- dizziness
- constipation
- upset stomach

Time Required for Drug to Take Effect: Starts
working 3 to 12 hours after taking a dose.

Symptoms of Overdose:
- blurred vision
- hallucinations
- racing heartbeat
- chest pain

Special Notes:
- This medication can cause dizziness, so avoid driving or engaging in tasks that require alertness until you know how your body responds to this drug.
- Chewing gum, sucking on hard candy, or brushing your teeth may help with the side effect of dry mouth.
- Drink plenty of noncaffeinated liquids, unless told otherwise by your health-care provider.

valproic acid

Brand Names:
Depakene
Depakote
Depakote ER

Generic Available: yes

Type of Drug: antiepileptic

Used for: Treatment of epilepsy, migraine headaches, and bipolar disorder.

How This Medication Works: Believed to increase the amount of the chemical gamma-

aminobutyric acid (GABA) to stabilize and calm the brain.

Dosage Form and Strength:
- tablets (125 mg, 250 mg, 500 mg)
- capsules (250 mg)
- delayed-release capsules (125 mg)
- oral syrup (250 mg/5 mL)
- sprinkles in capsules (125 mg)

Storage:
- room temperature
- protect from moisture—do not store in bathroom or kitchen

Administration:
- Swallow tablets, capsules, and delayed-release capsules whole; do not break, crush, or chew.
- Depakote Sprinkle capsules may be opened and the contents sprinkled on soft food or into liquid.
- Take syrup as is or mix with other liquids such as water or juice.
- Take with food to avoid stomach upset.
- Take a missed dose as soon as possible. However, if it is almost time for the next dose, skip the missed dose and return to your dosing schedule.

Precautions:
Do not use if:
- you've had an allergic reaction to valproic acid.
- you have severe liver disease.

Talk to your doctor if:
- you are taking any other medication, especially any other seizure medicine, chlorpromazine, cimetidine, rifampin, a salicylate (such as aspirin),

a benzodiazepine (such as diazepam, clonazepam, or lorazepam), warfarin, or zidovudine.

- you have kidney disease, liver disease, or a history of pancreatitis.

Side Effects:

Contact your health-care provider immediately if you experience:

- **continued nausea, vomiting, or stomach pain.**
- **yellowing of the skin or eyes.**
- extreme tiredness or weakness.
- mood changes or confusion.
- unusual bleeding or bruising.
- dark urine.
- a rash or facial swelling.

Commonly reported side effects:

- weakness or drowsiness
- hair loss
- nausea, vomiting, diarrhea, or stomach pain
- trembling of the hands
- weight loss or gain
- dizziness
- nervousness or trouble sleeping

Time Required for Drug to Take Effect:

Decreases the number and/or frequency of seizures and migraines as long as it is taken.

Symptoms of Overdose:

- hallucinations
- sedation or deep sleep
- double vision or spots before the eyes
- incoordination

Special Notes:

- This medication may cause drowsiness. Use caution when driving a motor vehicle or operating dangerous machinery.
- Do not discontinue this medication without first talking with your doctor.
- You will need to have periodic blood tests to monitor your blood counts and liver function.

valsartan

Brand Name: Diovan

Generic Available: no

Type of Drug: angiotensin II receptor blocker

Used for: Treatment of high blood pressure (hypertension) or heart failure.

How This Medication Works: Lowers blood pressure by blocking the effects of angiotensin, a strong chemical that causes blood vessels to constrict.

Dosage Form and Strength: tablets (40 mg, 80 mg, 160 mg, 320 mg)

Storage:

- room temperature
- protect from heat, light, and moisture—do not store in bathroom or kitchen

Administration:

- Usually taken once or twice daily.

- May be taken without regard to meals, but take with food if stomach upset occurs.
- Avoid antacids for 2 hours after taking this drug.
- Take a missed dose as soon as possible. However, if it is almost time for the next dose, skip the missed dose and return to your regular dosing schedule.

Precautions:

Do not use if:

- **you are pregnant or could become pregnant.**
- you are allergic to valsartan or have had adverse reactions to other drugs in this class, such as irbesartan or candesartan.
- you have bilateral renal artery stenosis (blockage of the kidney's blood vessels), severe kidney disease, or hyperaldosteronism.

Talk to your doctor if:

- you are taking a potassium-containing salt substitute, potassium-sparing diuretic, or a potassium supplement.
- you are allergic to any angiotensin-converting enzyme (ACE) inhibitor.
- you have liver or kidney disease.
- you are taking lithium or allopurinol.
- you have low blood pressure.
- you become dehydrated.

Side Effects:

Contact your health-care provider immediately if you experience:

- signs of a life-threatening reaction, which include fever; wheezing; chest tightness; and itching or swelling of face, lips, tongue, or throat.

- severe headache that does not go away.
- severe dizziness or fainting.
- chest pain or palpitations.
- swelling in the hands, ankles, or feet.
- a rash.

Commonly reported side effects:
- dizziness and fatigue
- low blood pressure
- cough
- diarrhea

Time Required for Drug to Take Effect:

This medication begins to lower your blood pressure within 2 to 6 hours after you take the first dose; however it may take 4 to 8 weeks of continued treatment for the medication to reach its maximum effectiveness.

Symptoms of Overdose:

- low blood pressure
- slow heart rate
- high potassium levels

Special Notes:

- Do not consume salt subsitutes that contain potassium while you are taking this drug (ask your pharmacist about what you are using if you are not sure).
- Follow a diet plan and exercise program recommended by your health-care provider.
- Consult your health-care provider before using over-the-counter products, because some can increase blood pressure.

- Avoid driving or other tasks that require alertness until you see how this medicine affects you.
- To avoid dizziness, rise slowly over several minutes from a sitting or lying position.
- Drink plenty of fluids in hot weather to prevent dehydration.

valsartan and hydrochlorothiazide combination

Brand Name: Diovan HCT

Generic Available: no

Type of Drug: antihypertensive combination (angiotensin II receptor blocker and thiazide diuretic)

Used for: Treatment of high blood pressure (hypertension).

How This Medication Works: Valsartan and hydrochlorothiazide is a combination of two drugs that work together to lower blood pressure. Valsartan lowers blood pressure by blocking the effects of angiotensin, a strong chemical that causes blood vessels to constrict. Hydrochlorothiazide lowers blood pressure by decreasing the amount of excess fluid in the body, decreasing the amount of work the heart has to do.

Dosage Form and Strength: tablets (80 mg valsartan/12.5 mg hydrochlorothiazide, 160 mg/12.5 mg, 160 mg/25 mg)

Storage:
- room temperature
- protect from light and moisture—do not store in bathroom or kitchen

Administration:
- Usually taken once daily.
- Take at a similar time each day.
- May be taken without regard to meals, but take with food if stomach upset occurs.
- Take a missed dose as soon as possible. However, if it is almost time for the next dose, skip the missed dose and return to your dosing schedule.

Precautions:
Do not use if:
- **you are pregnant or could become pregnant.**
- you are allergic to valsartan (or related drugs such as candesartan, eprosartan, losartan, or olmesartan), thiazide diuretics, carbonic anhydrase inhibitors, loop diuretics, or sulfonamides.
- you have bilateral renal artery stenosis.

Talk to your doctor if:
- you have diabetes, gout, or liver or kidney disease.
- you have had angioedema (swelling of the face or mouth).
- you are taking allopurinol, lithium, potassium supplements, spironolactone, or triamterene.
- you have low blood pressure or become dehydrated.

Side Effects:

Contact your health-care provider immediately if you experience:

- signs of a life-threatening reaction, which include wheezing; chest tightness; and itching or swelling of face, lips, tongue, or throat.
- severe dizziness, headache, or fainting.
- chest pain or palpitations.
- a change in amount of urine or frequency of urination.
- severe dry mouth, increased thirst, and constant nausea or vomiting.
- numbness, tingling, or muscle cramps.

Commonly reported side effects:

- dizziness or light-headedness
- fatigue
- diarrhea

Time Required for Drug to Take Effect:

Starts lowering blood pressure within 24 hours of first dose, but may take 2 to 4 weeks of treatment to reach maximum effectiveness.

Symptoms of Overdose:

- low blood pressure
- slowed heart rate
- high potassium levels
- generalized weakness
- confusion
- muscle weakness

Special Notes:

- Do not use potassium-containing salt substitutes while taking this drug.

- Follow a diet plan and exercise program recommended by your health-care provider.
- Consult your health-care provider before using over-the-counter products, because some can increase blood pressure.
- Avoid driving or other tasks that require alertness until you see how this medicine affects you; it may cause drowsiness or dizziness.
- Limit alcohol intake while on this medication.
- To avoid dizziness, rise slowly over several minutes from a sitting or lying position.

venlafaxine

Brand Names: Effexor, Effexor XR

Generic Available: yes (tablet only)

Type of Drug: antidepressant

Used for: Treatment of depression, generalized anxiety disorder, and social anxiety disorder.

How This Medication Works: May prolong the action of the brain chemicals serotonin and norepinephrine.

Dosage Form and Strength:
- tablets (25 mg, 37.5 mg, 50 mg, 75 mg, 100 mg)
- 24-hour capsules (37.5 mg, 75 mg, 150 mg)

Storage:
- room temperature
- protect from moisture—do not store in bathroom or kitchen

Administration:

- Tablets usually taken 2 or 3 times daily; capsules taken once daily.
- Take with food.
- Swallow capsules whole; do not break, crush, or chew.
- Do not abruptly stop taking this medication.
- Take a missed dose as soon as possible. However, if it is almost time for the next dose, skip the missed dose and return to your regular dosing schedule.

Precautions:

Do not use if:

- you are allergic to venlafaxine.
- you have taken a monoamine oxidase (MAO) inhibitor, such as phenelzine or tranylcypromine, within the past 14 days.

Talk to your doctor if:

- you have ever had liver problems, kidney problems, seizures, or bipolar disorder.
- you have had a recent heart attack or have high blood pressure, heart disease, or thyroid disease.
- you drink alcoholic beverages.

Side Effects:

Contact your health-care provider immediately if you experience:

- **suicidal thoughts or a desire to harm yourself.**
- headache.
- seizures.
- dizziness or fainting when standing up.
- vision changes.

- chest pain or rapid heartbeat.
- suicidal thoughts.
- difficulty breathing.
- unusual restlessness, excitement, or confusion.
- severe nausea or vomiting.
- severe weakness.

Commonly reported side effects:
- drowsiness, dizziness, or light-headedness
- dry mouth
- nervousness, anxiety, or difficulty sleeping
- decreased sexual interest or ability
- decreased appetite or nausea
- diarrhea or constipation
- sweating

Time Required for Drug to Take Effect: Some patients may notice improved appetite or sleep within the first few weeks of treatment, but it may take 4 to 8 weeks to reach maximum effectiveness.

Symptoms of Overdose:
- extreme drowsiness or weakness
- seizures
- rapid heartbeat

Special Notes:
- Venlafaxine may interact with several other drugs commonly taken by older adults. To avoid interactions, show your doctor and pharmacist a list of all the drugs, including nonprescription ones, you take regularly or on occasion.
- Never increase your dose without the advice of your doctor. Even small changes in dose may increase the risk of unwanted effects. Contact

your health-care provider immediately if you take more of this medication than was prescribed.

- Venlafaxine may cause an increase in blood pressure. Have your blood pressure checked regularly.
- Know which "target symptoms" (restlessness, worry, fear, or changes in sleep, mood, or appetite) you are being treated for and be prepared to tell your doctor if your target symptoms are improving, worsening, or unchanged.
- Do not discontinue this drug without first talking with your doctor.
- Do not drink alcohol while taking this medication.

verapamil

Brand Names:

Calan
Calan SR
Covera-HS
Isoptin

Isoptin SR
Verelan
Verelan PM

Generic Available: yes

Type of Drug: cardiovascular (calcium channel blocker)

Used for: Treatment of angina, high blood pressure (hypertension), and abnormal heart rhythms (arrhythmias).

How This Medication Works: Inhibits smooth-muscle contraction and causes blood vessels to dilate.

Dosage Form and Strength:
- tablets (40 mg, 80 mg, 120 mg)
- sustained-release tablets, caplets, and capsules (120 mg, 180 mg, 240 mg)

Storage:
- room temperature
- protect from moisture—do not store in bathroom or kitchen

Administration:
- Take verapamil at the same time every day.
- Swallow sustained-release forms whole; do not crush or chew.
- Take sustained-release forms with food or milk.
- Take a missed dose as soon as possible. However, if it is almost time for the next dose, skip the missed dose and return to your dosing schedule.

Precautions:
Do not use if:
- you have had an allergic reaction to verapamil or another calcium channel blocker, such as amlodipine, diltiazem, or nifedipine.

Talk to your doctor if:
- you have heart disease, kidney disease, liver disease, or problems with your circulation or blood vessels.
- you are taking any other drugs, especially other blood pressure medicines, digoxin, carbamazepine, cyclosporine, or warfarin.

Side Effects:

Contact your health-care provider immediately if you experience:

- severe constipation.
- a skin rash, itching, or difficulty breathing.
- severe headache.
- slow heartbeat (fewer than 50 beats per minute).
- chest pressure or discomfort.
- severe dizziness or fainting.
- swelling of the ankles, feet, or lower legs.

Commonly reported side effects:

- low blood pressure
- headache
- constipation
- drowsiness or fatigue
- nausea
- bleeding or changes in the gums

Time Required for Drug to Take Effect: Starts
to work within 2 hours of taking a dose, but takes at least 2 to 4 weeks of treatment to reach maximum effectiveness.

Symptoms of Overdose:

- nausea and vomiting
- weakness
- dizziness, drowsiness, or loss of consciousness
- confusion or slurred speech
- heart palpitations or chest pain

Special Notes:

- Verapamil is not a cure, and you may have to take this medication for a long time.

- Changing positions slowly when sitting and/or standing up may help decrease dizziness caused by this medication.
- If this drug makes you dizzy, avoid tasks requiring alertness, such as driving or operating machinery.
- Check with your physician or pharmacist before using any over-the-counter medications while taking this drug.
- Ask your doctor to tell you the safe range for your heart rate, but call your doctor if your heart rate falls below 50 beats per minute.
- Be careful to avoid becoming dehydrated or overheated; drink plenty of fluids.
- The shell of the extended-release tablet may appear in your stool. This is normal and does not mean the medicine has not been absorbed.
- Getting extra fluids and dietary fiber and exercising regularly may help prevent constipation.

warfarin

Brand Name: Coumadin

Generic Available: yes

Type of Drug: anticoagulant

Used for: Prevention of blood-clot formation.

How This Medication Works: Inhibits the clotting ability of the blood. **This drug can cause major or fatal bleeding. Use exactly as directed and keep**

all appointments with your health-care provider for bloodwork.

Dosage Form and Strength: tablets (1 mg, 2 mg, 2.5 mg, 3 mg, 4 mg, 5 mg, 6 mg, 7.5 mg, 10 mg)

Storage:

- room temperature
- protect from light and moisture—do not store in bathroom or kitchen

Administration:

- Doses differ for each person and may change during therapy based on blood-test results.
- Take at a similar time each day.
- If you forget to take a dose, do not double the amount the next day; take the usual dose that your doctor has prescribed. Missing only one dose will not cause a clot to form.
- Missing more than one dose may cause problems; tell your doctor if you miss more than one dose.
- The dose required to keep a clot from forming is often very close to the dose that may cause bleeding; taking more than prescribed may cause bleeding.

Precautions:

Do not use if:

- you have had an allergic reaction to warfarin.
- you are or may be pregnant.
- you have bleeding problems, an aneurysm, diverticulitis, severe liver disease, extremely high blood pressure, or you recently had brain surgery.

Talk to your doctor if:
- you have a stomach ulcer or ever had a stroke.
- you are taking any other medication, because many drugs can affect warfarin's activity, including prescription and over-the-counter medicines, natural products, and supplements.

Side Effects:

Contact your health-care provider immediately if you experience:
- severe back pain.
- bleeding gums or nosebleeds.
- black, tarry stools or red blood in your stools.
- blue or purple skin or toes.
- unusual, frequent, or severe bruising.
- difficulty breathing.
- coughing up blood or material resembling coffee grounds.
- cuts or wounds that won't stop bleeding.
- decreased alertness or confusion.
- severe dizziness, falling, or fainting, especially if you hit your head.
- severe or persistent headache.
- heavy or unexpected menstrual bleeding.
- paralysis, weakness on only one side of the body, or speech difficulty.
- severe stomach pain or bloating.
- bloody, pink- or red-tinged urine.
- unusual tiredness, weakness, or unsteadiness.
- yellowing of the eyes or skin.

Commonly reported side effects:
- loss of appetite
- gas or bloated stomach

- nausea, vomiting, or diarrhea
- hair loss

Time Required for Drug to Take Effect: Varies by patient, dose, and reason for therapy.

Symptoms of Overdose: Internal and external bleeding (see first section of Side Effects for symptoms.)

Special Notes:
- While you are taking warfarin, your doctor will periodically monitor therapy with blood tests.
- It is important that all of your health-care providers be aware that you are taking warfarin.
- Avoid vitamins or products containing vitamin K.
- Check with your physician or pharmacist before using any over-the-counter drugs (including aspirin, aspirin-containing products, or other pain medicines), natural products (especially garlic, ginseng, or ginkgo supplements), or vitamins (especially vitamin E) while you are on warfarin.
- Changes in diet may affect the way warfarin works. Maintain a steady, well-balanced diet. Too many leafy green vegetables on consecutive days may alter your bleeding time; you should eat the same weekly balance of vegetables.
- Do not drink alcohol while taking this medication.
- Tell the doctor or dentist you are taking warfarin if you are going to have any medical procedure or emergency treatment.
- Wear identification that says you take warfarin, in case an accident or injury occurs.

- You should never take more or less of this medication than has been prescribed by your doctor.
- Talk with your health-care providers about the signs and symptoms of bleeding.

zolpidem

Brand Names: Ambien, Ambien CR

Generic Available: no

Type of Drug: sedative

Used for: Treatment of insomnia and sleep disorders.

How This Medication Works: Reduces electrical activity in the brain, thus calming the brain.

Dosage Form and Strength: tablets (5 mg, 10 mg)

Storage:
- room temperature
- protect from moisture—do not store in bathroom or kitchen

Administration:
- Take on an empty stomach, at least 1 hour before or 2 hours after a meal.
- Do not take more than the prescribed amount.
- This medication is often taken on an "as-needed" basis. Do not take it more often than once every 24 hours unless your prescriber directs otherwise.

- If you have been taking this drug every night for more than 2 weeks, do not abruptly stop taking it; contact your health-care provider first.
- Take a missed dose as soon as possible. However, if it is almost time for the next dose, skip the missed dose and return to your regular dosing schedule.

Precautions:

Do not use if:

- you have had an allergic reaction to zolpidem.

Talk to your doctor if:

- you are taking any other drug, especially an antipsychotic, antidepressant, narcotic, sedative, or other drug that may depress the central nervous system.
- you have liver disease or lung disease such as emphysema, asthma, or bronchitis.
- you feel you need to continue this medicine for more than 7 days.
- you have sleep apnea or have been told you snore.
- you have a history of drug dependence.

Side Effects:

Contact your health-care provider immediately if you experience:

- depression or suicidal thinking.
- difficulty breathing, itching, swelling of the face or throat, or a rash.
- clumsiness or falls.
- confusion or excessive sedation.
- chest pain or palpitations.
- irritability, nervousness, or suicidal thoughts.
- hallucinations

Commonly reported side effects:
- abnormal dreams
- dizziness or double vision
- dry mouth
- diarrhea, nausea, or vomiting
- feeling weak
- headache

Time Required for Drug to Take Effect:
Begins to work within 15 to 30 minutes after a dose.

Symptoms of Overdose:
- severe dizziness
- nausea and vomiting
- very low blood pressure
- coma

Special Notes:
- Do not drink alcohol while taking this medication.
- Use of zolpidem should be limited to 7 to 10 days.
- Older patients should start with a lower dose of 5 mg to avoid excessive side effects.
- If you develop an urge to harm yourself in any way, call 911 immediately.
- You should not use this medicine if you are unable to devote 7 to 8 hours to sleep before you need to be active again.
- Even when taking this medication, having good sleep habits is important: Avoid naps during the day, caffeine or large meals in the evening, and using the bed for anything (such as television viewing or working) but sleep and sexual activity.
- This medication may be habit forming.

Brand Names

BRAND NAME	GENERIC NAME
AccuNeb	albuterol
Accupril	quinapril
Aciphex	rabeprazole
Actiq	fentanyl
Actonel	risedronate
Actos	pioglitazone
Adalat	nifedipine
Adalat CC	nifedipine
Adoxa	doxycycline
Advair Diskus	salmeterol and fluticasone combination
Advil	ibuprofen
Afeditab	nifedipine
Aggrenox	aspirin and extended-release dipyridamole combination
Alavert	loratadine
Aldactone	spironolactone
Aleve	naproxen
Allegra	fexofenadine
Aloprim	allopurinol
Alphagan	brimonidine
Alphagan P	brimonidine
Altace	ramipril
Altoprev	lovastatin
Ambien	zolpidem
Ambien CR	zolpidem
Amoxil	amoxicillin
Anaprox	naproxen
Anaprox DS	naproxen
Anexsia	hydrocodone and acetaminophen combination
Antivert	meclizine
Apidra	insulin glulisine
Apresoline	hydralazine
Aquazide	hydrochlorothiazide

BRAND NAME	GENERIC NAME
Aricept	donepezil
Aricept ODT	donepezil
Arimidex	anastrozole
Ascriptin	aspirin
Asmanex	mometasone
Atacand	candesartan
Ativan	lorazepam
Atrovent	ipratropium
Atrovent HFA	ipratropium
Avalide	irbesartan and hydrochlorothiazide combination
Avandia	rosiglitazone
Avapro	irbesartan
Avinza	morphine
Avodart	dutasteride
Azo-Gesic	phenazopyridine
Azo-Standard	phenazopyridine
Bactrim	sulfamethoxazole and trimethoprim combination
Bactrim DS	sulfamethoxazole and trimethoprim combination
Bancap HC	hydrocodone and acetaminophen combination
Bayer	aspirin
Bentyl	dicyclomine
Biocef	cephalexin
Bonamine	meclizine
Bonine	meclizine
Boniva	ibandronate
Bufferin	aspirin
Bumex	bumetanide
BuSpar	buspirone
Calan	verapamil
Calan SR	verapamil
Capital with Codeine	codeine and acetaminophen combination
Capoten	captopril

BRAND NAME	GENERIC NAME
Carbatrol	carbamazepine
Cardizem	diltiazem
Cardizem CD	diltiazem
Cardizem LA	diltiazem
Cardizem SR	diltiazem
Cartia	diltiazem
Casodex	bicalutamide
Cataflam	diclofenac
Catapres	clonidine
Catapres-TTS	clonidine
Celebrex	celecoxib
Celexa	citalopram
Cipro	ciprofloxacin
Cipro XR	ciprofloxacin
Clarinex	desloratadine
Claritin	loratadine
Claritin Redi-Tabs	loratadine
Cogentin	benztropine
Colchicine	colchicine
Colyte	PEG 3350 and electrolyte solution (PEG-ES)
Combivent	ipratropium and albuterol combination
Commit	nicotine
Compazine	prochlorperazine
Compro	prochlorperazine
Concerta	methylphenidate
Congestac Caplets	pseudoephedrine and guaifenesin combination
Cordarone	amiodarone
Coreg	carvedilol
Coreg CR	carvedilol
Cosopt	dorzolamide and timolol combination
Coumadin	warfarin
Covera-HS	verapamil
Cozaar	losartan
Cymbalta	duloxetine

BRAND NAME	**GENERIC NAME**
Darvocet-N 50	propoxyphene napsylate and aceta-minophen combination
Darvocet-N 100	propoxyphene napsylate and aceta-minophen combination
Daytrana	methylphenidate
Deconsal II	pseudoephedrine and guaifenesin combination
Deltasone	prednisone
Depakene	valproic acid
Depakote	valproic acid
Depakote ER	valproic acid
Desyrel	trazodone
Detrol	tolterodine
Detrol LA	tolterodine
Diastat	diazepam
Diazepam Intensol	diazepam
Digitek	digoxin
Dilacor XR	diltiazem
Dilantin	phenytoin
Diovan	valsartan
Diovan HCT	valsartan and hydrochlorothiazide combination
Ditropan	oxybutynin
Ditropan XL	oxybutynin
Dopar	levodopa
Doryx	doxycycline
Dramamine Less Drowsy Formula	meclizine
DuoNeb	ipratropium and albuterol combination
Duragesic	fentanyl
Dyazide	triamterene and hydrochloro-thiazide combination
EC-Naprosyn	naproxen
Ecotrin	aspirin
Effexor	venlafaxine
Effexor XR	venlafaxine
Elavil	amitriptyline

BRAND NAME	**GENERIC NAME**
Haldol	haloperidol
Humalog	insulin lispro
Humulin	insulin
Hydralazine	hydralazine
HydroDiuril	hydrochlorothiazide
Hytrin	terazosin
Hyzaar	losartan and hydrochlorothiazide combination
Iletin	insulin
Imdur	isosorbide mononitrate
I-Prin	ibuprofen
ISMO	isosorbide mononitrate
Isoptin	verapamil
Isoptin SR	verapamil
Istalol	timolol
Kadian	morphine
K+8	potassium chloride
K+10	potassium chloride
Kay Ciel	potassium chloride
K+Care	potassium chloride
K-Dur 10	potassium chloride
K-Dur 20	potassium chloride
Keflex	cephalexin
Klonopin	clonazepam
K-Lor	potassium chloride
Klor-Con	potassium chloride
Klor-Con 8	potassium chloride
Klor-Con 10	potassium chloride
Klor-Con/25	potassium chloride
Klor-Con M	potassium chloride
Klotrix	potassium chloride
K-Tab	potassium chloride
Lanoxicaps	digoxin
Lanoxin	digoxin
Lantus	insulin glargine
Larodopa	levodopa

BRAND NAME	GENERIC NAME
Lasix	furosemide
Lescol	fluvastatin
Lescol XL	fluvastatin
Levaquin	levofloxacin
Levemir	insulin glargine
Levothroid	levothyroxine
Levoxyl	levothyroxine
Lexapro	escitalopram
Lipitor	atorvastatin
Lithobid	lithium
Lodosyn	carbidopa
Lofibra	fenofibrate
Lopid	gemfibrozil
Lopressor	metoprolol
Lorcet	hydrocodone and acetaminophen combination
Lortab	hydrocodone and acetaminophen combination
Lotensin	benazepril
Lotrel	amlodipine and benazepril combination
Lumigan	bimatoprost
Lunesta	eszopiclone
Lupron	leuprolide
Lupron Depot	leuprolide
Macrobid	nitrofurantoin
Macrodantin	nitrofurantoin
Maxifed	pseudoephedrine and guaifenesin combination
Maxzide	triamterene and hydrochloro-thiazide combination
Menadol	ibuprofen
Metadate CD	methylphenidate
Metadate ER	methylphenidate
Methylin	methylphenidate
Methylin ER	methylphenidate
Meticorten	prednisone
Mevacor	lovastatin

BRAND NAME	GENERIC NAME
Miacalcin	calcitonin
Micro-K	potassium chloride
Micro-K 10	potassium chloride
Micronase	glyburide
Microzide	hydrochlorothiazide
Midol	ibuprofen
Minitran	nitroglycerin
Miralax	polyethylene glycol (PEG 3350)
Mobic	meloxicam
Monodox	doxycycline
Monoket	isosorbide mononitrate
Monopril	fosinopril sodium
Motrin	ibuprofen
Moxilin	amoxicillin
MS Contin	morphine
MSIR	morphine
Mucinex-D	pseudoephedrine and guaifenesin combination
Namenda	memantine
Naprelan	naproxen
Naprosyn	naproxen
Nasonex	mometasone
Nexium	esomeprazole
Niacor	niacin
Niaspan	niacin
Nicobid	niacin
Nicoderm CQ	nicotine
Nicorette	nicotine
Nicotrol	nicotine
Nifediac CC	nifedipine
Nifedical XL	nifedipine
Niravam	alprazolam
Nitrek	nitroglycerin
Nitro-Bid	nitroglycerin
Nitro-Bid Ointment	nitroglycerin
Nitro-Dur	nitroglycerin
Nitrolingual Spray	nitroglycerin
NitroQuick	nitroglycerin

BRAND NAME	GENERIC NAME
Nitrostat	nitroglycerin
Nolvadex	tamoxifen
Norco	hydrocodone and acetaminophen combination
Normodyne	labetalol
Norvasc	amlodipine
Novolin	insulin
Novolog	insulin aspart
NuLYTELY	PEG 3350 and electrolyte solution (PEG-ES)
Oramorph SR	morphine
Oretic	hydrochlorothiazide
OxyContin	oxycodone
Oxydose	oxycodone
OxyFAST	oxycodone
OxyIR	oxycodone
Oxytrol	oxybutynin
Pacerone	amiodarone
Pamelor	nortriptyline
Pamprin Maximum Strength All Day Relief	naproxen
Parcopa	levodopa and carbidopa combination
Paxil	paroxetine
Paxil CR	paroxetine
Pen VK	penicillin
Pepcid	famotidine
Pepcid AC	famotidine
Percocet	oxycodone and acetaminophen combination
Periostat	doxycycline
Phenergan with Codeine	promethazine and codeine combination
Phenytek	phenytoin
Pherazine with Codeine	promethazine and codeine combination
Plavix	clopidogrel

BRAND NAME	GENERIC NAME
Plendil	felodipine
Pletal	cilostazol
Polymox	amoxicillin
Pravachol	pravastatin
Premarin	estrogens, conjugated
Prevacid	lansoprazole
Prevacid SoluTab	lansoprazole
Prilosec	omeprazole
Prilosec OTC	omeprazole
Principen	ampicillin
Prinivil	lisinopril
Procardia	nifedipine
Procardia XL	nifedipine
Prodium	phenazopyridine
Pronap-100	propoxyphene napsylate and acetaminophen combination
Propacet 100	propoxyphene napsylate and acetaminophen combination
Propecia	finasteride
Proscar	finasteride
Protonix	pantoprazole
Proventil	albuterol
Proventil HFA	albuterol
Proventil Repetabs	albuterol
Prozac	fluoxetine
Prozac Weekly	fluoxetine
Pseudovent	pseudoephedrine and guaifenesin combination
Pyridium	phenazopyridine
Quibron	theophylline
Razadyne	galantamine
Razadyne ER	galantamine
Reglan	metoclopramide
Remeron	mirtazapine
Remeron SolTab	mirtazapine
Respaire	pseudoephedrine and guaifenesin combination

BRAND NAME	GENERIC NAME
Restoril	temazepam
Risperdal	risperidone
Risperdal M-Tabs	risperidone
Ritalin	methylphenidate
Ritalin-LA	methylphenidate
Ritalin-SR	methylphenidate
RMS	morphine
Roxanol	morphine
Roxanol/100	morphine
Roxicet	oxycodone and acetaminophen combination
Roxicodone	oxycodone
Rozerem	ramelteon
Sanctura	trospium
Sarafem	fluoxetine
Septra	sulfamethoxazole and trimethoprim combination
Septra DS	sulfamethoxazole and trimethoprim combination
Serevent Diskus	salmeterol
Seroquel	quetiapine
Sinemet	levodopa and carbidopa combination
Sinemet CR	levodopa and carbidopa combination
Singulair	montelukast
Slo-bid	theophylline
Slo-Niacin	niacin
Slo-Phyllin	theophylline
Slow FE	ferrous sulfate
Spiriva	tiotropium
Sterapred	prednisone
Synthroid	levothyroxine
Tavist ND	loratadine
Taztia XT	diltiazem
Tegretol	carbamazepine
Tegretol-XR	carbamazepine

BRAND NAME	**GENERIC NAME**
Tenormin	atenolol
Theo–24	theophylline
Theo-Dur	theophylline
Tiazac	diltiazem
Timoptic	timolol
Timoptic-XE	timolol
Tofranil	imipramine
Tofranil-PM	imipramine
Toprol XL	metoprolol
T-Phyl	theophylline
Trandate	labetalol
Transderm-Nitro	nitroglycerin
Travatan	travoprost
TriCor	fenofibrate
Trimox	amoxicillin
Tylenol with Codeine	codeine and acetaminophen combination
Tylox	oxycodone and acetaminophen combination
Ultracet	tramadol and acetaminophen combination
Ultram	tramadol
Ultram ER	tramadol
Ultrapin	ibuprofen
Uniphyl	theophylline
Unithroid	levothyroxine
Uristat	phenazopyridine
Uroxatral	alfuzosin
Valium	diazepam
Vasotec	enalapril
Veetids	penicillin
Ventolin	albuterol
Ventolin HFA	albuterol
Verelan	verapamil
Verelan PM	verapamil
VESIcare	solifenacin
Viadur	leuprolide

BRAND NAME	GENERIC NAME
Viagra	sildenafil
Vibramycin	doxycycline
Vibra-Tabs	doxycycline
Vicodin	hydrocodone and acetaminophen combination
Vicodin ES	hydrocodone and acetaminophen combination
Volmax	albuterol
Voltaren	diclofenac
Voltaren-XR	diclofenac
VoSpire ER	albuterol
Xalatan	latanoprost
Xanax	alprazolam
Xanax XR	alprazolam
Zantac	ranitidine
Zantac 75	ranitidine
Zelapar	selegiline
Zestril	lisinopril
Zetia	ezetimibe
Zocor	simvastatin
Zoloft	sertraline
Zyloprim	allopurinol
Zyprexa	olanzapine
Zyrtec	cetirizine

Canadian Brand Names

BRAND NAME (MANUFACTURER)	GENERIC NAME
Adalat (Bayer)	nifedipine
Aldactone (Pfizer)	spironolactone
Amoxil (Wyeth-Ayerst)	amoxicillin
Apo-Allopurinol (Apotex)	allopurinol
Apo-Amitriptyline (Apotex)	amitriptyline
Apo-Amoxi (Apotex)	amoxicillin
Apo-Ampi (Apotex)	ampicillin
Apo-Atenolol (Apotex)	atenolol
Apo-Benztropine (Apotex)	benztropine
Apo-Carbamazepine (Apotex)	carbamazepine
Apo-Cephalex (Apotex)	cephalexin
Apo-Diazepam (Apotex)	diazepam
Apo-Dipyridamole (Apotex)	dipyridamole
Apo-Doxy (Apotex)	doxycycline
Apo-Ferrous Sulfate (Apotex)	ferrous sulfate
Apo-Folic (Apotex)	folic acid
Apo-Furosemide (Apotex)	furosemide
Apo-Hydro (Apotex)	hydrochlorothiazide
Apo-Hydroxyzine (Apotex)	hydroxyzine
Apo-Imipramine (Apotex)	imipramine
Apo-Lorazepam (Apotex)	lorazepam
Apo-Metoprolol (Apotex)	metoprolol
Apo-Naproxen (Apotex)	naproxen
Apo-Nifed (Apotex)	nifedipine
Apo-Nitrofurantoin (Apotex)	nitrofurantoin
Apo-Prednisone (Apotex)	prednisone
Apo-Propranolol (Apotex)	propranolol
Apo-Timol (Apotex)	timolol
Apo-Verap (Apotex)	verapamil
Apresoline (Novartis)	hydralazine
Atarax (Pfizer)	hydroxyzine
Ativan (Wyeth-Ayerst)	lorazepam
Avodart (GSK)	dutasteride
Bactrim (Roche)	sulfamethoxazole and trimethoprim
Bentylol (Aventis)	dicyclomine
Betaloc (AstraZeneca)	metoprolol
Blocadren (Merck Frosst)	timolol

BRAND NAME (MANUFACTURER)	GENERIC NAME
Novo-Furantoin (Novopharm)	nitrofurantoin
Novo-Hydrazide (Novopharm)	hydrochlorothiazide
Novo-Hydroxyzin (Novopharm)	hydroxyzine
Novo-Hylazin (Novopharm)	hydralazine
Novolin (Novo-Nordisk)	insulin
Novo-Lorazem (Novopharm)	lorazepam
Novo-Naprox (Novopharm)	naproxen
Novo-Nifedin (Novopharm)	nifedipine
Novo-Pramine (Novopharm)	imipramine
Novo-Pranol (Novopharm)	propranolol
Novo-Profen (Novopharm)	ibuprofen
Novo-Purol (Novopharm)	allopurinol
Novo-Semide (Novopharm)	furosemide
Novo-Sorbide (Novopharm)	isosorbide dinitrate
Novo-Spiroton (Novopharm)	spironolactone
Novo-Triamzide (Novopharm)	triamterene and hydrochlorothiazide
Peptol (Horner)	cimetidine
Phenazo (ICN)	phenazopyridine
Plendil (AstraZeneca)	felodipine
Premarin (Wyeth-Ayerst)	estrogens, conjugated
Reglan (Wyeth-Ayerst)	metoclopramide
Rozerem (Takeda)	ramelteon
Sanctura (Indevus)	trospium
Slow-Fe (Novartis)	ferrous sulfate
Spiriva (Boehringer Ingelheim)	tiotropium
Stemetil (Rhone-Poulenc Rorer)	prochlorperazine
Synthroid (Abbott)	levothyroxine
Tagamet (GSK)	cimetidine
Tarka (Abbott)	verapamil
Tegretol (Novartis)	carbamazepine
Tenormin (AstraZeneca)	atenolol
Tofranil (Novartis)	imipramine
Tylenol with codeine (Janssen-Ortho)	codeine and acetaminophen
Valium (Roche)	diazepam
Verelan (Wyeth-Ayerst)	verapamil
VESIcare (GSK)	solifenacin
Vibramycin (Pfizer)	doxycycline
Xatral (Sanofi Synthelabo)	alfuzosin
Zyloprim (GSK)	allopurinol

General Index